The Spirits of Neoliberal Reforms
and Everyday Politics of the State in Africa

THE SPIRITS OF NEOLIBERAL REFORMS AND EVERYDAY POLITICS OF THE STATE IN AFRICA

Edited by

Béatrice Hibou, Boris Samuel

& Laurent Fourchard

ACPA
Politique africaine

KARTHALA

AMALION
PUBLISHING

Published by Amalion Publishing in association with Association des
Chercheurs de Politique Africaine (ACPA) and Éditions Karthala 2017

Amalion Publishing
BP 5637 Dakar-Fann
Dakar CP 10700
Senegal
www.amalion.net

Association des Chercheurs de Politique Africaine (ACPA),
Fondation nationale des sciences politique, Les Afriques dans le monde
(LAM), IEP de Bordeaux, 11 Allée Ausone,
Domaine Universitaire, 33607 Pessac Cedex, France

Éditions Karthala
22-24, boulevard Arago, 75013 Paris, France
www.karthala.com

ISBN 978-2-35926-067-0 PB
ISBN 978-2-35926-068-7 Ebook

Cover designed by Will McCarty

Cover image, a detail of *La Ronde d'Egungun II* (2009) by Julien Sinzogan.
Used by permission and courtesy of the artist.

Contents

✳

Contributors

Amin Allal is CNRS Research Fellow at the Centre d'Etudes et de Recherches Administratives, Politiques et Sociales (CERAPS) in Lille, France. He holds a PhD in Political Science from Sciences-Po Aix en Provence in 2013 and was a WAFAW post-doctoral fellow in 2014. His research interests include mobilisation, public and social policies. He has edited *(In)disciplines et sanctions partisanes. Perspectives comparées* with N. Bué (Presses Universitaires du Septentrion, 2016) and *Devenir révolutionnaires. Au cœur des révoltes arabes,* with T. Pierret (Armand Colin, 2013).

Sidy Cissokho is a PhD candidate in political science and assistant lecturer at Université Paris 1 Pantheon Sorbonne. He works on professional drivers' union formation and the relationship between the representatives of this group and political party movements and government administration at the local level in Senegal. His main area concerns the period from the 1980s and the implementation of the structural adjustment reforms till date, using mainly an ethnographic approach on motor parks. He recently published two articles in the journals *Revue Tiers monde* (2015) and *Terrains et Travaux* (2014) respectively on the drivers' union organization and elections in motor parks.

Jeroen Cuvelier holds a PhD in social and cultural anthropology from Leuven University. His dissertation, which earned him the 2013 prize of the Belgian Royal Academy for Overseas Sciences, dealt with the construction of masculine identities among artisanal miners in the former province of Katanga, situated in the southeastern part of the Democratic Republic of Congo. Cuvelier has held research positions at the International Peace

Information Service in Antwerp, and the Royal Museum for Central Africa in Tervuren. Between January 2012 and December 2015, he was a postdoctoral fellow for the Special Chair for Humanitarian Aid and Reconstruction at Wageningen University, coordinating a research project on the impact of mining reforms on Congo's artisanal mining sector. At the same time, he was also involved in a research project about the relationship between artisanal mining, urbanization and access to land in Eastern Democratic Republic of Congo at the Conflict Research Group of Ghent University. Between September 2015 and September 2016, he served as a visiting professor at the department of anthropology of Leuven University. His current research project focuses on the impact of mining-induced displacement and resettlement on the dynamics of belonging among displaced people in Katanga.

Mamadou Diouf is one of the important historians of Western Africa today. His research on colonial and postcolonial research cover subjects ranging from Senegalese brotherhoods to new theoretical tool for African historiography. Diouf holds a PhD from the Université Paris-Sorbonne, France. He leads the Columbia University Institute for African Studies at the School of International and Public Affairs and is also a professor in Columbia's Department of Middle East and Asian Languages and Cultures (MEALAC). His research interests include urban, political, social and intellectual history in colonial and postcolonial Africa. His publications include *Tolerance, Democracy, and Sufis in Senegal* (ed. 2013), *New Perspectives on Islam in Senegal: Conversion, Migration, Wealth, and Power* (with Mara A. Leichtman) (2009); *Academic Freedom in Africa* (with Mahmood Mamdani) (CODESRIA, 1993).

Pierre Englebert is the H. Russell Smith Professor of International Relations and professor of African politics at Pomona College in Claremont, California, where he also directs the International Relations Program and the African Politics Lab. His most recent books include *Inside African Politics* (2013, with Kevin Dunn) and *Africa: Unity, Sovereignty and Sorrow* (2009), which won the 2010 Best Book Award of the African Politics Conference Group. Englebert was a Fulbright Scholar at Bordeaux Institut d'Études Politiques in 2010–2011. His work focuses on state formation and decay in Francophone West and Central Africa, including issues of governance and decentralization, with a particular emphasis on the DR Congo since 2001.

Laurent Fourchard is Senior Research Fellow at the National Foundation for Political Science at the Centre d'Études et de Recherches Internationales (CERI) at Sciences Po Paris, France. He holds a PhD in history from Université Paris 7 and has been accredited to supervise PhD research from Sciences Po Paris from 2014. His research is located at the crossroads of African history and African politics. His interests focus on the regulation of violence, citizenship and belonging, everyday working of the state and urban comparative research. He has published twenty articles and edited five books on these issues, the last one on *Governing Cities in Africa: Politics and Policies* (with Simon Bekker) (HSRC Press, 2013). He has taught at Sciences Po Paris, Sciences Po Bordeaux, Université Paris 7 and the University of Cape Town. He is currently the director of publication of the journal *Politique africaine* and editorial board member of *Africa, The Journal of African History* and *International Journal of Urban and Regional Research*.

Béatrice Hibou is CNRS Senior Research Fellow at the Centre d'Études et de Recherches Internationales (CERI) in Paris, France. She holds a PhD in political economy from the École des Hautes Études en Sciences Sociales (EHESS, 1995) and has been accredited to supervise PhD research from Sciences Po, Paris since 2005. She is the author of many books on her comparative research in political economy, from a Weberian perspective, on the political significance of economic reform, on state trajectories, and on the exercise of domination in Africa and Europe, including *Political Anatomy of Domination* (Palgrave, 2017); *The Force of Obedience: The Political Economy of Repression in Tunisia* (Polity Press 2011); *The Bureaucratization of the World in the Neoliberal Era. An International Perspective* (Palgrave, 2015), *Privatizing the State* (ed., Hurst 2004) and *The Criminalization of the State in Africa* (co-authored with Jean-François Bayart and Stephen Ellis) (IUP, 1998). Since 2015, she is co-director of the Centre de Recherche, Économie, Société, et Culture (CRESC), Mohamed VI Polytechnic, University of Rabat (Morocco).

Achille Mbembe is a historian, political scientist, and public intellectual. He obtained his doctoral degree at the Université Paris 1 (Panthéon-Sorbonne) and subsequently obtained the DEA in Political Science at the Institut d'Études Politiques, Paris. He is a Research Professor of History and Politics at the Wits Institute for Social and Economic Research in Johannesburg, South Africa and a Visiting Professor in the Department of Romance Studies at the Franklin Humanities Institute, Duke University, USA. Between 1996 and 2001, he was Executive Secretary of the Council for the Development of Social Science Research in Africa, Dakar, Senegal. Achille Mbembe's research interests lie in the social sciences and African history and politics. More precisely, Mbembe investigates the "postcolony" that comes after decolonization. He is especially interested in the emergence of Afro-cosmopolitan cultures, together with the artistic practices that are associated with it. His publications include: *La naissance du maquis dans le Sud-Cameroun* (Karthala, 1996), *On the Postcolony* (California Univ. Press, 2001) and *Critique de la raison nègre* (La Decouverte, 2013).

Philémon Muamba Mumbunda is Professor and Dean of the Faculty of Political Sciences at the Université Catholique du Congo. He has published several papers and book chapters on state formation, conflicts, elections, party politics and lately on gender in the Democratic Republic of Congo. His most recent books include *Géopolitique identitaire en RDC. Cas de l'identité Kasaïenne* (L'Harmattan, 2010) and *Étude sur la masculinité en RD Congo* (AGB, 2015).

Boris Samuel is a researcher at the Chaire d'études africaines comparées, Ecole de Gouvernance et d'Economie de Rabat, Morocco. He holds à masters degree in economics and statistics from the École nationale de la statistique et de l'administration économique (ENSAE) and a doctorate in political science from Sciences Po Paris, France. He has over a decade experience as an expert in statistics, public finance and macroeconomics for various international organizations and governments in Africa. Samuel's research and publications examine technocratic practices across Africa and the Caribbean, to provide a historicized analysis of modes of government, power relations, and the politics of pricing and planning practices in Africa. He has taught at the Université Paris 1, Sorbonne and Sciences Po, Paris.

Lamia Zaki is a political scientist. She was a researcher at the Institut de Recherche sur le Maghreb Contemporain in Tunis between February 2007 and August 2010 and a visiting researcher at the Center for Contemporary

Arab Studies at Georgetown University in the US. Her work concerns the evolution of urban action in North Africa, including *Enjeux politiques et professionnels de l'action urbaine au Maghreb* (Karthala, 2010), *Terrains de campagne au Maroc. Les élections législatives de 2007 au Maroc* (Karthala-IRMC, 2009) and with Pierre-Arnaud Barthel *Expérimenter la ville durable au sud de la Méditerranée* (De L'aube, 2011).

Foreword

Laurent Fourchard

Politique africaine was launched in 1981 by a team of French and African scholars notably Jean-François Bayart, Christian Coulon, Jean Copans, Comi Toulabor, Yves-André Fauré, Jean-François Médard and Alain Ricard among many others. Founded as a clear departure from conventional approaches on Africa, it quickly established itself as the leading francophone journal in African studies. It has effectively been instrumental in de-exoticising Western academic perceptions about African politics and since the beginning has combined work that have transcended the narrow boundaries of disciplines like political science, anthropology, sociology, history and geography. Its most famous strengths is an emphasis on the historical and sociological basis of politics and its "politics from below" approach.

With 140 issues published, the journal offers articles that combine fresh empirical data and theoretical approaches. It gives priority to unpublished fieldworks, is wide open to African authors and aims to bridge the gap between in-depth academic researches and current affairs analysis. It wishes to provide a larger readership outside the academia with keys to understanding the vagaries of the continent. In the last decade, the journal has become more open to North Africa and has published special issues on Egypt, Libya, Tunisia, Morocco and Algeria contributing to bridge the gap between academic communities on the two sides of the Sahara as well as providing new original literature on Arabic-speaking countries, a not so common stance in African studies journals. For long devoted to French-speaking countries, the journal has eventually made significant efforts to reach out to the non-French speaking academic world: authors have come from a more diverse background from other European, African, American and Arabic countries: in the last two years, two-thirds of articles were published by non-French academics, a sign of the international popularity of the journal.

A number of colleagues outside France actually consider *Politique afric-aine* as one of the most influential non-English language journals in the field. Some of its founding fathers and academics – who have been key contributors to African studies and to social sciences in general – have used the journal as an open, provocative and imaginative arena (Jean-François Bayart, Mamadou Diouf, Béatrice Hibou, Achille Mbembe, Jean-François Médard to mention just a few) and their works originally published in *Politique africaine* have very often been translated into English. Yet despite its solid reputation the journal as a whole remains poorly read outside French-speaking communities.

As former co-editor of the journal with Marie-Emmanuelle Pommerolle (2009–2013), as director of publication and of the Association des chercheurs de *Politique africaine* (ACPA) since 2013 and in close collaboration with the editorial board and with Richard Banégas, former director of the journal, we thought it was time, after 35 years of existence, to broaden the journal to a larger English-speaking audience. Offering current scholarly contributions from the Francophone world to other Africanists and social scientists would not only help to expand the circulation and readership of *Politique africaine*'s landmark articles, but we also hope would strengthen academic dialogue between French- and English-speaking traditions in African studies.

This is the first book in English of articles initially published in French in *Politique africaine*. Within the board we initially imagined that the structure of the journal could be kept as such translating the four major sections (topical issue, briefing, research articles and debates of one specific book) which gives the journal its particularity, but we ended up in concentrating on one core theme and excluding other sections. We thought that several issues were worth of note when they first appeared in French: "Homosexuality and transgender", "Street parliaments", and the "France-Afrique" issues, for instance were published before similar papers came up in other African studies journals or were questions poorly covered in English-speaking countries.[1] However, we decided not to revisit these issues for now and chose the present collection because it reflects what we above all would like the reader to

consider as a reflection of our editorial line, providing fresh and original empirical data on countries usually less covered by other journals published in
English (Tunisia, Morocco, Burkina Faso, Mauritania, and to a lesser extent
DRC and Senegal) as well as to open a dialogue with more theoretical papers
published by the journal. Instead of adding papers to an existing issue we decided to select key empirical and theoretical articles published between 1999
and 2013 on the effects of neoliberal reforms in Africa. If there is an obvious
heterogeneity among papers published over a 12-year period, they however
have some common points which reflect a general editorial line focusing on
the historicity of daily practices backed by strong empirical evidences.

As suggested by Béatrice Hibou and Boris Samuel in the introduction of
the book, the authors do not take neoliberalism and the state as abstractions
but as historical processes. Most of them analyse neoliberalism through the
everyday practice of reform, expertise and process of rationalisation. The
emphasis on empirical exploration of concrete situations shows processes
more complex and ambivalent than a mere shrinking of state power:as suggested by the authors the shifts that transform modes of government might
be barely discernible with no clear-cut results, objectives of neoliberal reforms usually end up being of secondary importance and international recommendations are constantly being reinvented in each national situation.
Additionally, if neoliberalism has its own repertoire most of the time it clashes or is simultaneously shaped by other narratives (modernisation, development, reconstruction, nationalism....).

As such the book adopts a critical distance from the emerging literature
against a univocal neoliberal ideology or against neoliberalism seen as an
abstraction and not always distinguished from liberalism or capitalism. With
Marxists lamenting and neoliberal thinkers praising the shrinking of the state,
the idea of a vanishing state has become a powerful narrative in many parts of
the world and in the continent in particular. In highlighting empirical analysis
and political reconfigurations through the everyday politics of the state the
articles support the argument that there is nothing special about neoliberal
reforms. They refuse to consider *a priori* that the state is in any particular
danger but rather try to find the reasons for its transformations. This was
another key argument to decide to include in the collection landmark articles published in the late 1990s by Achille Mbembe on "On Private Indirect
Government", by Béatrice Hibou on "Privatising the State" and by Mamadou

Diouf on "Privatisation of African State and Economies". These articles help rethink the history of the colonial and postcolonial state through an on-going and far to be linear history of privatisation of modes and practices of government over a longer period of time.

This book could not have been possible without the support of a number of organisations and academics. We would like to thank the Agence Française de Développement (AFD) for its financial support and our publisher Karthala, co-owner of the journal with ACPA, for its intellectual assistance as well as to acknowledge the careful work of Susann Taponier for translating the papers from French to English. Yet a number of expressions so common in French (like *décharge*) remains difficult to translate. The *Politique africaine* editorial board from 2012 to 2016 has always supported the project despite several delays and failures with a number of British-based journals: thanks to the board members and to the current editors (Didier Péclard and Sandrine Perrot) for their advice and their analytical work on the articles in French. Thanks also to two specific board members, the secretary of ACPA, Séverine Awenengo d'Alberto, and the treasurer, Hélène Charton, for their time and energy: this book would not have been possible without their assistance. Richard Banégas, former editor and director of the journal till 2013 has been instrumental since the project took off. Thanks to Béatrice Hibou (another former editor of the journal) as well as Boris Samuel for accepting the challenge of writing an original introduction and in helping me with editorial guidance of the book. Eventually, it was not easy to find an English based publisher to accept a reader made up of articles formerly published in French. On behalf of the board, I would like to thank Amalion and his director Sulaiman Adebowale for his openness, his patience and for making this initiative possible. We look forward to renew this experience.

Endnote

1. "France-Afrique : sortir du pacte colonial", *Politique africaine*, 105, 1, 2007; "Les parlements de la rue. Espaces publics de la parole et citoyenneté en Afrique", 127, 3, 2012; and "La question homosexuelle et transgenre", *Politique africaine*, 126, 2, 2012.

1

✳

Introduction: Neoliberal Reforms and Everyday Politics of the State in Africa

Béatrice Hibou & Boris Samuel

This book of articles first published in French in the journal *Politique africaine* between 1999 and 2013 proposes an original interpretation of neoliberalism on the African continent. Several of these diverse articles are theoretical, pertaining to Africa as a whole, and were conceived through collective thinking about the dynamics of privatisation and delegation of public services (Béatrice Hibou, Achille Mbembe and Mamadou Diouf); whereas others focus on specific geographical areas, emphasising administrative techniques and procedures (Boris Samuel, Jeroen Cuvelier and Philémon Muamba Mumbunda); or expose the social dynamics arising from the pressures of neoliberal reforms (Amin Allal, Lamia Zaki, Pierre Englebert and Sidy Cissokho). Nevertheless, they all share the same basic approach: starting from everyday practices grounded in prevailing neoliberal discourse, they paint a picture of some of the different ways these reforms can play out over time. To help us understand this particular historical moment, the authors provide a broad overview of neoliberal variations by describing a variety of cases (decentralisation, reorganisation of state-owned companies according to managerial principles, macroeconomic management, urban transport, reforms of public services); a variety of countries and regions (Burkina Faso, Mauritania, Senegal, Morocco, Tunisia and Congo, the latter two instances underlining the contrast between the state capital and remote regions); a variety of actors (state actors at the local, national and international levels, private actors in the form of major companies or petty traders, etc.); and a variety of historical timeframes (ranging from a few decades to dynamics dating back several centuries), and even to present-day ethnographic studies.

Neoliberal systems and politics

The texts presented here grasp neoliberalism through reforms, such as privatisation, outsourcing or a managerialist approach to the economy, and their effects. They also approach neoliberalism by examining how particular economic or administrative techniques such as economic planning, decentralisation or tax collection are used. Usually the techniques described here are justified by rhetoric about the inadequacies and dysfunction of the state – the crisis of the nation-state, the state's inability to assert effective control over the economy, the diminishing role of the state in globalisation – in its attempt to cope with the rise of the private sector, the market, transnational players and networks, and the processes of commodification.[1]

Without necessarily challenging those claims, this book argues against univocal interpretations by widening the scope of analysis beyond discourse and ideologies and by maintaining a critical view of the terms used. The practices discussed here involve processes far more complex and ambivalent than mere readjustments between the seemingly natural and self-evident "public" and "private" actors or between the "state", the "market" and "society". On the contrary, our work shows that these interpretations are underpinned by methodological biases that underestimate the processes of reappropriation and conflicts between differing conceptions of power, they adopt narrow and normative definitions of the state, and they ignore historical trajectories. By taking a detached view regarding the use of the concept of "neoliberalism", the authors demonstrate that the discourses promoted by donors, the "international community" and the "organic intellectuals" (Gramsci) of liberalisation, management planning or privatisation, and even their pre-packaged ideas and highly standardised recipes, actually authorise very diverse practices that are sometimes totally out of line with their explicit objectives.

This does not mean that liberal discourse need not be taken seriously; indeed, all the studies in this book pay close attention to it. After all, it is a major component of the discourse employed by state authorities. It reveals, more than one might suspect, the intentions and strategies of the state and of the non-state actors who refer to it. It is employed not only by dominant governmental actors but also by protest leaders and opposition movements. Public debates, controversies and conflicts are framed in terms of the cognitive schemes of neoliberalism. In this sense, neoliberal conceptions are indeed hegemonic. Moreover, they express a profound break from the accepted references and assessment standards of the preceding decades, even when that break has interrupted the continuity of quite different historical trajectories. The break also concerns the management of the international environment and all its constraints and opportunities.

However, the essays in this book offer a socio-political analysis of the practices surrounding the systems, instruments and policies viewed as the embodiment of neoliberalism. They show how these new techniques have transformed social and political relationships and the power balance within African societies. More specifically, they reveal how neoliberal engineering, armed with its instruments and recommendations, helps bring about a new social reality that is also "co-constructed" by state action.[2] We see this in tax reforms in Congo, macroeconomic management techniques in Burkina Faso and Mauritania, decentralisation reforms in Congo, the outsourcing of utilities (electricity) in Morocco, reforms of public companies (mining) in Tunisia and the overall logic of privatisation on the African continent. The mechanisms (dispositifs)[3] introduced in the name of neoliberal rationality have led to new modes of government by modifying the prerequisites for access to administrative departments, reformulating relationships between citizens, private actors and the state or overseeing the construction of knowledge about the economy. In defining ways of thinking about the economy or the role of the quest for economic efficiency in policymaking, these mechanisms are framed by the limits of what is politically thinkable, which they themselves help to shape. At the same time, the mechanisms, though implemented in the name of instrumental rationality, seem to be embedded in the relationships of power and domination that they reappropriate. They may be directly subject to the authority of regime dignitaries or exploited by local Big Men, by central authorities that maintain order (Morocco, Tunisia, Congo) or by a regime's strong men (Burkina Faso). This does not keep them from being criticised and opposed (as Amin Allal shows in the case of the Gafsa mining basin), but such opposition does not necessarily call longstanding political configurations into question.

This attention to technical mechanism suggests something else. By focusing on actual practices, the chapters in this book reveal the wealth of information that can be obtained by emphasising the concrete, everyday aspects of reforms rather than the abstract reasoning used to analyse the rationality of these neoliberal systems and, more broadly, neoliberalism as an ideology. The way GDP growth rate is calculated, the way people in a Moroccan slum or in a remote region of Congo have access to public services or the way a company is privatised help to shape socio-political relations. These practices should not be evaluated normatively; they should not be described as "good" or "bad". The technical approach that consists of weighing the merits of policy options and assessing the adequacy or inadequacy of policies according to supposedly neutral or universal principles (such as economic efficiency) implicitly conveys value judgments and makes it difficult to take social relations into account.

In contrast, the chapters presented here shed light on the actors, their logics, their interests and their strategies, their ways of doing things and the different ways of operating that make up neoliberalism in practice.[4] In short, this approach aims to understand neoliberal reform as a set of procedures, codes and interactions specific to places, circumstances and historical contexts. The approach enables us to rethink traditional questions such as the role of expertise. When we consider the technical aspects of reform implementation and neoliberal engineering in political terms, we can give a better account of the relations between expertise and politics. Expertise reformulates existing social relations and gives rise to new forms of political enunciation. It is in no way akin to a depoliticising process, as has frequently been argued in reference to neoliberalism in Africa.[5] On the contrary, many of the articles here (notably those by Lamia Zaki, Boris Samuel, Jeroen Cuvelier and Philémon Muamba Mumbunda, and Sidy Cissokho) show that expert work redefines longstanding social relations and that, conversely, social relations invade expertise. For example, the relations of power and politics are in no way obscure in the rationalisation of transport in Dakar; the actors who adopt the new methods of motor park management reposition themselves in the sector. In the Tunisian case analysed by Amin Allal, the relation between international expertise and local interests is less obvious but just as present. To a certain extent, one can explain the "revolt" in the Gafsa mining basin by the encounter between social and political relations shaped by a specific trajectory of modes of government and the technical instructions issued by international experts.

In other words, neoliberal dynamics rely on technical processes that may be inconsistent, even though they are presented as resulting from one and the same process of rationalisation. These technical processes are simultaneously coupled with multiple social processes and thereby help to reshape them and give them new meanings. One of the postulates of the studies presented here is precisely that neoliberalism cannot be analysed in itself, as if it were a known essence, thing or dynamic. This means that neoliberalism is always specific. To understand it requires not only analysing the practices and processes involved but also accounting for how they are understood locally by the actors on the ground and how the specific meanings attached to the measures are adopted.

Reform is the leitmotif of neoliberalism in action

This book analyses a number of different reforms that can be considered neoliberal, such as the retreat of state authority, the promotion of economic stability, the maximisation of the profitability of major companies, the promotion of initiatives to improve bureaucratic and administrative efficiency, etc. Permanent reform is the chief embodiment of neoliberal forms of government. As the work of Michel Foucault has shown, reforms orient and control the actors' conduct. These reforms are also produced by neoliberal "doctrine". For economists such as Hayek, "failures" of the state make it necessary to supervise administrative authorities by introducing management rules. Such statements claim to be neutral and depoliticised, because they pretend to achieve the collective well-being.[6] However, while neoliberal reform reflects a new view of the role, importance and economic dimension of the state – until now viewed mainly in terms of its political dimension – it is also an expression of the voice of the state or even of state thinking. Indeed, neoliberalism thinks in terms of "governance", in other words, in terms of leadership or technocratic management supposedly enlightened by orthodox economic theories or administrative engineering. Most of the chapters deal with reconfigurations under way in the name of "efficiency", but all of them show the benefits – licit or illicit – that the state or certain central organisations gain from the reforms, even when they generate protest.

This is not to say that all neoliberal policies express one and the same conception of the relationship between the state and the economy – far from it. In the neoliberal era, the processes used to manage the economy reveal different ways of acting upon the economy and different ways of governing, even when they use the same instruments. The shared reference to neoliberalism and its reforms does not prevent diverse modes of government. The reforms set forth in the name of managerial rationality or efficiency are based on concrete reconfigurations and arrangements that make them different, negotiated and specific in each case. For example, the decentralisation of Congo may appear to reflect the context and balance of power that predated it, while structural adjustment may seem to coincide with a political trajectory of African states characterised by widespread use of indirect methods of government exercising power through intermediaries (Mamadou Diouf, Achille Mbembe). However, neoliberalism must not be understood in terms of a single regime or system; the empirical research presented here brings out its processes and politics-in-the-making and therefore its necessarily incomplete, unfinished, hybrid forms. That is why interpreting neoliberalism (with its "discharge",[7] "privatisation" or "liberalisation") as an ideal type or model is partly contradictory. Current situations should be understood not as illustrations of a supposedly new "paradigm", but as illustrations of this multiplicity of allegiances, levels of formality, ways of managing complexity and multiple references, standards and regulatory methods (Béatrice Hibou). "Discharge", "administrative rationalisation" and "economic stability" are only some of its forms. They enter into – and overlap with – a number of other reformist repertoires such as Sankarist modernisation in Burkina Faso, *beylicat* in Tunisia or the engineering of post-conflict reconstruction of the state in Congo. Of course, in all these configurations, there are always multiple styles of government, and neoliberal reforms are merely one modality. They are prominent, to be sure, and sometimes dominant, highly visible, "new" or considered as such, but absolutely not unique.

To say there is no neoliberal template also means that one should not seek to determine which form of state action – public or private – is preferable. The chapters in this book do not claim to analyse a change of hegemony. Instead, they show that the very notions of "private" and "public" can and do vary over time and space. Sometimes the shifts that transform modes of government are barely discernible, yielding no clear-cut results. However, they do have one point in common; contrary to the interpretations of state power in terms of "sharing, "dilution" or "resilience", [8] these chapters show that the keys to change and transformation are mostly in the hands of the state. This does not mean the state orchestrates such transformations or controls the changes. On the contrary, there is a variety of unforeseen processes of circumventing, appropriating and reinterpretation, along with a largely unconscious and contradictory historical process of conflict, negotiation and compromise among various groups and actors. The contributions to this book underscore the plurality of conditions that brought the state into being and made it evolve; they never underestimate the debates and clashes between different positions, standards or conceptions of state power that motivate the actors, public and private, state or non-state, that are stakeholders in this process.

Thus, neoliberal reforms are not analysed here for themselves but as material that can help us understand state logics, political concerns, power mechanisms and techniques of knowledge. Reform must be analysed within a set of social relations in which the state is, of course, always present, perhaps even central, yet nevertheless fluid, shifting, diverse and often narrowly institutionalised, depending on how power is exercised. This historical approach to political sociology therefore rejects any substantialist view of the state; the state is not presupposed and defined a priori but grasped in multiple forms of political and economic arrangements and their transformations. The reforms currently under way should be understood as a mutation in modes of government; they modify the forms and places of state intervention and reshape the values or norms linked to specific historical contexts.

The social and political processes discussed in the various contributions suggest that the objectives of neoliberal reforms and processes usually end up being of secondary importance. The new management methods – giving priority to efficiency and profitability, to transforming the relationship between citizens and institutions and to privatisation – are seldom the most important result of reforms. On the other hand, the way reforms are carried out and their outcomes always reflect political systems, historical trajectories and modes of international integration. They reveal the state of political societies insofar as the political game is also (and sometimes above all) played out in the field of management, economics and administrative processes.

Meanings of neoliberalism and historical trajectories of the state

In Africa, politics, at least since colonisation, has been founded on straddling positions of power and accumulation, the public and private sectors, legality and illegality.[9] Neoliberalism in Africa must be understood within this configuration. This does not exclude the existence of significant transformations. As Mamadou Diouf's chapter reminds us, neoliberal reforms have brought about changes in the relationship between economics and politics and between the citizen and the state. Moreover, they have altered the very meaning of the notions of public, private, market, state, and so on. Achille Mbembe conceptualises these configurations as "private indirect government" and Béatrice Hibou, following Weber, as "discharge". Moreover, as the texts presented here make clear, although neoliberal reforms may result in identical or nearly identical practices, they take on different meanings depending on the country (Senegal, Congo, Morocco, Tunisia, Burkina Faso and Mauritania), the region (Tunis, Gafsa), the sector (customs, electric power, transport) and the institution (national or local).

In this historical trajectory, "extraversion"– the processes, according to Bayart,[10] that transform situations of dependence on the outside into opportunities to exercise power and domination within political societies – is one of the key characteristics of African political societies. Neoliberal reform is necessarily incorporated into this specific way of understanding international integration. It is the prime locus of the relationships between the dominant actors in what is called the "international community" and African states, particularly in the wake of the conditionalities of the structural adjustment period. Although they appear to be uniform and ideologically univocal, the resulting policies and recommendations are in fact fluctuating, open-ended and unstable. They are appropriated by each country according to the political demands of the moment, the existing power struggles and the national actors involved. These policies are often seen as imposed from outside and opposed to the interests and logic of the state, but, when observed in the concrete, they reveal numerous interactions between the "international community" and African states. These interactions no doubt include open confrontation, pressure and blackmail but, even more, compliance, negotiation, latent or implicit opposition, insidious transformations and allowances for reinterpretation and leeway. Indeed, one cannot help but note that international recommendations are constantly being reinvented in each national situation. As Boris Samuel shows, at the end of the 1990s, Burkina Faso helped to strengthen the World Bank's case for intervention citing a "tradition of participation",[11] which suggests that their relationship cannot be adequately described solely in terms of international injunctions met by Burkinabe opposition. In the 1990s, a number of countries and segments of African societies began massively rejecting adjustment programmes, more on political than on economic grounds. They were thus expressing a sort of nationalism, playing on colonial recollections and the rejection of a certain form of domination. Gradually, however, they embraced, at least partially, certain aspects of neoliberal dogma and, in any case, adopted some aspects, particularly the macroeconomic dimension. Economic arguments (market vitality, recognition of certain advantages in dynamic international integration) were instrumental in introducing macroeconomic orthodoxy into the African world, leading, for instance, to the adoption of neoliberal African programmes such as NEPAD.[12] But its socio-political impact was also fundamental, as shown in the successful fight against corruption, scepticism regarding state intervention and criticism of state inefficiency or the strategic decision to form alliances with leading world powers. Similarly, neoliberalism today, in the sense of a managerial rationalisation or a set of norms and reforms to promote state efficiency and transparency, takes shape not only through globally established techniques but also through the dynamics and desires of whole segments of African political societies, such as demands for social inclusion and greater social justice or expectations of state accountability through performance assessment.

Contrary to what most of the literature on globalisation tends to argue, the contributions to this book highlight political reconfigurations, which would support the idea that there is nothing special about neoliberal reforms. Indeed, the political history of the modern period is usually read as a reflection on the crisis of the state, emphasising the tension between the nation-state and inter- or trans-national dynamics. For the most part, this history has been analysed as the dismantling of the state by exogenous phenomena – war, imperialism, international markets and free trade. Recent research, however, tends to view these phenomena as the intertwining of two distinct realities. The state is largely a product of globalisation,[13] developing in Africa through international injunctions, which it re-appropriates, and extending its authority through creative adaptation. That is precisely what is borne out, in different ways, by all the chapters in this book; they share a common research position in refusing to consider a priori that the state is in any particular danger. Instead, they turn to empirical observation to find the reasons for its transformations. The banality of neoliberalism lies, in fact, in the commonly expressed fear that the very existence of the African state is threatened by international constraints.

Studies of African societies have shown that transformations of modes of government and rearrangements between public and private are common-place. This book emphasises the geographical and historical recurrence of modes of government normally considered neoliberal, such as "discharge" or "private indirect government". One of our arguments, put forward especially in the texts of Mamadou Diouf and Béatrice Hibou, is that, far from being an umpteenth crisis of the state, modes of government are simply undergoing modifications "as usual". These modifications simultaneously transform the relationships between public and private, the economy and politics, licit and illicit and legal and illegal that result from the increased use of contracts, as the texts of Sidy Cissokho on public transport in Dakar and Jeroen Cuvelier and Philémon Muamba Mumbunda on customs in Congo clearly illustrate. Weber – and Locke before him – pointed out that the essential characteristic of modern law in action was the centrality of legal transactions, particularly contracts. More broadly, such modes of government were commonly used in the past, as historical works on premodern societies testify. "Discharge" was a recurrent method of exercising power for Roman publicans, in delegations by feudal societies, in land tenures granted by European royalty and in the Ottoman Empire. Conversely, by underlining these facts, we can understand the extent to which the ordinary conception of the state today – intervening directly and continuously through a bureaucratic apparatus – is normative. The configurations and arrangements are specific to each historical situa-tion due to globalisation itself, which enables techniques and processes to circulate and each national or regional situation to write its own history, incorporating some of these standard tools to produce a singular situation and meaning.

Endnotes

1 S. Strange, *The Retreat of the State. Diffusion of Power in the World Economy,* Cambridge: Cambridge University Press, 1996; I. Zartman (ed.), *Collapsed States. The Disintegration and Restoration of Legitimate Authority,* Boulder, London, Lynne Rienner, 1995; R.D. Kaplan, "The Coming Anarchy", *The Atlantic Monthly,* 273(2), Feb. 1994, pp. 44–76.

2 A. Desrosières, *Gouverner par les nombres. L'argument statistique II.* Presses des Mines, 2008; Pierre Lascoumes and Patrick le Galès, *Gouverner par les Instruments,* Paris: Presses de Sciences Po, 2004.

3 In keeping with Foucauldian terminology.

4 Michel de Certeau, *L'invention du quotidien. 1. Arts de faire,* Paris: Le Seuil, 1990 (1980). (Cf. the English translation by Steven Randall entitled *The Practice of Every Day Life*).

5 J. Ferguson, "From African Socialism to Scientific Capitalism: Reflexion on the Legitimation crisis in IMF-Ruled Africa", in D. Moore, G. Schmitz, *Debating Development Discourse: Institutional and Popular Perspectives,* London: Macmillan, 1995; J. Ferguson, *Global Shadows. Africa in the Neoliberal World Order,* Durham, NC: Duke University Press, 2006; T. Mitchell, *Rule of Experts: Egypt, Techno-Politics, Modernity,* Berkeley: The University of California Press, 2002; B. Campbell, "La bonne gouvernance, une notion éminemment politique" in *Les non-dits de la bonne gouvernance,* Paris: Karthala, 2001, pp.119–49; J. Elyachar, *Markets of Dispossession: NGOs, Economic Development, and the State in Cairo*, Durham, NC: Duke University Press, 2005.

6 B. Jobert, "Le mythe de la gouvernance dépolitisée", in P. Favre et al., *Être gouverné. Études en l'honneur de Jean Leca,* Paris: Presses de Sciences Po "Académique", 2003, pp. 273–85.

7 The term *décharge* was forged by Béatrice Hibou from her reading of Weber (French translations of the German terms Verpachtung and Überweisung found in *General Economic History* (trans. F. H. Knight), London: George Allen & Unwin, 1927). The term has since been adopted by a whole series of French works in the historical sociology of politics. It was translated as "discharge" in the English-language version of *La privatisation des États* (Privatizing the State). For this reason, we have used the same word here, even if it is not altogether felicitous.

8 S. Strange, *The Retreat of the State…,* op. cit; D. Chandler, *Resilience, the Governance of Complexity,* New York: Routledge, 2014; J.M. Châtaigner (ed.), *Fragilités et résilience. Les nouvelles frontières de la mondialisation,* Paris: Karthala, 2014.

9 J.-F. Bayart, *The State in Africa. The Politics of the Belly,* trans. by Mary Harper, Christopher and Elizabeth Harrison, 2nd edition, Cambridge: Polity Press, 2009.

10 J.F. Bayart, "Africa in the world. A history of extraversion", *African Affairs,* no. 99, 2000, pp. 217–67.

11 B. Samuel, *La production macroéconomique du réel. Formalités et pouvoir au Burkina Faso, en Mauritanie et en Guadeloupe,* doctoral thesis, Institut d'Etudes Politiques de Paris, December 2013.

12 J. Coussy, "Etats africains, programmes d'ajustement et consensus de Washington", *L'Economie politique,* no. 32, 2006/4, pp. 29–40.

13 J.F. Bayart, *Global Subjects. A Political Critique of Globalization,* Cambridge: Polity Press, 2007.

2

✳

Uncertainty, Autonomy and Parasitism: Decentralised Territorial Entities and the State in the Democratic Republic of Congo

Pierre Englebert

Introduction

Decentralisation reforms[1] have made great strides in Africa since the 1990s.[2] The reforms, dear to the hearts of donors, ostensibly aim to achieve good governance and democratisation by bringing administrations close to the people they manage.[3] But what happens when the reforms are only partially introduced in a predatory state with weak administrative capabilities and little interest in decentralising?

This chapter draws on the experience of the Democratic Republic of Congo to answer that question. It argues that the implementation of decentralisation reforms in Congo has been characterised by uncertainty stemming from the weakness of the state. This uncertainty is reflected in the simultaneous production – by act or omission – of both decentralising and recentralising rules; a tendency to multiply laws and institutions through negligence, sedimentation or adaptation; arbitrary financial transfers; and confusion over the powers and status of local state agents. However, while this uncertainty limits the capacity of decentralised authorities to perform the administrative duties in the areas that fall within their competence, it also creates opportunities for autonomy, which local agents seize upon to provide for themselves. Contrary to the expected outcomes of decentralisation, widespread uncertainty has produced a local state of exception, largely free of legal constraints, self-serving and incapable of offering services (in fact, a miniature replica of the Congolese state). However "failed" it may appear, Congolese decentralisation has consequently helped to develop a social and political compromise between central and local elites and between government leaders and civil servants, creating a sort of power-sharing arrangement that underpins the state. Its administration is undoubtedly weak, but it is not itself a failed state, inasmuch as its very formation depends on these practices.

In the light of decentralisation reforms, this article presents a local view of the internal dysfunction of a weak state and how the dysfunction distorts those reforms. It shows that certain characteristics of weakness, such as uncertainty about the rules and how they are supposed to be implemented, can be combined with the precarious situation of state agents not only to rob the state of its administrative capacity but also to promote a governance of exception. Thus, paradoxically, the very reforms that were intended to serve local populations end up exposing them to even greater predation. The aspect of uncertainty has been neglected in the depiction of state fragility. This article endeavours to show that it is intrinsic to the operation of weak states and shapes the kind of power they engender.

My analysis focuses, above all, on the functioning of "decentralised territorial entities" (DTE), i.e. cities, communes sectors and chiefdoms, which are at the heart of Congolese decentralisation. The examples come from fieldwork conducted in 2010 and 2011 in two communes in the southern part of Kinshasa (Kimbanseke and Lemba) as well as in the territory of Mbanza-Ngungu and the district of Boko in the Bas Congo. Although this material is not sufficiently in-depth to qualify as a full-blown ethnographic study, it is in line with recent research on decentralisation in the DR Congo.[4]

A system of uncertainty

Decentralisation was introduced in the DR Congo through the 2006 constitution and two organic laws adopted in 2008, one relating to free administration of the provinces, the other detailing the organisation and operation of the DTEs and their relationship to the central government and the provinces. The provinces, cities, communes, sectors and chiefdoms already existed prior to decentralisation, but they were considered deconcentrated institutions, i.e. their personnel were appointed by the central government, and they enjoyed no legal, administrative, financial or political autonomy. Decentralisation gave them this autonomy, along with numerous powers. The law provides for 29 exclusive areas of responsibility, including health care, education and provincial administration, and 25 areas of joint responsibility with the government, among them domestic security, the administration of courts and tribunals, taxation, the media, land and mining rights, territorial management, the regime of waters and forests, and cooperation with international partners. As for the DTEs, their areas of responsibility extend to the construction, management and maintenance of local roads and car parks, public works and contracts, local police, sanitation, drainage and sewerage systems, public health, public buildings, power distribution, child care and schools, public lighting, literacy courses and social centres, etc. The mayors (cities), *bourgmestres* (communes) and heads of sectors and chiefdoms are also officers of the judicial police and the civil registrar.

To finance their actions, the constitution authorises the provinces to withhold 40 percent of the national tax revenues levied on their administrative subdivision and impose other local taxes. In turn, the DTE are entitled to a 40 percent retrocession of the 40 percent granted to the provinces (i.e. 16 percent of national revenue). They also have the authority to impose local taxes, including patent and other taxes on road traffic, beer and tobacco consumption, market stands and land taxes based on the surface area of mining and forestry concessions. To ensure democratic decentralisation, the law provides for the election by universal suffrage of provincial assemblies (which then elect the governors) and city, commune, sector and chiefdom councils (which in turn elect their own executive colleges).

In reality, Congolese decentralisation bears little resemblance to these legal provisions. Instead, it revolves around a wobbly system of contradictory policies, obsolete, non-existent or unenforced laws, an unpredictable, precarious situation for its agents and a chaotic profusion of institutions. The result is widespread uncertainty regarding the enforcement of laws, the actual powers of certain bodies and institutions and the legal value of decisions emanating from various sources of authority.

This uncertainty manifests itself first by omission – the failure to implement decentralisation by a government that prefers centralisation. Many constitutional and legal provisions go unheeded or are ambiguously enforced. Provincial elections were indeed held in 2006, but elections for the DTEs, originally planned for 2008, were postponed to 2010 and later to 2013, and mayors, *bourgmestres* and other heads of sectors and chiefdoms continue to be appointed by Kinshasa. The government has also ignored a constitutional clause that expanded the number of provinces from 11 to 26. A law mandating the transfer of public administration and finance powers has yet to be implemented, leaving the provinces and DTEs unable to fully assume their new responsibilities. Even more seriously, virtually none of the financial measures in support of decentralisation has been implemented. The government is still very far from allocating 40 percent of its revenue to the provinces and DTEs, and the small amount that it does allocate is not withheld by provincial tax offices but retroceded by the central administration. Between 2007 and 2011, the amount of annual retrocession to the provinces accounted for between 6 and 15 percent of their budgets,[5] compared with about 20 percent prior to decentralisation.[6]

In addition to these omissions, certain actions have been carried out with the aim and/or effect of suppressing decentralisation. In January 2011, a hasty revision of the constitution withdrew the question of expanding territorial subdivision to 26 provinces from the scope of constitutional authority and placed it in the hands of the legislature, which relegated it to an indefinite future. The same revision also gave the president the right to remove governors from office and dissolve provincial assemblies, thereby depriving these bodies of political independence and weakening their local autonomy. In the past, the government had already revoked edicts adopted by the provincial assemblies. The post of minister of decentralisation was also abolished in 2011, no doubt in part because the minister at the time, Mbusa Nyamwisi, had decided to run in the presidential elections.

Lack of enforcement of decentralisation measures, whether total or only partial, has generated considerable ambiguity concerning the location of official authority, the validity of its actions and the question of which administrative and political system is actually in force. It is true that a similar tendency to recentralise authority has been observed in other instances of decentralisation in Africa.[7] Elsewhere on the continent, decentralisation has fallen short of the law just as frequently through "strategic or partial" implementation".[8] Moreover, decentralisation reforms arising from post-conflict agreements or democratic transition, as in Congo, are also more likely to be violated wherever they are implemented, particularly once political stability has been achieved. However, the situation in Congo far exceeds these common features. In this case, partial or inconsistent decentralisation has resulted in a pronounced pluralism and even profusion of Congolese laws, institutions and regulations, creating an unusually high degree of uncertainty in the country's administration. I am not referring to the type of pluralism generally found in African political systems due to the importance of customary law,[9] the application of multiple standards by administrations[10] or the hybrid nature of modes of governance.[11] In Congo, the multiplicity of laws and institutions takes on an entirely different dimension, forming a largely chaotic system within the "modern", formal sphere of the state itself.

For example, not only are the constitutional provisions regarding decentralisation seldom implemented, but they contradict previous laws that have not been revised. Thus, "territories" that have now become deconcentrated entities were decentralised in 1998 during a reform implemented by the regime of Laurent-Désiré Kabila. At the time, they had authority over the sectors. Today, the sectors are decentralised and therefore, in principle, independent of the territories. Yet, in the absence of implementation legislation, the territories often continue exercising their authority over the sectors.[12] The provinces and DTEs are thus forced to compete with the deconcentrated administrations under their jurisdiction (district commissaries, territorial administrators or provincial delegations of national ministries) that once had *de jure* (and, until now, partly *de facto*) authority over their areas of responsibility. Similarly, as the World Bank notes:

> The division heads of the (local) public administration still maintain the same relationships with their supervisors in Kinshasa as the ones they had before the provinces were introduced and therefore neglect to develop ties with the supervisory minister at the provincial level.[13]

The 2008 organic laws also contradict other laws relating to state operations, such as the one concerning the establishment of a tax system that does not recognise either the provinces or their governors. Decentralisation actors are therefore working in a legal muddle; they are always on shaky ground, and everything is open to interpretation.

The confusion is compounded by the hybrid status of local civil servants. Indeed, the provinces and DTEs are mainly made up of deconcentrated personnel. Lacking resources, they resort to using staff from provincial or local extensions of national ministries,[14] resulting in the creation of largely semi-legal, ad hoc administrative frameworks developed through adaptation and improvisation. This suits the national government, which tends to use the DTEs to "discharge" inflated staff, making "decentralisation look like a dumping ground".[15] In the commune of Lemba in Kinshasa, for instance, there are about 600 civil servants of the central government, comprising approximately 80 percent of commune personnel.[16] In the commune of Kimbanseke, based on the figures provided by the *bourgmestre*, local personnel account for fewer than 200 of the commune's 700 state agents, along with around 500 police officers for this poor, densely populated commune where the government fears that violence will erupt.[17] In Bas-Congo, the territory of Mbanza-Ngungu and its seven sectors also have about 700 civil servants, a "large majority" of whom are deconcentrated.[18] Boko, one of the seven sectors, has 40 deconcentrated and 18 local agents.[19] As for the provincial administration of Kinshasa, it has 6,080 deconcentrated agents and 1,682 "new units" hired directly by the province.[20]

The preponderance of central government agents in decentralised entities is not unique to Congo. It is especially confusing in this case, however, where it is intensified by the ambiguous status and remuneration of these civil servants. Most of the deconcentrated agents are "registered" or "mechanised", to borrow the Congolese expressions. In other words, they are officially employed by the state, which is responsible for paying their salaries. That does not mean much, however, as the base salary of Congolese civil servants is very low (5–10 percent of their actual salary); it is increased by adding multiple bonuses and other forms of compensation known as *primes* (allowances).[21] When the central government "discharges" personnel to the provinces and DTEs, it also transfers the responsibility for paying their allowances and operating expenses. Though salaries and allowances are not always paid on time at the national level either, this transfer increases the agents' precarious condition and makes their compensation even more uncertain.

Many civil servants are not yet (or no longer) registered. This is true of most agents directly recruited by the provinces and DTEs. In the hope of achieving greater job security, these agents spend much of their time applying for registration by the central administration. Few applications are success-ful, given the constraints imposed on public employment by the country's financial partners. These civil servants are thus left with no clear-cut status and receive only the allowances that the local authorities can grant them. They are by no means the only ones in this situation. As allowances make up most of their income, many agents of the state avoid retirement because pen-sions are based solely on one's official salary. Moreover, during the past two decades, in the regions outside state control at one time or another, "new units" have been regularly hired in the local branches of the administration without the approval of the central government. In Orientale Province, for example, 48 percent of the public administration is made up of "non-mech-anised" new units.[22] When the new units are combined with non-retirees, up to 60 percent of state agents in some provinces are "non-registered".[23] As a result, all these agents, together with the administrations for which they work, operate in an extremely precarious, uncertain atmosphere in which a great deal of energy is expended trying to resolve personnel and remunera-tion issues.

Finally, Congolese decentralisation has also led to institutional prolifera-tion, raising doubts about the force of rules and the legality of decisions.[24] Decentralisation inherently generates a multiplication of institutions. It gives rise to a new ministry and decentralisation support units in other ministries such as the Ministry of Planning and Development and a sizeable number of projects with development partners. It also leads to the formation of new assemblies with legislative powers and new executives in each province. Moreover, although the constitutionally mandated councils and executive colleges of the DTEs have not yet been set up, their formal legal autonomy already represents a diffraction of the state.

Beyond this multiplication of the state, there is further semi-official in-stitutional pluralism stemming from the problems linked to implementing decentralisation. For example, in the context of the 40 percent retrocession of national revenues to the provinces and DTEs, the question soon arose as to the meaning of "national resources" and how they could be fairly allocated to each province. The government was taking advantage of these uncertain-ties to limit its retrocession, but the new governors succeeded in convening a National Forum on Decentralisation in 2007. The forum brought together 300 delegates representing the central government, the National Assembly, the Senate, provincial assemblies, provincial governments, civil society, traditional leaders and technical and financial partners. Numerous inter-ministerial preparatory commissions, technical working groups, provincial workshops and "coordinating interfaces" between ministries were organised.[25]

The Forum adopted a "solidarity formula" that divided national resources into different categories according to their origin and territoriality, each with a different retrocession rate.[26] The government agreed to apply this formula in the 2008 budget, but this promise ran counter to its 2006 commitment to the IMF to implement "corrective measures" that excluded retrocession of certain revenues included in the Forum plan.[27] It also contravened a 2007 "governance contract" limiting transfers to the provinces on the pretext that they lacked adequate budgetary capacity.[28] In the end, the 2008 transfers were well below the amounts agreed by the Forum, and in 2009 the government returned to its own "arbitrary" criteria.[29] The outcome of the Forum illustrates the confusion surrounding the validity of public decisions ensuing from institutional multiplication. The fact that the government could ignore these decisions raised doubts about their legal value. In its actions or omissions, the government (and to a lesser extent local administrations) could therefore choose whether or not to take advantage of the constitution, current or previous laws, decrees, decisions by bodies such as the Forum and international commitments to financial partners, all of them largely contradictory.

The Forum, itself an institution with an ambiguous status, gave rise to others, including the National Council to Implement and Monitor the Decentralisation Process (CNMD), an inter-ministerial committee to manage, coordinate and monitor the CNMD and a technical unit to support decentralisation. Further bodies included the Council of Governors, a body set up in 2008 to "harmonise" the actions of the national government with those taken by the governors of the provinces;[30] the Association of Communes and Sectors provided for by the Ministry of Decentralisation in 2009;[31] the provincial technical units organised to support decentralisation; and provincial revenue-collection departments such as the Kinshasa Revenue Department or the Provincial Revenue Department of the Bas Congo that are in competition with the national bodies.

Sources of uncertainty

It should be noted that uncertainty is not specific to the decentralisation sector or even to Congo. Théodore Trefon has discussed the widespread tendency of Congolese state agents to instrumentalise uncertainty in order to maximise their power and autonomy.[32] Dominique Darbon and Ivan Crouzel invoke the tendency of African administrations to "accumulate strata", reflecting adaptation and negotiation by the state.[33] It is also true that the instability of the law is a condition naturally associated with the dynamics of decentralisation. Guy Braibant notes that during decentralisation reform in France in 1982:

> the number and length of the documents published in the Official Journal doubled at least [...]. Very often, the new documents did not replace the old ones but were added to them. This proliferation was accompanied by instability [...]. The documents were difficult to understand, sometimes contradictory and often ambiguous.[34]

That said, certain conditions in Congo have reinforced these tendencies and made it easier to turn uncertainty into a system. The first condition has been the government's determination to backtrack. Congolese decentralisation came out of the 2003–2006 post-conflict transition government, which included political figures committed to federalism, and was supervised by financial "partners" who preferred such a system. On the other hand, its implementation has depended on the regime of Joseph Kabila, which is more homogeneous, more emancipated from its partners and professes a distinctly more unitarist approach.[35] Thus, the government's failure to implement commitments was in all likelihood a foot-dragging strategy to slow down or avoid decentralisation,[36] and it has been part of a broader retreat from democracy that began as soon as the transition period was over.[37] The leadership's tendency to recentralise was partly due to their fear of renewed fragmentation of the country, which is barely reunited after years of war.[38] Moreover, the degree to which Congo's "partners" actually preferred decentralisation added to the confusion; they often lacked a common vision (the World Bank and the IMF were far less enthusiastic than certain bilateral partners), and some of their other objectives, such as rebuilding the state, might conflict with decentralisation.

Second, the weak administrative and synchronising capacity of Congo's state apparatus is patently obvious. Congolese public administration is chaotic at every level of the state. The government has a hard time designing and implementing public policies, and the quality of Congolese governance is widely considered one of the poorest in the world. In the "Worldwide Governance Indicators" project, the Congolese administration and public services received a score of -1.7 (on a scale of -2.5 to 2.5), nearly the lowest on the continent (just ahead of Somalia).[39] To a large extent, the incompetence and lack of coordination of government action is responsible for the confusion and gradual sedimentation of arrangements, rules and institutions that, in turn, clutter up the public space and scramble even more the signals needed to take rational collective or individual action.[40]

Third, although the state suffers from its own weaknesses, the surrounding confusion can sometimes prove useful as a method of political management. There are few incentives for the government to eliminate uncertainties that give it leverage over numerous actors it cannot control otherwise. Confusion has other advantages. First of all, it accelerates the deterioration or "decay" of political situations, thus giving the regime a chance to make a "clean sweep" from time to time, which accomplishes little but gives the impression of governing.[41] This accounts for the prime minister's suspension of provincial edicts and the clause authorising the removal of governors that was included in the constitutional revision. Institutional uncertainty also helps deprive local governance of its main prerogatives and representative functions and ultimately befits a desire to recentralise the government. By making the status and actions of decentralised actors precarious, it allows the government to maintain effective control in spite of its own weaknesses. This logic is not specific to Congo. As Papa Faye has shown, the decentralisation of forest resources in Senegal resulted in a similar profusion of institutions, generating confusion as to who was responsible for what. Central government bodies took advantage of the situation by reigning in the prerogatives of the rural councils in favour of those representing national priorities.[42]

Finally, confusion facilitates state impunity by depriving citizens of any clear legal redress. Decentralisation enables the central government to redirect popular discontent towards new targets. Ernest Harsch points out that the urban demonstrations following decentralisation in Burkina Faso were targeted at communes more than at the national government.[43] But if the communes can claim they lack resources and power, they are exonerated, leaving citizens with nowhere to turn, as no one can be held accountable. J.

Tyler Dickovick and Rachel Beatty Riedl note that even when decentralisation is successful in Africa, "many devolved responsibilities have not been clearly assigned to the local administrations or they are inadequately funded", allowing the governments to create "an often intentional problem of responsibility".[44] Uncertainty is therefore not only a disorder afflicting governance in the Congo; it is also an intrinsic component of that governance.

Uncertainty's propensity to reproduce itself through adaptation deserves special attention. The social actors who have to cope with uncertainty seek to minimise the attendant material and political risks. In a weak institutional environment, negotiation and transaction are used to adapt and mitigate those risks. This corresponds to what Anastase Bilakila calls the "*coop*", identified as an individual survival strategy.[45] It is characterised by informal bargaining, trickery, negotiation and innovative survival solutions that require "wheeling and dealing". For Bilakila, the "*coop*" is an illustration of Congolese perseverance in the face of adversity. At the collective level, transactions are visible in the creation of new arenas, such as the 2007 Forum, or in commitments such as the 2007 "governance contract" or "letters of intent" to donors. Each group of social actors tries to limit the uncertainty it faces, in other words, to clarify and stabilise the parameters of its action, but this local management of uncertainty generates negative externalities. In the end, it multiplies the causes of collective uncertainty by producing more institutional and regulatory layers that are equally ambiguous, because they are developed outside the institutions and laws of the state. Uncertainty reproduces itself by shifting the focus to questions about the validity of arrangements and the equivalency of rules. The regulation of political and social relationships gives rise to uncontrolled institutional sedimentation that generalises the system of uncertainty. The actors devote a great deal of their time to devising institutional solutions to existing blockages, but those solutions end up fostering a system of inertia through confusion.

Precariousness

Uncertainty plays a role in shaping Congolese governance first by engendering material precariousness within local administrations. Wherever decentralisation reforms have been introduced in Africa, local authorities are financed primarily through a system of intergovernmental transfers to compensate for an insufficient local tax base.[46] The low rate of retrocession in

Congo means the provinces are unable to assume their new areas of responsibility. They react in part by frequently failing to make the required transfers to the DTEs and appropriating the latter's tax revenues for themselves, leading to situations of financial distress at the local level. In the commune of Lemba (250,000 inhabitants) in Kinshasa, the total amount of transfers from the province was 55 million Congolese francs (about EUR 45,000) in 2009, compared with the budgeted amount of 1 billion (a realisation rate of 0.55 percent). In 2010, the commune of Kimbanseke (1.4 million inhabitants) received only 9 million Congolese francs (about EUR 7,300), compared with a budgeted amount of 6 billion (a realisation rate of 0.15%). In Mbanza-Ngungu in Bas-Congo, the territory is supposed to receive 1.5 million per month from the province, but in May 2011, the total amount paid by the latter was only equivalent to the month of January.[47] As a result, DTE budgets are woefully inadequate. For the year 2008, the revenues of the 24 communes of Kinshasa ranged from EUR 11,000 (e.g. Kalamu, Matete) to EUR 67,000 per commune (e.g. Limete).[48] Lack of money is a real problem, but so is the unpredictability of its arrival: provincial transfers arrive out of the blue and cannot be budgeted. The provinces increasingly prefer to replace them by "gifts" granted "against retrocession" in the future.[49]

The provinces not only shirk their transfer obligations, but they also take advantage of the uncertainty to help themselves to the revenues collected by the DTEs. Whereas the Law of 2008 (Article 112) gives DTEs the right to levy numerous taxes, some provinces make use of their legislative autonomy to pass edicts contradicting the law and appropriating most of the taxes normally reserved for the DTEs.[50] The latter are left with nothing but daily "remunerative" taxes on market stands, the sale of civil registration documents, the celebration of marriages, the hiring of public venues for certain events and taxes that are harder to recover such as bicycle licences (relatively uncommon in Kinshasa) and taxes on wood-cutting or grazing animals (forcing the commune first to catch the animals and then wait for their owners to come and claim them), which at best bring in a few hundred euros a day.[51]

Autocentric, partial administrations

Theoretically, the meagre revenues left to DTEs are supposed to provide for the salaries of local agents, the allowances and operating expenses of all locally assigned civil servants (sometimes several hundred individuals) and DTE services and responsibilities. In reality, they cover only part of the salaries, allowances and expenses. In Lemba, around 40 percent of commune revenues go to pay the agents that collect market stand taxes, 20 percent go to local agents' transport expenses and the rest to various items such as meals, spare parts, postage and the per diems for security agents. The commune cannot provide public services or implement its areas of responsibility. In Kimbanseke, where the commune is responsible for paying the allowances and expenses of 500 police officers, covering the allowances alone exhausts local revenue. Whatever is left goes to transport expenses. In Mbanza-Ngungu, the salaries of non-mechanised employees, allowances and mission expenses account for 40 percent of the budget (out of EUR 30,000). In 2010, the rest was used to finance the construction of a new civil registration building and meeting hall (for hire from the territory) and office renovations.

Given the communes' broad areas of responsibility, there is a pronounced fiscal imbalance between their resources and their service obligations. This conflict is resolved in large part by not providing the services for which they are responsible (except for producing civil registration documents, which is remunerated). About 90 percent of the expenditure of the communes of Kinshasa go to operating expenses, 3 percent to social services and 6 percent to investments.[52] The only public investment made in Lemba was to install toilets next to the *bourgmestre*'s office. In Kimbanseke, the commune does not undertake any infrastructure projects and almost no sanitation works. The *bourgmestre* admits: "I didn't do anything. I didn't have the means [...]. All the money goes to paying allowances".[53] His interventions were limited to "one-off actions" typically carried out by foreign-based NGOs. In Mbanza-Ngungu, the small amount allocated to public investment pays for itself; constructing the civil registration building and the meeting hall (for hire) are investments that bring in territorial revenue.

The commune tax system is thus almost completely monopolised by its own reproduction. The state is self-serving as well as partial. The only services it offers are those that allow the providers to extract resources. Even in Katanga, which has a reputation of being more functional than other provinces, the World Bank notes: "Several public services are not available in many of the districts and territories. Many services that fail to generate revenue are deserted".[54]

The self-service state implies not only a limited array of activities but also the corruption of their very nature. Local agents, who receive little or no payment, perform their work in such a way as to pay themselves. They take advantage of grey areas to create zones of freedom or administrative autonomy where they can operate with few constraints and fend for themselves. Decoupled from the law, this autonomy manifests itself in a tendency to engage in parasitic and predatory practices. In Lemba, the financial reports from 2009 and 2011 show that a large percentage of the commune's revenue was used to finance tax collection; 30 percent of the revenue from stand taxes went to "the effort to collect" those taxes and 10 percent to "tax collector allowances". The *bourgmestre* of Kimbanseke acknowledges that the "lack of incentives" (i.e. resources) encourages the predatory actions of its agents. The head of Lemba's Cultural Promotion Fund (she herself is a deconcentrated agent) explains that "she goes into the field", sometimes with the help of the police, to tax people for the commune's (non-existent) cultural services.[55] As taxes in the Congo are not automatically paid by taxpayers but collected directly by local agents at the taxpayer's home or head office, the agent "goes into the neighbourhoods", armed with the legal document confirming the existence of a cultural services tax to obtain payment. Her visits result in disputes, absconding taxpayers or various negotiations. The fact remains that her department, like the others in Lemba, levies its own taxes, which is a full-time job.

Officially, local agent-collectors are entitled to 10 percent of the revenue they generate. If a tree is felled in the commune, they draw up a payment receipt for 10,000 francs and a tax receipt for 9,000. And in all likelihood, the collection of these taxes also entails additional payments that go unrecorded. The World Bank notes that "most of the new units are engaged in collecting tax revenues for the provinces and districts and their 'salaries' are based on the amount of revenue they generate",[56] highlighting the harassment and corruption that ensues from this process. As there are many local taxes (e.g. taxes on bicycles, homemade alcohol, transporting the dead, livestock, the sale of planters' identity documents, cooking oil production licences, etc.), local agents and their revenue demands on the local populations have become omnipresent.

The greater the vulnerability of the DTEs, the farther they must extend their reach. In fact, the decentralised authorities are forced to go out in person into the territories they administer and exercise their prerogatives simply to meet their own needs. Out of sheer necessity, the exercise of public authority and the practice of state power become virtual subsistence strategies. Thus, the very weakness of the state helps shapes its predatory nature and enables its decentralised reproduction through the chaotic process of sovereign revenue-sharing with local elites. It is worth pointing out here that this system does make it (barely) possible to feed many mouths. The cities, communes, territories and sectors employ as many as several hundred civil servants who depend on the regulatory and fiscal authority of the DTEs for their survival. This authority is multiplied all the way down to the most local level. In Kimbanseke, in addition to its own personnel, the commune's authority is relayed by 46 neighbourhood chiefs, 46 deputy neighbourhood chiefs, 46 neighbourhood secretaries, 46 "population officers" and 276 "census agents" (6 per neighbourhood), who operate along the same lines.[57]

A local state of oddity

Instead of the "local governance" called for by its promoters, Congolese de-centralisation encourages the predatory empowerment of local authorities and the formation of a sort of atypical state in which the force of the law is called into question. The state becomes diffracted rather than decentralised. Its absolutism, predatory practices and lack of effective administration at the local level mirror the image of the state at the national level. Decentralisation creates more sovereign units, both numerically and by transferring the state's legal personality, while uncertainty encourages their autonomy.

The local agents of the state set themselves up as predators living off local populations, but in the case of Congo, it does not imply the domina-tion of a hegemonic, monolithic state whose areas of responsibility are being cynically used by its agents. Rather, what we are witnessing is a decentralised system of domination based on the precarious situation of the dominating agents themselves. In the end, it is partly this precariousness that prevents them from performing other duties besides revenue extraction. The notion of "zones of uncertainty" developed by Michel Crozier and Erhard Friedberg is useful here. In every organisation, the power of a social actor "depends on the extent of the zone of uncertainty he can control as a result of his own unpredictability towards his partners".[58] Though the local actors are not the cause of the uncertainty that surrounds them in Congo, the uncertainty allows them to mitigate their precarious condition and protect themselves from the domination of the provinces and the central government.

In this way, DR Congo is rebuilding itself by universalising predatory practices. The "discharge" of civil servants to the local level represents a sort of social contract of indirect patronage. The central government puts its clients in the local state, where its own weakness allows them to produce a livelihood for themselves by preying on the local populations. It is only partially patronage in the traditional sense in which political leaders compensate their political allies by offering them positions of local authority, as has been the case in several decentralisation experiments in Africa.[59] In the case of Congo, being a member of the ruling political family is of minor importance. It is true that the *bourgmestres* and deputy *bourgmestres* of the communes of Kinshasa all belong to the Alliance for the Presidential Majority (AMP), whereas the city is primarily in the opposition, as the results of the 2011 presidential and legislative elections show. This means in part that positions of authority are given to political clients. However, it also means that the individuals who are chosen typically repay the leaders' investment by aligning themselves with the regime, if they were not previously members of a coalition party (which probably makes it easier to perform their duties and simplifies their relations with the state). Elsewhere in the country, the mayors and *bourgmestres*, appointed during the 2003–2006 transition, reflect the political pluralism of the transition institutions. Sector heads and territorial administrators are career civil servants, most of them from the Ministry of the Interior. They are government agents but not necessarily members of the ruling party. Indeed, some of them belong to different political families.

Hence, at a more fundamental level, it is a system of class- or even caste-based patronage between state agents. The clients are the civil servants, impoverished by two decades of crisis and war. Unable to provide for their families, no doubt partly due to the astounding amount of resources apparently being privately appropriated by the country's leadership, they are left to take care of themselves. The state is being rebuilt through its weakness. Unable to streamline or control its administration, the government capitalises on the existing uncertainty (which it helps to create) by delegating zones of autonomy to these civil servants and local elites. Hence, it is a limited form of patronage, in which the clients are left to their own devices.[60]

Congolese decentralisation has tended to consolidate the powers of a state undergoing reform rather than devolve its areas of responsibility and resources to territorial communities. It has helped to stabilise the regime by sacrificing the local governing agents' accountability to the local population. The state's administrative weakness is thus at the core of its failed decentralisation. It has contributed to confusion over rules and decisions, legal and institutional pluralism, the failure to complete reforms and the vulnerability of local actors. However, this weakness is not merely a matter of capacity, and its effects on the state are not neutral. It has allowed the regime to seize control of the state and of the decentralisation process. The regime has consolidated its power while engendering poor governance in an institutional environment that remains fragile.

This brings to mind the notion of "masquerade" used by Théodore Trefon to describe Congolese politics, according to which the country's rulers have willingly sought to mystify their international partners. Insofar as it pertains to decentralisation, however, it is doubtless more valid in fact than as a deliberate strategy.[61] Though the regime has resisted decentralisation, it is neither directly nor solely responsible for the hybrid, uncertain system that prevails today. As this article has shown, the current system is the combined result of a multitude of dynamics linked to the weakness of the state, which has nevertheless adapted to it quite well.

Endnotes

1   This article is an outgrowth of work undertaken when the author was a Fulbright scholar at the research laboratory *Les Afriques dans le monde* (LAM) in Bordeaux (2010–2011). The fieldwork was made possible by a grant from the Earhart Foundation (Michigan). The author wishes to thank LAM for its hospitality, the Fulbright and Earhart Foundations for their funding and Emmanuel Kasongo for his help, along with Michel Cahen, Dominique Darbon, Tom De Herdt, Mohamed Kanja Sesay, Denis Tull, the editors of *Politique africaine* and three anonymous reviewers for their comments and suggestions.

2   J. T. Dickovick and R. B. Riedl, *Comparative Assessment of Decentralization in Africa: Final Report and Summary of Findings*, Washington: USAID, 2010.

3   D. Olowu and J. Wunsch (eds.), "Local governance in Africa. The challenges of democratic decentralization', Boulder: Lynne Rienner, 2004; J. Ribot, "Democratic decentralization of natural resources. Institutional choice and discretionary power transfers in Sub-Saharan Africa", *Public Administration and Development,* vol. 23, no.

1, 2003, pp. 53–65; A. Agrawal and J. Ribot, "Accountability in decentralization. A framework with South Asian and West African Cases", *Journal of Developing Areas*, vol. 33, no. 4, 1999, pp. 473–502.

4   E. Kasongo, "La Gouvernance des entités territoriales décentralisées: défis et enjeux de la gestion des finances publiques communales à Kinshasa (2002–2008)", doctoral thesis in political and administrative sciences, Université de Kinshasa, 2009; World Bank, *République démocratique du Congo. Etude sur le découpage.* Joint study with the European Commission, Belgian Cooperation and the United Nations Development Programme, Washington, 2010.

5   World Bank, *République démocratique du Congo: étude sur le découpage....,* op. cit., p. 22; Democratic Republic of Congo, "Tableaux de synthèse. Projet du budget de l'État 2011. CDMT (indicative)", Kinshasa, Budget Ministry, September 2010.

6   K. Kaiser, "Decentralization in the Democratic Republic of Congo: Opportunities and risks", Atlanta: Andrew Young School of Policy Studies, Georgia State University, International Studies Program Working Paper 8–31 December 2008; interview with J. Mabi, World Bank, Kinshasa, November 2010. There has been a decline in retrocession despite the fact that the national budget increased in real terms by 15 percent in 2009, 89 percent in 2010 and 10 percent in 2011, partly due to commodity prices.

7   See J. Ribot, A. Agrawal and A. M. Larson, "Recentralizing while decentralizing. How national governments reappropriate forest resources", *World Development*, vol. 34, no. 11, 2006, p. 1864–1886.

8   J. T. Dickovick and R. B. Riedl, *Comparative Assessment...*, op. cit., p. 59.

9   M. Mamdani, *Citizen and Subject: Contemporary Africa and the Legacy of Late Colonialism*, Princeton: Princeton University Press, 1996; C. Ntampaka, *Introduction aux systèmes juridiques africains*, Namur: Presses universitaires de Namur, 2004.

10 D. Darbon, "La culture administrative en Afrique: La Construction historique des significations du phénomène bureaucratique", *Cadernos de Estudos Africanos*, no. 3, 2002, p. 65–92; G. Blundo and P.-Y. Le Meur (eds.), *The Governance of Daily Life in Africa*, Leiden, Brill, 2009.

11 M. Poncelet, G. André and T. De Herdt, "La survie de l'école primaire congolaise (RDC): héritage colonial, hybridité et résilience", *Autrepart*, no. 54, 2010, p. 23–42; J.-P. Olivier de Sardan, "Les huit modes de gouvernance locale en Afrique de l'Ouest", London: Programme "Afrique: pouvoir et politique", working paper no. 4, 2009.

12 Interview with J. Kilay, territory administrator, Mbanza-Ngungu, May 2011.

13 World Bank, *République démocratique du Congo: études ur le découpage...*, op. cit., p. 15.

14 Ibid., p. 47.

15 Interview with E. Kasongo, professor at the University of Kinshasa, November 2010.

16 Interview with D. Lubo, *bourgmestre* of Lemba, November 2010.

17 Interview with E. Gatembo nu-Kaké, *bourgmestre* of Kimbanseke, May 2011.

18 Interview with J. Kilay, territory administrator, Mbanza-Ngungu, May 2011.

19 Interview with K. Simba, secretary of the sector of Boko, May 2011.

20 Interview with O. Ndoko, chief of staff of the executive secretariat of the provincial cabinet of Kinshasa, May 2011.

21 K. Kaiser, "Decentralization in the Democratic Republic of Congo…", op. cit., p. 21. For example, *primes* are granted for travel expenses, advanced degrees, housing, etc.

22 Ibid., p. 48.

23 C. Millet and J. Nkongolo, *DRC Case Study for the Informal Development PartnersWorking Group on Decentralisation and Local Governance*, Washington: World Bank, 2010, p. 7.

24 A similar profusion was observed in the area of national education. Cf. G. André, T. De Herdt et al., "L'école primaire congolaise entre héritage, hybridité et résilience", in T. De Herdt (ed.), *À la recherche de l'État en République démocratique du Congo. Acteurs et enjeux d'une reconstruction post-conflit*, Paris: L'Harmattan, 2011, pp. 115–58.

25 Democratic Republic of Congo, "Cadre stratégique de mise en œuvre de la décentralisation (CSMOD)", réalisé avec l'appui du Pnud, Kinshasa, Ministry of Decentralisation and Territorial Management, 2009, p. 11–12.

26 Cf. World Bank, *République démocratique du Congo: étude sur le découpage…*, op. cit., p. 26.

27 D. Johnson, "R.D.C.: la décentralisation en danger?", Goma, Pole Institute, 2006, available at www.pole-institute.org.

28 D. Tull, "Troubled state-building in the Democratic Republic of Congo. The challenge from the margins", *Journal of Modern African Studies*, vol. 48, no. 4, 2010, p. 654.

29 World Bank, *République démocratique du Congo: étude sur le découpage…*, op. cit., p. 22.

30 By law, this body must meet at least twice a year; in fact, it has not met once since 2008.

31 République démocratique du Congo, Cadre stratégique…, op. cit., p. 39.

32 T. Trefon, "Administrative obstacles to reform in the Democratic Republic of Congo", *International Review of Administrative Sciences*, vol. 76, no. 4, 2010, p. 714.

33 D. Darbon and I. Crouzel, "Administrations publiques et politiques publiques des Afriques", in M. Gazibo and C. Thiriot (eds.), *Le Politique en Afrique: état des débats et pistes de recherche*, Paris, Karthala, 2009, p. 76.

34 G. Braibant, "Restaurer la stabilité de la règle de droit", in M. Crozier and S. Trosa (eds.), *La décentralisation: réforme de l'État*, Boulogne-Billancourt, Éditions Pouvoirs Locaux, 1992, pp. 152–3.

35 Laurent-Désiré Kabila was in power from 1997 until his assassination in January 2001. His son, Joseph, succeeded him and shared power with the opposition during the transition period from 2003 to 2006. Elected president in 2006 (and officially

re-elected in 2011), he has since governed on the basis of a vague coalition, at first called the "Alliance for the Presidential Majority" (AMP), and later "Presidential Majority" (MP), dominated by his party, the People's Party for Reconstruction and Democracy.

36 See J. Omasombo, "Décentralisation au Congo: L'Echec?", *La Libre Belgique*, 14 April 2010.

37 See T. Trefon, *Réforme au Congo (RDC). Attente et désillusion*, Tervuren/Paris, Mrac/ L'Harmattan, 2009; International Crisis Group, "Congo: A Stalled Democratic Agenda", *Africa Briefing*, no. 73, April 2010; "RDC: Joseph Kabila: Mobutu Light?", *Jeune Afrique*, 30 January–5 February 2010.

38 In this regard, see Kabila's remarks assimilating the centralisation-decentralisation dichotomy to the strong opposition in Congo between territorial integrity and separatism. The official condemnation of separatism suggests the central authorities' attitude towards decentralisation. See International Crisis Group, "Congo: A Stalled Democratic Agenda", op. cit., p. 14.

39 See www.govindicators.org, Based on a factorial analysis of several governance indicators, this index is standardised and normally distributed, i.e. it has an average value of 0 and its standard deviation a value of 1. Congo is thus 1.7 standard deviations below the global average.

40 The work of Inge Wagemaekers et al. and Marc Poncelet et al. also reveals the prevalence of a regime of uncertainty in the areas of land and education, respectively, whereas the multiple revisions and terminations of mining contracts suggest that this sector is not immune either. See I. Wagemaekers et al., "Lutte foncière dans la ville. Gouvernance de la terre agricole urbaine à Kinshasa et Kikwit", in T. De Herdt (ed.), *À la recherche de l'État en République démocratique du Congo...*, op. cit., pp. 73–113; M. Poncelet, G. André and T. De Herdt, "La survie de l'école primaire congolaise...", op. cit.

41 I wish to thank a participant in the LAM seminar for suggesting this hypothesis.

42 P. Faye, *Décentralisation, pluralisme institutionnel et démocratie locale: Etude de cas de la gestion du massif forestier Missirah/Kothiary (région de Tambacounda, Sénégal)*, Dakar: Codesria, 2005.

43 E. Harsch, "Urban Protest in Burkina Faso", *African Affairs*, 2009, vol. 108, no. 431, pp. 263–88.

44 J. T. Dickovick and R. B. Riedl, *Comparative Assessment...*, op. cit., p. 10 and p. 26.

45 A. N. Bilakila, "La 'coop' à Kinshasa: survie et marchandage", in T. Trefon (ed.), *Ordre et désordre à Kinshasa. Réponses populaires à la faillite de l'État*, Paris: L'Harmattan, 2004, pp. 33–46.

46 J. T. Dickovick and R. B. Riedl, *Comparative Assessment...*, op. cit., p. 24.

47 Interviews with the *bourgmestres* of Lemba and Kimbanseke and the territorial administrator of Mbanza-Ngungu, November 2010 and May 2011.

48 E. Kasongo, *La Gouvernance des entités territoriales décentralisées...*, op. cit.

49 Interview with the *bourgmestre* of Lemba, November 2010.

50 For example, City [Province] of Kinshasa, "Édit No. 0005/08 du 11 octobre 2008 relatif aux impôts, taxes et droits provinciaux et locaux dus à la ville de Kinshasa", *Journal officiel*, special issue, 25 October 2008.

51 Commune of Lemba, "Financial Report", 5 May 2011. Jules Kilay, territorial administrator of Mbanza-Ngungu (province of Bas Congo), tells a similar story.

52 E. Kasongo, *La Gouvernance des entités territoriales décentralisées...*, op. cit.

53 Interview with E. Gatembo nu-Kaké, *bourgmestre* de Kimbanseke, mai 2011.

54 World Bank, *République démocratique du Congo. Etude sur le découpage...*, op. cit., p. 53.

55 Group discussion with local civil servants, Lemba, May 2011.

56 World Bank, *République démocratique du Congo. Etude sur le découpage...*, op. cit., p. 49.

57 The commune has 30 official neighbourhoods and 16 "new" neighbourhoods, which are also affected by uncertainty.

58 M. Crozier and E. Friedberg, *L'Acteur et le système*, Paris: Seuil, 1977, p. 72. I would like to thank Dominique Darbon for suggesting the relevance of this notion.

59 J. T. Dickovick and R. B. Riedl, *Comparative Assessment...*, op. cit.; see also G. Lambright, *Decentralization in Uganda: Explaining Successes and Failures in Local Governance*, Boulder: L. Rienner, 2010, which links this type of patronage to poor local governance.

60 For example, although the *bourgmestre* of Kimbanseke belongs to the Unified Lumumbist Party (PALU), like the two prime ministers since 2006, he complains that his two visits to present his grievances at the prime minister's office yielded nothing.

61 T. Trefon, *Congo Masquerade: The Political Culture of Aid Inefficiency and Reform Failure*, London, Zed Books, 2011.

3

✳

Neoliberal Customs Reform, State Weaknesses and Legal Pluralism: The Case of the Single-Window System in Kasumbalesa, DR Congo

Jeroen Cuvelier
& Philémon Muamba Mumbunda

Introduction

November 11, 2011, was a day of celebration in Kasumbalesa, a Congolese border town located opposite the Zambian town of Chililabombwe, 85 kilometres from the provincial capital, Lubumbashi. On that day, a formal ceremony was held to inaugurate a new, ultra-modern customs complex that cost several million dollars and comprised, among other facilities, a large, four-storey building housing the main customs services, six entrance lanes, parking lots, a clinic, showers and toilets.[1] Several prominent figures had come to Kasumbalesa to attend the ceremony: Joseph Kabila, the president of the republic, as well as Moïse Katumbi Chapwe, governor of the province of Katanga, Albert Kasongo Mukonzo, director general of the Office Congolais de Contrôle (OCC) [Congolese Control Agency] and Gabriel Mwepu, deputy director of the Direction générale des Douanes et Accises (DGDA) [Directorate General of Customs and Excise].[2]

Clearly, Kabila's presence at the inauguration ceremony was hardly a coincidence. It signalled, first of all, the strategic importance of Kasumbalesa as the country's first land border crossing – second only to Kinshasa in traffic volume.[3] It also stemmed from the fact that the completion of the building project on the border between Congo and Zambia provided an excellent opportunity to demonstrate the goodwill of the Congolese government, often criticised by Western donors and Congolese civil society for its lack of dynamism in conducting political and administrative reform. When interviewed by *Digital Congo*, a privately-owned television station belonging to Kabila's sister, Governor Katumbi of Katanga said the projects carried out in Kasumbalesa should be considered proof of the effectiveness of the reconstruction policy initiated by the president: "All five projects are now under way in the Democratic Republic of Congo, especially in the province of Katanga".[4]

In his inaugural speech in 2006, President Kabila had indeed outlined five priority projects for the country's development in the areas of housing, job creation, water and energy, education and health, and infrastructure.[5] As Katrien Pype noted in her analysis of the propaganda of the Parti pour la Reconstruction et la Démocratie (PPRD) [Party for Reconstruction and Democracy][6], the campaign surrounding the five projects was primarily designed to show that the president and his team were capable of concrete achievements and ready to explain to Congolese taxpayers how their money was spent. Thus, it is not surprising that the team of Digital Congo journalists reporting on the inauguration of the new building were careful to show a large billboard with a picture of the president, along with the following slogan: "If you do not believe my words, at least believe my works". By referring to the biblical words of Jesus, Kabila's spin doctors were seeking to highlight the fact that the president was following the example of the Messiah in trying to convince unbelievers through concrete acts and results.

Yet, when we look at the track record of Joseph Kabila's twelve years in power, the indicators prove disappointing in almost every area. In 2011, Congo ranked last among the 187 countries in the Human Development Index drawn up by the United Nations Development Programme (UNDP). Life expectancy at birth in the former Belgian colony was 48.4 years, the average length of schooling 3.5 years and per capita gross national income USD280. Again according to the UNDP, 78 percent of the Congolese population complained about the quality of water;[7] their dissatisfaction was corroborated by a 2012 World Bank report stating that the Congolese economy loses USD208 million per year due to poor water purification.[8] Transparency International claims the Congolese government totally lacks transparency in its management of the national budget; it ranks Congo 160th among 176 countries perceived as least corrupt.[9] Should we then conclude that the inauguration ceremony of the new building in Kasumbalesa was pure show,[10] a masquerade in a bankrupt state? Not necessarily.

The customs world in Kasumbalesa: a semi-autonomous social field

While it is widely recognised that the Congolese state is very weak and bears virtually no resemblance to the Weberian ideal of the modern state, we think it would be an exaggeration to say it is moribund or on the verge of disappearing. As Fredrik Söderbaum points out,[11] many African states manage to survive through recognition of their sovereignty by the international community. According to this author, the strategic importance of sovereignty explains in turn why so many African policymakers are quick to support neoliberal regional initiatives such as the Southern African Development Community (SADC) and the Common Market for Eastern and Southern Africa (COMESA), despite their goal of reducing the role of the state in the economies of the region. Söderbaum believes African leaders are well aware that, by participating in such initiatives, they can present themselves as leaders of real, solid states, recognised and supported by the international community.[12]

Brenda Chalfin's research on customs reform in Ghana shows that Söderbaum is right in arguing that neoliberal projects do not necessarily lead to a weakening of African states. Chalfin found that, contrary to what one might think, the Ghanaian authorities were able to use the neoliberal reform program to strengthen the presence and influence of the state, especially at its borders. The Accra government took advantage of financial support from multinational companies to increase the efficiency of customs services through a whole range of technical innovations and thus strengthen its authority in the outlying areas of Ghanaian territory.[13]

Chalfin's analysis of the situation in Ghana provides a template for questioning the effects of neoliberal customs reform in Congo, which involved a two-pronged plan to create new infrastructures and introduce a "single-window" system. The idea behind this innovation was that automated import and export procedures would help increase the level of transparency, reduce the number of agents involved in customs clearance and, in the long run, substantially reduce fraud. However, despite the international community's attempt to interfere in the affairs of the Kasumbalesa customs world, the latter has not lost the ability to generate its own rules and enforce them. As a result, cross-border traffic still fails to comply fully with official legislation. The continuation of legal pluralism is the root cause of a wide range of informal arrangements between customs officials and users.

As in the Lake Chad Basin, where Janet Roitman conducted her investigations of cross-border trade, a "code of officialdom" and a "code of trafficking"[14] coexist in Kasumbalesa. This is why, in our analysis, we consider the Kasumbalesa customs world a "semi-autonomous social field", defined by Sally Falk Moore as:

> a small field that can be studied by an anthropologist, which has the ability to generate rules and customs and symbols internally, but which is also vulnerable to rules and decisions and other forces emanating from the larger world surrounding it. The semi-autonomous social field has rule-making capabilities and the means to induce or coerce compliance; but it is simultaneously set in a wider social matrix that can and does affect and invade it, sometimes at the invitation of persons inside the field, sometimes on its own initiative.[15]

Nevertheless, it is important not to overestimate the autonomy of the Kasumbalesa customs world as a social field nor to overstate the antagonism between the Kinshasa regime and the border town customs services. In a book focussing on the survival of the African state in the postcolonial era, Pierre Englebert has shown that, in many states considered weak or failed in Africa, regional elites prefer not to openly oppose the power of the central government. Instead of resisting or rebelling, these elites try to keep up good relations with certain key players in the central government. According to Englebert, this attitude stems from the fact that, even in a state on the verge of bankruptcy and with few remaining financial resources for the central government to distribute to its clients, it is always in the interests of regional elites to obtain and hold on to good positions within state institutions. They can use the authority deriving from such positions to dominate the local population and/or extract revenue, but they can gain access to such positions only with the support of policymakers at the national level.

In Congo, the Kinshasa government entrusts segments of state power to regional elites who can then access revenue directly and with considerable flexibility. They are thus free to invent their own rules and pursue their corrupt practices, despite attempts by donors to promote good governance in Congolese public institutions.[16] If the social field of the Kasumbalesa customs world enjoys a certain degree of autonomy, it is largely due to the prebendal politics introduced by the Kabila regime.[17]

We will begin the following discussion by explaining how and why the Congolese government introduced a single-window system as part of a neoliberal customs reform imposed by the international community. We will then show that the introduction of this new system has had four main consequences: increased competition between the different customs services for access to illicit revenue; the resurgence of a number of old corruption techniques that allow regional elites and customs officials to avoid certain restrictions imposed by the single-window system; stepped-up requests by state authorities and their clients for the services of non-governmental customs brokers to facilitate informal negotiations and fraud; and the emergence of a shadow organisation allowing the provincial authorities to raise tax revenues from cross-border trade outside the single-window system.

Introduction of the single-window system

According to Ibrahima Diagne, the concept of the single window can be defined as "a facility allowing the parties involved in trade and transport to submit standardised data and documents at a single entry point to complete all official formalities relating to import, export or transit."[18] Congo is not the only African country to have introduced a single-window system. Several countries in Africa have taken similar steps, encouraged or even compelled by the realities of economic globalisation and the requirements of donors and international institutions such as the World Trade Organisation, the World Customs Organisation, the World Bank and the United Nations.[19]

A 2009 World Bank report revealed that transport costs in Africa are the highest in the world.[20] The report observed that the problem stemmed from, among other things, extremely burdensome, slow and costly bureaucratic procedures that delayed carriers crossing international borders. The single-window system is an attempt to solve this problem. In Cameroon, for example, as Thomas Cantens has noted, there are several advantages in using

Sydonia, the software developed by the United Nations Conference on Trade and Development (UNCTAD) to help developing countries modernise their customs services and establish single-window systems. The program makes it possible to eliminate useless customs formalities, increase traffic flow, reduce costs and improve the transparency of the system.[21] Furthermore, Sydonia enables the production of harmonised statistics and facilitates the collection of custom duties by the state.[22]

In Congo, policymakers in Kinshasa and the provinces all have their own reasons for supporting the computerisation of customs clearance procedures, a key component of the programme for the reform and modernisation of Congolese customs launched in 2003 and funded by the International Monetary Fund and the World Bank as part of the effort to achieve economic stability and national reconstruction.[23] Under the terms of its collaboration with these financial institutions, the national government in Kinshasa was required to increase the country's revenue, improve public finance management and the business environment, combat fraud in the public sector and attract private investors.[24] For its part, the government of Katanga saw the measures announced in the context of customs reform as a first step towards greater financial autonomy for the provinces. The people of Katanga and policymakers at the provincial level eagerly awaited the beginning of the decentralisation process foreseen under the new constitution of 18 February 2006.[25]

Donors to the DRC have invested heavily in customs reform. In 2006, the European Union and the French government co-funded three pilot projects to reform the Office des Douanes et Accises (OFIDA) [Office of Customs and Excise], the main Congolese customs service, which operates in the port of Matadi in East Kinshasa and in Kasumbalesa. By financing the project in Kasumbalesa at an estimated cost of EUR2.5 million to 3 million, the donors sought to reorganise and streamline OFIDA's operations by providing new premises, equipment and computer hardware as well as technical and organisational assistance and capacity-building for customs personnel.[26]

On 10 May 2010, the minister of finance inaugurated the single-window system in Kasumbalesa.[27] Since then, the new software (called Sydonia ++) has enabled customs officials to communicate internally via email and exchange data on the quantity and nature of import-export goods. In theory, they need only rely on the data received electronically as well as the online version of the tariffs of duties and taxes to do their work.[28] The system is managed by the DGDA, which succeeded OFIDA.

Four consequences of the single-window system in Kasumbalesa

Kasumbalesa is one of the most strategic transit hubs between Central Africa and Southern Africa. The border town is the main gateway for all incoming goods intended for the provinces of Katanga and East and West Kasai and also serves as an exit point for outgoing Congolese products intended for Southern Africa and outside the continent. The Congolese government never misses an opportunity to emphasise that the introduction of the single-window system has boosted cross-border traffic and significantly increased customs revenue in Kasumbalesa. Whereas truck drivers once had to wait 4 to 7 days for permission to cross the border, the average waiting time today is reportedly 2 days.[29] According to Xavérine Karomba, Vice-Minister of Foreign trade in the national government between February 2010 and March 2012, the introduction of the single-window system has raised monthly customs revenues in Kasumbalesa from USD1.2m to USD32m.[30]

Growing competition between the various customs services

However, not everything is rosy in Kasumbalesa. During our fieldwork in Lubumbashi and Kasumbalesa in October 2011 and January 2012, we noted that some public officials had trouble accepting the single-window system. They saw it as a threat that challenged a whole set of practices specific to the "semi-autonomous field" of the Kasumbalesa customs world. Before customs reform, the work was done manually, and large numbers of agents were involved in processing customs data. Furthermore, each customs service enjoyed considerable freedom in doing its job and managing its own revenues. Customs reform, especially automated data processing, has significantly changed the relationship between the various customs services.

In particular, complications have arisen in the relationship between the Office Congolais de Contrôle (OCC) [Congolese Control Agency] and the Direction Générale des Douanes et Accises (DGDA) [Directorate General of Customs and Excise]. Both institutions were created in the 1970s under President Mobutu. The OCC, set up in January 1974, has always been responsible for monitoring the quantity, quality, compliance with legal requirements and prices of all consumer goods.[31] The DGDA, on the other hand, succeeded OFIDA, an institution founded in 1979 that had been in charge of collecting customs duty on all goods imported and exported by the DRC.[32] Distrust between the two institutions has grown significantly since the introduction of the single-window system, which is run by the DGDA. For example, when the DGDA began accusing OCC officers of fraud, the OCC responded by claiming the DGDA was undervaluing goods.[33]

The OCC found itself increasingly marginalised by the reform. It was not granted access to the Sydonia server[34] and was criticised by the Fédération des entreprises du Congo (FEC) [Congolese Business Federation] for imposing excessive duties on imported products.[35] Local OCC officials had to organise several meetings with their DGDA colleagues in an effort to preserve their organisation's legal prerogatives,[36] but, in May 2012, Albert Mukonzo Kasongo, the director general of the OCC, was forced to sign a memorandum of understanding recognising the supremacy of the DGDA. The text of the agreement stated, among other things, that the DGDA had a legal mandate to "collect, in the name and on behalf of the OCC, the OCC costs and related VAT due on the import or export of goods" (Article 1), that the costs related to joint inspections would be borne by the OCC (Article 8) and, finally, that the OCC should provide the equipment and funding needed to operate the agreement's monitoring committee (Article 9).[37] Thus, OCC lost the right to collect duty in its own name and was forced to bear all costs associated with the implementation of the memorandum of understanding.

The asymmetry in the balance of power between the DGDA and the OCC seems to be due, at least in part, to political relations at the national level. In an article on administrative reform in Congo, Theodore Trefon explains that the selection of candidates for managerial positions in public enterprises such as the DGDA and the OCC depends on actors at the top of the political pyramid, who make these appointments using the logic of paternalism and political patronage.[38] Given that the political elites protecting the interests of the DGDA at the national level seem to have more power and influence than those who defend the interests of the OCC, it is not surprising that the terms of the memorandum of understanding are to the advantage of the DGDA.

The shift in the balance of power between the DGDA and the OCC also seems to have affected their interactions with Bivac, a company with which the Congolese government signed an agreement in December 2005.[39]

Congo is among the developing countries that have adopted Pre-shipment Inspection Programmes (PSI) to minimise the risk of corruption and secure customs revenues.[40] Bivac International, a subsidiary of Bureau Veritas, is responsible for pre-shipment inspection of all goods to be imported into Congolese territory "whose FOB (Free on Board) value is equal to or greater than USD2,500".[41] In theory, the inspection reports drawn up by Bivac are supposed to limit the discretionary power of customs officials,[42] but, according to information obtained from sources at the OCC, the DGDA has developed strategies to generate illicit revenues. For example, it is said that some goods arrive in Congo without their Bivac certificate and that DGDA officials then negotiate with the importer by offering them an opportunity to avoid the penalties provided by law for failure to produce the certificate.[43]

G.K., a senior OCC official in Kasumbalesa, noted that his agency's revenues have dropped dramatically since the DGDA took over in Kasumbalesa. Furthermore, he complained about the permissive attitude of the DGDA agents who, according to him, often turn a blind eye to unacceptable practices:

> Nowadays, it's open warfare on a daily basis. Last Saturday, three trucks were stopped for lack of proper labelling. They were carrying large quantities of sugar packed in big bags, which were unmarked. Yet the DGDA decided to let the trucks go through because they were afraid of losing revenue. To combat fraud by DGDA agents, we have decided in some cases to open additional files.[44]

G.K.'s testimony suggests that OCC employees are defending themselves tooth and nail against DGDA domination. As they see it, the DGDA is taking advantage of its position as head of the single-window system to prevent other customs services from doing their job properly. Because the OCC has no faith in the neutrality of the DGDA, it has refused to accept the computerisation of all customs data and remains opposed to the concentration of payment and billing within a single-window system. In order to preserve some of their power, OCC agents have got into the habit of opening parallel files, which they manage manually: this allows them to impose informal taxes that do not appear in the Sydonia system. As for the importers, most of them prefer to keep quiet and pay whatever they are asked in order to avoid wasting time in discussions with OCC agents.

Recycling old corruption practices

Players in the Kasumbalesa customs world have resurrected a number of old corruption techniques to circumvent the restrictions of the single-window system. A good example of such techniques is the "laboratory", a term that emphasises the experimental, creative side of corruption, the art of concealment and deception. In the customs environment of Kasumbalesa, the word refers to the process of falsifying commercial documents submitted to customs in order to underestimate the value, change the tariff description and modify the origin of the goods.[45] Before customs data is entered into the computer, there is still plenty of room for negotiation, and falsified documents are difficult to detect. At first glance, they present all the characteristics of authentic documents, and the seals affixed in transit countries give them a high degree of credibility. Therefore, the only sure way to uncover document falsification is to physically check the goods. However, customs officials only stop those who do not comply with the rules established in this semi-autonomous field of customs in Kasumbalesa. If the trader has paid informal duty through its customs broker, the customs agent feels a moral obligation to sign the papers and let the goods go through.

Another example is the "invisibility" phenomenon. After lowering the value of the goods, the customs broker must "hand something over" to the customs official so that s/he will not "look" too closely. The amount used for the invisible transaction depends on the overall impression given by the agent, the goods to be cleared and the broker's connections within the customs services. The whole idea is that the money must not leave any traces, hence its "invisibility".[46] This operation requires that the broker be familiar with the customs environment and, in particular, friendly with the customs officials in order to keep the informal fee as low as possible.

Growing importance of mediation practices: The example of bilanga

A third effect of the introduction of the single-window system is the growing importance of brokering practices. As Nassirou Bako-Arifari has noted with regard to customs corruption in West Africa, customs officials often negotiate with users (importers/exporters) through intermediaries. In many border areas in Africa, customs brokers act as specialists in organizing fraudulent transactions such as the "invisibility' practice described above, thereby mitigating the risk for state officials and their clients. In exchange for a commission, these intermediaries are prepared to recover or give out cash bribes, intimidate those who refuse to follow the "rules" and impose informal taxes.[47] The introduction of the single-window system in Kasumbalesa has led to an increase in such mediation practices.

Bilanga is a Lingala word meaning "field". The term refers to any fraudulent activity that generates profits, just as an agricultural field produces food for its owner. Thus, when a bureaucrat cashes in on a special favour, s/he will refer to it as his/her *bilanga*.[48] In Kasumbalesa, the term refers to illicit cross-border trafficking. Since the Mobutu era, people have been moving goods across the borders without paying customs duty by using small bush paths a few kilometres from the Kasumbalesa border crossing. To avoid trouble, traffickers make arrangements with the various agencies responsible for security along the border.

Illegal cross-border trade is controlled fairly strictly by members of the Congolese national army, which shows once again that the social field of the Kasumbalesa customs world is not entirely autonomous. Indeed, it depends for its very existence on the tacit approval of certain strategic players in the Kabila regime. According to several sources in Kasumbalesa, certain members of the presidential family are involved in illicit cross-border trade between Zambia and Congo. One person who is often mentioned is Laurent-Désiré Kabila's elder sister Mama Kibawa, who died in September 2010. According to information we received, Mama Kibawa and her associates allegedly enjoyed distinct privileges, including not having to pay bribes either to Zambian or Congolese authorities. After the death of Mama Kibawa, her family is believed to have continued playing a leading role in the *bilanga*.

With regard to importing goods into Congo through the *bilanga*, it should be kept in mind that some trucks from Southern Africa do not cross the border; drivers prefer to avoid the official border crossing in Kasumbalesa because they know the modernisation of customs services has made it very difficult to avoid inspections. Instead, they stop on the Zambian side of the border, where their trucks are unloaded in a district dubbed the "Comesa" in reference to the regional organisation that promotes international trade in Southern and Eastern Africa. Before crossing the border, the products are stored in warehouses managed by Congolese entrepreneurs (who rent them from Zambian owners). There are about 100 such warehouses.

In most cases, the goods leaving "Comesa" are transported by bicycle, which makes it possible to cross the border more or less unnoticed, thereby avoiding formal procedures for the payment of duties and taxes on imports and the requirement to obtain permits for the import of food products. The cyclists, called *bakatako*, work in teams of 10–20. Each team member is paid according to the number of bags he carries. On average, a cyclist can carry fourteen to fifteen 25-kg bags per ride. Since the distance between the starting point – a warehouse in the "Comesa" district – and the end point – a parking lot in Kasumbalesa – is 4–5 kilometres, we estimate that each cyclist can make up to five rides a day, transporting a total of 75 bags. Normally, *bakatako* receive between 150 and 200 Congolese francs (EUR0.12 to 0.16) per bag. Another group of players, called "customs brokers", ensures that the cycling teams cross the border through negotiated arrangements with representatives of all state agencies. Truck drivers hand money over to them to "grease everyone's palm". Public service officials also use intermediaries. Known as *per civils* (civilian persons), their job is to stop traffickers and fine them between 2,000 and 5,000 Congolese francs (EUR1.65 to 4).

Truck drivers ("Canters") and taxi-bus drivers ("Dubai") who transport goods that entered via the bilanga need a document called the Déclaration Simplifiée à l'Importation (DSI) [Simplified Import Declaration] to travel from Kasumbalesa to Lubumbashi. This declaration is an official document obtained from customs agents in the new building in Kasumbalesa; it is indispensable for importing small quantities of goods such as sugar, oil, eggs, rice and cement. However, even truck drivers with a DSI are forced to pay bribes to DGDA and OCC officials, who have erected an illegal barrier nearby the village of Whisky.[49]

The informal arrangements of the *bilanga* are a good illustration of what Tobias Hagmann and Didier Péclard have called "negotiated statehood".[50] We are dealing here with government actors who continue to create and enforce their own rules at the local level despite attempts by the international community to take over their "semi-autonomous social field" through legislation and imposition of top-down customs reform such as the single-window system. What has changed since the reform is that the people involved in the *bilanga* have become more cautious. Almost all the players resort to the services of intermediaries; customs officials and the military use *per civils*, while truck drivers and *bakatako* use customs brokers. Another striking fact is the way formal and informal procedures are intertwined. Whereas the carriers of goods coming from the *bilanga* are careful to obtain a DSI document at the new customs building, DGDA and OCC agents have put up an illegal barrier to impose informal taxes on the same individuals.

Emergence of a shadow institution

The last effect of neoliberal customs reform in Kasumbalesa is the creation of an unofficial anti-fraud brigade. According to our sources, this brigade allows the provincial government to generate tax revenues from cross-border trade outside of the single-window system managed by the DGDA under the supervision of the Ministry of Finance. As we mentioned earlier, the provincial authorities of Katanga have been waiting a long time for the implementation of decentralisation, which would give them greater financial autonomy.[51]

The official anti-fraud brigade of Katanga is known as Cosefkat (Coordination de surveillance économique et financière) [Coordination for economic and financial surveillance]. It is supervised by Edmond Mbaz-A-Bang, Minister to Governor Moïse Katumbi. The brigade is coordinated by Gabin Tshinabu, son of a former player in Tout Puissant (TP) Mazembe, a football club headed by Katumbi. The governor set up Cosefkat in July 2007 with a mission to "detect and record violations of customs, mining, oil and immigration laws".[52] In its 2009 annual report, Cosefkat stated that its main priority was to fight "tax fraud in the form of document fraud committed by the members of the state-run financial system [...] who manage state revenue".[53] The official anti-fraud brigade thus appears to have been established to support the efforts of the Kinshasa government to clean up public finances. In 2007, Prime Minister Antoine Gizenga's team was under strong pressure from the International Monetary Fund and other international donors to put an end to dysfunction in the country's financial management.[54] Creating Cosefkat allowed Katumbi to demonstrate that he was serious about taking the national government's tax concerns into account.

However, according to several reliable sources in the business environment,[55] there is also an unofficial anti-fraud brigade operating in the shadows. It carries out searches of individuals and vehicles on the three main roads leading to the border between Congo and Zambia. This brigade is known to the general public as the "cent pour cent" [100 percent], a nickname reserved for fanatical supporters of the TP Mazembe football club. In

Lubumbashi, a taxi driver compared the unofficial anti-fraud brigade to the Jeunesse du Mouvement Populaire de la Révolution (JMPR) [Youth of the Popular Movement of the Revolution] in the Mobutu era, insofar as both consisted, for the most part, of unemployed youths mobilised by a strong-man to protect his interests and intimidate his opponents.[56] In the view of one member of Katangese civil society, the brigade occupies a position of considerable power:

> This service has more authority than any other state organisation [...]. It checks all customs documents (incoming and outgoing), that is to say, import and export. And if it finds an anomaly, it is fully empowered by the provincial authorities to seize and send the disputed goods to the governorate or wherever they please instead of the customs warehouses. No one else has the authority to release the goods aside from the provincial authority or its representative. [...] The organisation operates according to the specifications given by its founder. They obey their leader and no one else. Sometimes these youths take drugs and are called the leader's militia. They are the young people called the "cent pour cent" [...]. The provincial authorities send police forces to assist them in performing their duties. This gives them a great deal of power.[57]

Another source close to the Katangese political opposition gave a similar account:

> The offices of their chief leaders are housed in the provincial governorate of Katanga, along with the impounds for vehicles supposedly seized for customs fraud. This is also the place where the owners of seized goods are fined with no legal grounds or jurisdiction, and no human rights lawyers are allowed to enter the governorate offices to defend the rights of those accused of something. Sometimes the individuals concerned [...] give cash bribes even before they are brought to the impound at the provincial governorate; [...] [T]his money never reaches the state since it goes right into the pockets of these unsupervised individuals who are not registered as state officials. For instance, a businessman [...] had all five of his minibuses seized. Admittedly, they had illegally entered Congo via Kasenga and were headed towards Lubumbashi. The minibuses were sent to the provincial governorate where the owner was asked to pay fines and penalties of approximately USD100,000, whereas he would have paid only USD15,000 had the vehicles entered legally.[58]

It is not surprising that Katumbi is suspected of calling upon TP Mazembe supporters to staff the unofficial anti-fraud brigade. As Arnold Pannenborg has noted, the Governor of Katanga is part of a group of "Big Men" who understand that the presidency of a football club has several advantages. It helps them boost their popularity, find business opportunities and gain political influence.[59] After making his fortune in fishing, shipping and mining, Katumbi became president of TP Mazembe in 1998. He invested a great deal of his own money in the club, putting TP Mazembe in a position to achieve the greatest successes in its history. As one might expect, Katumbi's success in the world of sports had a very positive impact on his political career. For several years,[60] he was considered a close friend of President Kabila and a member of his famous "Katangese clan", a group of powerful men from the province where Kabila had grown up, who advised him in political and economic matters.

Katumbi's career confirms Englebert's theory about the ambivalent attitude of the regional elites *vis-à-vis* the central government. Even though the governor of Katanga may not always agree with the way Congo is run, he is careful not to openly oppose the Kinshasa regime; he knows that his support for Kabila gives him considerable freedom in managing his own province. Kinshasa deliberately overlooks the way Katumbi appears to use the unofficial anti-fraud brigade to keep a tight grip on cross-border trade and increase tax revenues for the province in an unorthodox manner.[61]

Conclusion

The purpose of this chapter was to analyze the implications of neoliberal customs reform in the border town of Kasumbalesa. We have used the concept of the "semi-autonomous social field" developed by Moore to examine how different groups of players within the customs world have tried to preserve some of their freedom to establish informal rules governing cross-border trade. All the same, it would be simplistic to present the implementation of customs reform in Kasumbalesa as a total failure. Although the introduction of the single-window system has not totally eradicated corruption in the border town, the modernisation of the border crossing has nevertheless helped to reinforce the fiscal capacity of the Congolese state. As Chalfin suggested in her study of customs reform in Ghana, African governments can intentionally exploit the international community's aversion to corruption, knowing that, in the current neoliberal climate, donors are likely to consider customs corruption as a technical problem that can be solved by technological intervention. Governments can therefore seek technical and financial support to bolster the state apparatus in borderlands that have previously been difficult to keep in line. The Kabila regime has perfectly understood the twofold advantage of international support for customs reform in Congo. Not only has this support strengthened state control over the rich province of Katanga, it has also created the impression that the government is prepared to comply with international standards of "good governance". Thus, Kinshasa has been able to continue its prebendal politics while leaving a certain amount of freedom to the players in the semi-autonomous social field of the Kasumbalesa customs world to (re)-organise their corrupt practices without worrying about the "terror of transparency"[62] imposed by the international community.

Endnotes

1   Daily news on *Digital Congo TV*, 11 November 2011.

2   "Inauguration of the new building of the border crossing in Kasumbalesa", information from the website of the Congolese Office of Control, <www.occ-rdc.cd/article702.html>, accessed on 5 December 2012.

3   M. Devey, "Katanga – Carnet de route: stratégique Kasumbalesa", *Jeune Afrique*, 30 May 2012.

4   Daily news on *Digital Congo TV*, 11 November 2011.

5   T. Vircoulon, "La Chine, nouvel acteur de la reconstruction congolaise", *Afrique Contemporaine*, vol. 3, no. 227, 2008, p.110.

6   K. Pype, "Political billboards as contact zones. Reflections on urban space, the visual and political affect in Kabila's Kinshasa", in R. Vokes (ed.), *Photography in Africa: Ethnographic Perspectives*, Suffolk: Boydell and Brewer, 2012, pp. 187–204.

7   DRC profile in 2011, established by UNDP, <http://hdrstats.undp.org/fr/pays/profils/COD.html>, accessed 6 December 2012.

8   Water and Sanitation Program of the World Bank, *Economic Impacts of Poor Sanitation in Africa*, <www.wsp.org/content/africa-economic-impacts-sanitation#DRC>, accessed 17 March 2013.

9   Information available on the website of Transparency International, <www.transparency.org/country #COD>, accessed 7 December 2012.

10   See T. Trefon, *Congo Masquerade: The Political Culture of Aid Inefficiency and Reform Failure*, London: Zed Books, 2011.

11   F. Söderbaum, "Modes of regional governance in Africa. Neoliberalism, sovereignty boosting, and shadow networks", *Global Governance*, vol. 10, no. 4, October–December 2004, pp. 419–36 (in particular p. 426).

12   Ibid., pp. 423–5.

13 B. Chalfin, *Neoliberal frontiers: An Ethnography of Sovereignty in West Africa*, Chicago: University of Chicago Press, 2010.

14 J. Roitman, *Fiscal Disobedience: An Anthropology of Economic Regulation in Central Africa*, Princeton: Princeton University Press, 2005, p. 188.

15 S.F. Moore, "Law and social change. The semi-autonomous social field as an appropriate subject of study", *Law & Society*, vol. 7, no. 1, 1972, p. 720.

16 P. Englebert, *Africa: Unity, Sovereignty and Sorrow*, Boulder, CO: Lynne Rienner, 2009 (in particular, Chapter 4).

17 See also *The State Versus the People: Governance, Mining and the Transitional Regime in the Democratic Republic of Congo*, Amsterdam: Netherlands Institute for Southern Africa and International Peace Information Service, 2006, pp. 59-65, <http://fataltransactions.org>; T. Trefon, "Public service provision in a failed state. Looking beyond predation in the Democratic Republic of Congo", *Review of African Political Economy*, No. 119, May 2009, pp. 9–21.

18 I. Diagne, *L'exemple du Sénégal: facilitation des échanges et coopération Sud Sud*, OECD, 2006, <www.oecd.org/dac/aft/37479766.pdf> , accessed 21 February 2013.

19 B. Chalfin, *Neoliberal Frontiers...*, op. cit.

20 S. Teravaninthorn and G. Raballand, *Transport Prices and Costs in Africa: A Review of the Main International Corridors*, Washington: World Bank, July 2008.

21 T. Cantens, "La réforme de la douane camerounaise à l'aide d'un logiciel des Nations unies ou l'appropriation d'un outil de finances publique", *Afrique contemporaine*, vol. 3–4, no. 223–4, 2007, p. 290.

22 F. Saudubray, "Les vertus de l'intégration régionale en Afrique", *Afrique contemporaine*, vol. 3, no. 227, 2008, p. 181.

23 "Inauguration du 'guichet unique' au port de Matadi. L'Adg Kasongo: "apprenons à faire la douane autrement", *Le Potentiel*, 1 July 2003. The decree on the establishment of the single-window system for import and export has been signed by the president on 30 December 2005, <www.leganet.cd>, accessed 22 February 2013.

24 T. Trefon, *Congo Masquerade...*, op. cit., p. 25; J. Tshibwabwa Kuditshini, "Global governance and local government in the Congo. The role of the IMF, World Bank, the multinationals and the political elites", *International Review of Administrative Sciences*, vol. 74, no. 2, June 2008, pp. 195–216.

25 Government of the DRC/World Bank, *Etude diagnostique sur l'intégration*, Government of the DRC/World Bank, July 2010, p. 39.

26 Global Witness, *Une corruption profonde: fraude, abus et exploitation dans les mines de cuivre et du cobalt du Katanga*, report, Global Witness Publishing, July 2006, p. 12 <http://www.global witness.org/sites/default/files/import/kat-doc-fr-lowres.pdf>.

27 "Inauguration guichet unique à Kasumbalesa" website of the government of the Katanga Province, 11 May 2010, <www.katanga.cd>, accessed 12 December 2012.

28 M. Mwamba, "Katanga: l'informatisation fait gagner du temps et de l'argent", *Syfia Grands Lacs*, 25 November 2011.

29 AECOM International Development, "Integrated border management (IBM). Border operations assessment", Kasumbalesa, report submitted to USAID/ Southern Africa, October 2011, p. 21.

30 Mr. Mwamba, "Katanga...", op. cit.

31 The OCC monitors not only imported and exported products but also those produced and consumed locally. See P. Englebert, *Africa...*, op. cit., pp. 69–70.

32 T. Trefon and B. Ngoy, *Parcours administratifs dans un État en faillite. Récits populaires de Lubumbashi (RDC)*, Paris: L'Harmattan, 2007, pp. 70–1.

33 "Kasumbalesa: guichet unique, l'OCC et la DGDA à couteaux tires", *Radio Okapi*, 22 August 2010.

34 Interview with OCC officials, Kasumbalesa, January 2012.

35 "Vent de panique dans le monde des affaires: la FEC à couteaux tirés avec l'OCC", *Le Potentiel*, 30 April 2010.

36 "Kasumbalesa: guichet unique...", op. cit.

37 Memorandum of understanding for cooperation as part of the single-window system for import and export, signed in Kinshasa, 16 May 2012, http://www.occ-rdc.cd/article822.html, accessed 17 March 2013.

38 T. Trefon, "Public service provision in a failed state: Looking beyond predation in the DRC", *Review of African Political Economy*, vol. 36, no. 119, 2009, p. 11. The DGDA reports to the Ministry of Finance, which was led between February 2010 and November 2011 by Matata Ponyo, the current prime minister and a member of President Kabila's Parti du Peuple pour la Reconstruction et le Développement (PPRD) [People's Party for Reconstruction and Development], as is his replacement, Deputy Finance Minister Patrice Kitebi. The Director General of the DGDA is Deo Rugwiza Magera, who was appointed to this position by the former RCD-Goma rebel movement during the transition period. The OCC, on the other hand, reports to the Ministry of Economy and Trade, currently headed by Jean-Paul Nemoyato Bagebole. Before the elections, the latter was a member of the Convention des Démocrates Chrétiens [Christian Democrats Convention], a political opposition party, but he was excluded from his political family after deciding to join the government of Matata Ponyo. The Acting Director General of the OCC is Albert Kasongo Mukonzo, whose reputation was tarnished in 2010 after he was charged with fraud. Suspended from his duties since 25 October 2010, he was rehabilitated on 2 February 2011.

39 "Signature d'un contrat de vérification avant embarquement des importations en RDC", Digitalcongo, 1 December 2005.

40 V. Dequiedt, A.-M. Geourjon and G. Rota-Graziosi, "Les Programmes de Vérification des Importations (PVI) à la lumière de la théorie de l'agence", *Afrique contemporaine*, vol. 2, no. 230, 2009, p. 152.

41 The contract signed in December 2005 provides that Bivac shall verify, on behalf of the OCC, the compliance of invoices and the quality of goods in accordance with the standards applicable in the DRC and the specifications submitted by the OCC. On behalf of the DGDA, the company must check the prices and quantities of goods. Information obtained from the OCC website, <www.occ-rdc.cd>, accessed on 12 December 2012.

42 V. Dequiedt, A.-M. Geourjon and G. Rota-Graziosi, "Les Programmes de Vérification…", op. cit., p. 152.

43 World Bank, *Étude diagnostique…*, op. cit., p. 69.

44 Interview with G.K., OCC agent, Kasumbalesa, 30 January 2012.

45 Interview with P. D., from Ogefrem (*Office de gestion du fret multimodal*), and F. L., from the DGDA, Lubumbashi, 10 September 2011.

46 Idem.

47 N. Bako-Arifari, "We don't eat the papers: Corruption in transport, customs and the civil forces", in G. Blundo and J.-P. Olivier de Sardan (eds.), *Everyday Corruption and the State: Citizens and Public Officials*, London: Zed Books, October 2006, pp. 183–5.

48 Interview by email with Georges Mulumbwa Mutambwa, linguist at the University of Lubumbashi, 14 June 2012.

49 Whisky is located 7 kilometres from the border. The village owes its name to the local production of *lutuku,* a native alcoholic drink made from fermented corn and cassava.

50 T. Hagmann and D. Péclard, "Negotiating statehood: Dynamics of power and domination in Africa", *Development and Change,* vol. 41, no. 4, July 2010, pp. 539–62.

51 M.-F. Cros, "La décentralisation en panne", *La Libre Belgique,* 19 March 2008; L. Essolomwa, "Décentralisation: le Katanga réclame une hausse de la rétrocession après le reprise minière", Radio Okapi, 27 April 2011.

52 Report of the Provincial Coordination of Economic and Financial Surveillance of Katanga, 9 February 2010, <www.katanga.cd>, accessed 14 February 2013.

53 Ibid. p. 2.

54 OECD and African Development Bank, *Perspectives économiques en Afrique* 2008, Paris: OECD, May 2008, p. 260.

55 Interviews with businessmen, Lubumbashi, January 2012.

56 Interview with a taxi driver, Lubumbashi, 2 February 2012.

57 Email from a member of Katangese civil society, received 18 January 2013.

58 Email from a source close to the Katangese political opposition, received on 16 February 2013.

59 A. Pannenborg, *Big Men Playing Football: Money, Politics and Foul Play in the African Game,* Leiden: African Studies Centre, vol. 43, 2010, pp. 1–14.

60 Since 2011, relations between Kabila and Katumbi have cooled a bit. See "War, Diamonds and Football: The Amazing Story of Congo's TP Mazembe", *CNN,* 21 December 2010.

61 We tried several times to contact the entourage of Moïse Katumbi by phone and email for his reaction to the evidence we had collected concerning the existence of the unofficial anti-fraud brigade. So far, we have had no reply [Authors' note].

62 B. Chalfin, *Neoliberal Frontiers…,* op. cit., p. 126.

4

✳

Outsourcing the State? Public Transport Reform in Dakar under President Abdoulaye Wade

Sidy Cissokho

Introduction

Following the changeover of political power in Senegal in 2000, public transport reform was introduced in the capital.[1] Planning for reform had begun in the 1990s with the support of the World Bank, which defined the overall direction and financing mechanisms. At the time, the city of Dakar was heralded as a "pilot city" in Africa.[2] The reform measures gave priority to "private" management of urban transport over the "public" management system in place until then. Yet an analysis solely in terms of "privatising" public action would not give us the full picture of the turmoil the reform generated in the sector. In Senegal, transport is dominated by so-called "informal" companies with close ties to the state, a situation that rules out any reform approach radically opposing the state. In this context, liberal reform does not always imply withdrawal of the state. On the contrary, it may give the state an opportunity to reaffirm or renegotiate the framework in which it intervenes. Contrary to the notion of privatisation, the notion of "discharge"[3] allows for mutual dependence between private and public actors. It points to the growing importance of private actors in state intervention but suggests that these changes should be analysed as a restructuring of public action rather than simply as the retreat of the state. Therefore, this article does not intend to examine the shift in the boundary line between public and private but rather the nature of the ongoing negotiations between the two sectors in a context of reform.

Motor parks [*gare routière*] in the Dakar region were the main sites of the government restructuring of transport services in Senegal. The relationship between the transport sector and the state originally grew out of management issues in these stations, so it was logical for the reforms to take place there. This relationship was forged primarily within and in reference to "unions" that grouped together all the drivers working out of the same station and that had long been responsible for station management in place of the municipal government. Implementing the reform in the motor parks meant "privatising" the management of these spaces, thereby calling into question the role of the unions. In addition, the parks were where the new vehicles required by the reform were installed. We will therefore base our analysis on the data collected in two of the so-called "urban" motor parks affected by the reform: Petersen and Colobane motor parks. The first is close to the city centre and serves the suburbs of Dakar. Opened in 1996, it was formed by combining three different stations previously separated from each other in the capital. Petersen was the first motor park in the capital to have its management privatised, and the first renewal of bus fleet took place on the lines served by this station. Colobane station also serves the Dakar suburbs. It is located along the National 1 highway at the entrance to the city. The privatisation of its management was announced in 2008. Part of the fleet operating out of Colobane also underwent vehicle renovation. For purposes of comparison, we will also include observations carried out at Pompiers station, the oldest and one of the main motor parks in Senegal. It takes its name from the site where it was set up in 1962, near a fire station [in French: *caserne de pompiers*]. Pompiers serves the other cities and the lower region of Senegal. It is described as an "intercity" motor park. At the time of writing, it has not yet been affected by the reforms, which so far have concerned only "urban" traffic.[4]

The data used in writing this article was collected during a two-month study conducted in March and April 2010.[5] Analysis of the interviews, observations and documents produced by the various entities managing the motor parks reveals the logic that helped to shape the successive state policies in the transport sector. After the regime change, state intervention through the reform promoted by the country's donors has merely recycled the logic introduced during the Socialist Party era. Accordingly, the affirmation of the state's authority has not been the result of its proactive intervention alone, but rather of a series of arrangements that suited its interests and those of the various actors in the transport world. Transport reform has not questioned the role of the state but rather that of its representatives in the sector, in this case the drivers' unions.

The successive representatives of the state in the transport sector

Unlike peasant organisations during the liberalisation of Senegal's agricultural sector, the trade unions, formed first by hauliers and then by drivers, succeeded in becoming representatives of the state in the transport sector.[6] The reform of the transport sector ushered in by the World Bank in the early 2000s was merely an updated version of previous reforms carried out when the socialists were in power during the 1970s. Transport sector reform was one of the areas in which a socialist "hegemonic bloc" took hold in the first decade after decolonisation. Initially, it was set up for the benefit of hauliers and subsequently for drivers after the peaceful handover of political power from Senghor to Diouf. The reforms and the converging interests of the government and major hauliers and later drivers resulted in the creation of the unions. This is the structure inherited from the socialist era that post-changeover reform called into question.

The major hauliers

In the early years after decolonisation, Senegalese hauliers gradually ceased to be marginalised by transport initiatives promoted by foreigners. They continued to be marginalised by the state, however, until the "Senegalisation" of the economy began in the 1970s, when hauliers obtained government recognition.

Under colonial rule, intercity transport of goods and passengers was largely dominated by hauliers of Lebanese extraction. The *Régie du transport du gouvernement general* [General Government Transport Authority], which became the *Régie des transports du Mali* [Mali Transport Authority] in 1959 and then the *Régie des transports du Sénégal* [Senegal Transport Authority] in 1961, controlled urban transport. This public company was at first responsible for the transport of civil servants but eventually widened its scope of action to serve the entire population. In addition to public transport, there were also private *"cars rapides"* buses, first in Saint-Louis and then in Dakar, belonging to Senegalese operators, each of whom owned a fleet of a dozen vehicles. Although the novelty of the new *cars rapides* buses and the obsolescence of horse-drawn carriages worked to the advantage of such initiatives,[7] the economic policy pursued during the 1960s favoured the public transport network in the capital, whereas Lebanese hauliers maintained their dominant position in intercity transport throughout the country.

At the end of the 1960s, the regime of Léopold Sédar Senghor drew widespread criticism for its economic strategy of continuity with the colonial period. The opposition came in particular from Senegalese businessmen, among them the hauliers belonging to the *Union des groupements économiques sénégalais* [Union of Senegalese Economic Groupings] or UNIGES. They attacked Senghor for continuing the preferential treatment given to French economic interests over those of Senegalese entrepreneurs. After promoting the creation of a more moderate hauliers' trade union, the state finally managed to meet their demands.[8] The "Senegalisation" of the economy thus began in the early 1970s.

The state generated a new clientele for itself through financial institutions empowered to make loans – which were seldom repaid – to revitalise Senegalese business activities. Financing was made available in all sectors of the economy, including transport. Loans were granted mainly on the basis of the entrepreneurs' degree of proximity to the ruling power.[9] The new policy led to the gradual reintroduction of rapid coaches and their owners, who received de facto recognition from an inter-ministerial advisory board in 1973. These hauliers were incorporated into institutions such as the Transport Management Committee, responsible for jointly defining transport policy.[10] In 1976, they benefitted from a plan to revamp their fleet of vehicles and, in 1980, *l'opération maitrisards,* an internship scheme offered young graduates jobs in the transport field and provided an initial opportunity to streamline the sector.[11]

Some of the major hauliers combined their dominant economic positions with advantageous positions in religious and political spheres. The success of these businessmen earned them considerable status in the Mouride Brotherhood, even when they had no family ties with the *marabouts*.[12] On the political side, certain large hauliers such as Bamba Sourang and Lobatt Fall won seats in parliament. They became members of state bodies such as the Economic and Social Council. They were also awarded numerous public procurement contracts to transport civil servants.

The community of drivers

The transport world was gradually integrated into government networks through individuals belonging to the many "unions" and collective of drivers scattered throughout the country. In 1985, the *Fédération nationale des groupements de transporteurs du Sénégal* [National Federation of Senegalese Haulier Unions], the longstanding trade union of hauliers set up in 1963, was weakened by a split resulting in the creation of a second federation, the *Fédération nationale des transporteurs du Sénégal* [National Federation of Senegalese Hauliers]. In 1991, the hauliers were divided by a further split that produced a third trade union, the *Syndicat national des transporteurs et chauffeurs du Sénégal* [National Union of Senegalese Hauliers and Drivers].[13] During the same period, the drivers were increasingly challenging the legitimacy and ability of major hauliers to represent them. They decided to organise on their own within the country's various motor parks. President Abdou Diouf used these internal divisions to achieve his own political objective: to bring the drivers unions into the urban network of the Socialist Party.

At first, the splits between major organisations within the haulier confederation arose from the initial measures for the liberalisation of the sector; the debate was focused on how much tax they had to pay. But the large hauliers were also competing within the Socialist Party for seats in parliament or appointments in various administrative bodies. Cracks gradually appeared in trade union representation of the hauliers, weakening the overall ties between trade unionism and the ruling party.

The first versions of the structural adjustment plans in the transport sector modified the relationships between hauliers and drivers, thereby helping to generate opposition on the part of the drivers. In 1985, the longstanding practice of delivering licences according to itinerary was eliminated. In 1986, vehicle imports were liberalised. The number of hauliers grew and, with them, the number of drivers. The profiles of investors in the transport world diversified. During the 1990s, a growing percentage of hauliers had no experience as drivers, mechanics or apprentices. This "de-professionalisation" of the sector created turmoil in labour relations between drivers and hauliers. Drivers were no longer assured of fixed wages or compensation for travel expenses; instead they were regularly required to pay a flat fee to the haulier for the use of vehicles.[14] In this context, the drivers also accused the hauliers who represented them of thinking only about their own personal advantage and not "intervening" sufficiently on their behalf. Abdou Diouf sought to break up the partisan blocs established during the Senghor regime and used the drivers' demands for this purpose. In exchange, the drivers seized upon the president's ideas to create their own trade union representation. The alliances – religious, trade union and partisan – formed with the major hauliers on a national scale developed into local alliances within the motor parks.

Originally, the drivers' unions were *dahiras*, an urban version of *daaras*, the rural associations of Mourides. Drivers operating from the same park contributed to a *dahira* contingency fund. Even today, the unions are presented as social welfare organisations. They serve as channels to communicate instructions (*N'diguel*) from *marabouts*.[15] The unions therefore help to perpetuate the "Senegalese social contract".[16] They also oversee fundraising for the *marabouts*. Indeed, each *dahira* is required to make an annual offering to its *marabout*. The transport sector appears to have become a haven for the Mouride Brotherhood weakened by the agricultural crisis in the mid-1970s.

In the 1990s, this network of mutualist associations progressively integrated the Confédération Nationale des Travailleurs du Sénégal (CNTS) [National Confederation of Trade Unions of Senegal] through the leader of the transport branch's organization. The unionist used these associations as a resource both to gain support from the presidential party and to secure his own position within the confederation. As a counterpart, the associations used the Trade Union as an additional way to connect the presidential party.

In their dealings with the Dakar municipality, the "committees" or *dahiras* were called "management committees". Despite early decentralising measures, the municipality remained attached to the central government.[17] Relations with city authorities took the form of direct, personal relationships between the mayor and the most influential members of the unions. Thus, the Pompiers union obtained new lighting as well as a paved boarding area from the mayor.

The unions were therefore not unconsciously ruled out by the state and the municipality, nor were they a sign of a "failure" to manage public space on the part of the authorities. On the contrary, the unions emerged "from a functional collaboration that ensured the link between the state's role in controlling space and social groups using potential political ploys to achieve their ends".[18] In the transport sector, this special arrangement took concrete form in the unions. It is these structures that have been undermined by the recent transport reform.

Motor parks in the Socialist Party era

The drivers' unions are "twilight institutions".[19] Though private, they exercise state authority in the motor parks. They are incorporated into the municipal and national administrative network mainly through the practice of "brokering".[20] This set of daily interactions has been called into question by the reform. To describe day-to-day station management by driver unions, we have mainly used the example of Pompiers motor park today. As an "intercity" station, it has not yet been affected by the reforms mentioned above and thus reflects the "discharge" methods adopted at the end of the 1980s.[21]

The board and its "constituency"

The unions have a pyramid organisation with ordinary drivers at the bottom and a "board" at the top. Board members are the only ones with direct links to the *marabouts,* the trade union confederation and political parties. The method of union affiliation to the CNTS clearly illustrates these relationships. Only a handful of board members have a card proving their affiliation with the CNTS. In the case of a call for strike action, for example, the heads of the confederation telephone their representatives on the board, who in turn relay the instructions within the station. Each week, the union as a whole pays the CNTS a fee drawn from station operating revenues. The amount of the fee varies according to the number of drivers affiliated by the union to the CNTS.

The board president is elected at a general assembly. The other board members are appointed by the president or recommended by his circle. These positions are coveted because they carry both prestige and fixed wages. Appointments to the posts are made in keeping with "factionalist"[22] logic. The board members justify their positions on the basis of know-how, seniority or personal success, but this rhetoric partly conceals family or regional ties. At Pompiers park, the secretary general of the union justifies his position by his level of education. However, he is also the brother of a union member and had never worked in the transport sector prior to occupying this post.[23] The distribution of posts and aid thus leaves some station players on the sidelines, and those sidelined view the selective distribution system as a form of graft.

Indeed, the board members have resources at their disposal, which they distribute in the form of posts or material advantages to various groups that use the site. Motor parks comprise several sectors of activity. There are, of course, boarding platforms, divided up according to the types of vehicles present in the market, and areas set aside for mechanics, hawkers and cheap restaurants. Others are reserved for vendors with fixed locations. The clientele of the union and its board is made up of all these sectors, each one operating in a well-defined territory of the station.

The board takes part in appointing the personnel in charge of passenger boarding. The station areas assigned to boarding are divided into "lines". Each line corresponds to a destination and a type of vehicle. There is a "line chief" at the head of each line, along with his team of "coaxers" responsible for drumming up customers.[24] The line chiefs and the coaxers are usually former drivers. Coaxers are hired at the discretion of the line chief or board members, depending on the charisma of the line chief. The line chiefs, on the other hand, are elected. Only the coaxers and drivers working on the line are allowed to vote. Elections are overseen by the union and its secretary general.

The personnel in charge of boarding pay a percentage of their daily income to the union. The customer pays the coaxer the price of the ride. The line chief centralises the money before the bus leaves the station and pays out a specified portion to the driver and the other coaxers. The amounts vary from one line to the next. By the end of the day, each line has taken in a considerable amount of revenue, a percentage of which goes directly to the union. The union members present the contribution process as a system of sharing the risks incurred by the drivers and coaxers. The payment must be sufficient to cover expenses arising from unforeseeable events such as death or illness. This "withholding tax" is the union's chief source of revenue, which accounts for their fear of internal dissension or "tendencies". Allowing the lines and their personnel too much autonomy would limit union revenue.

Union rules therefore stipulate that "[a]ny member who seeks to break up the order and unity of the union shall be excluded".[25]

In addition to posts, the board assigns spaces inside the station. Alhough the situation is seldom acknowledged, it appears to be impossible to engage peacefully in commercial activity in the motor park without union authorisation. Any business activity undertaken without prior approval from the union runs the risk of having its storefront obstructed by vehicles. This applies not only to mechanics, shopkeepers and hawkers, but also to business activities without any connection to transport that simply have their premises located inside the station. To obtain a parking place at Pompiers station, for example, the manager of an insurance agency had to pay a tax to the union as well as to the coaxers working in the vicinity of the parking place. In addition, the agency occasionally lends its more spacious premises to the union for its meetings.

The board and administration

Everyday corruption, informal practices and privatised public services are different types of "arrangements" worked out between the board and the authorities. The daily management of the motor parks is based on such "arrangements". These interactions concern exclusively the board members, state representatives and municipal authorities.

The union and its board appear, first of all, to act as an interface between the police, the gendarmes and site users. At Pompiers, the police occupy the same premises as the board members, where they share the telephone and their archives. The location and sharing of offices belonging to the union is a corollary of the inadequate resources available to civil servants in the police force present on the site and corresponds to an evergetism practice. It enables the police to have premises inside the motor park and is a corruptive investment for board members. The union premises are divided into two parts separated by a half-closed curtain, which shows the police agent's desk but hides the bench on which drivers charged with violations are made to wait.[26] Police officers and board members spend their time in the same space and hence develop privileged relationships. They eat at the same place and joke together. The same police officers appear to work at the station for years. The proximity and longevity of these relationships lead to a sort of symbiosis between the police and board members. Behind this daily routine and harmony – whether sincere or feigned – administrative relationships become personalised, and a series of corruptive investments are made, resulting in the informal privatisation of public services.[27] This proximity takes concrete form particularly in the repression of traffic violations.

Roadside interaction between drivers and the police or gendarmes can lead to one of two types of monetary penalty. The police agent may impose a direct monetary penalty on the driver by making him pay a fine immediately. On the other hand, the police agent may impose an indirect monetary penalty on the driver by confiscating his driver's licence, which he can recover only by paying a fine at the police premises. The transactions involving direct monetary penalties take place on the road and often allow some leeway for traditional bribery practices. They do not require the intervention of the union. In the case of indirect penalties, the board, like its counterparts in Benin or Nigeria, plays a central role.[28] Only one or two board members – the representatives of the CNTS within the union – are authorised to deal with the police. Their membership in the confederation allows them to brandish the threat of a strike or the support of high-placed connections, putting them on equal footing in their dealings. The trade union representatives recover all the driving permits seized by the police from drivers using the motor park. The drivers involved then have to file past the desk of the union secretary general to recover their permits after handing out financial payment, which is intended to remunerate both the union's brokering activity and the police officers. This auxiliary function comes into play only on such occasions. It may also pertain to other types of certification such as "off-road" permits required to transport passengers on unpaved roads or extensions of certification in the event of temporary licence withdrawal. The unions are thus seamlessly inserted into "the chain of transport corruption".[29]

The partnership may go so far as to designate targets and point out violations to the police officer on duty in the motor park, whose manager can "take disciplinary action against coaxers and their roster supervisors[30] who owe him obedience";[31] he must also "ensure the smooth operation of the union".[32] Within the scope of his attributions, he therefore brings coaxers lacking union accreditation to the police for punishment. The secretary general of the union and the police officer assigned to station surveillance conduct joint rounds. Together, they settle parking and traffic problems around the station and combat "poaching", defined as boarding or disembarking customers outside the station walls. Poaching represents not only a financial loss for the union but it is interpreted first and foremost as an act of secession. The fight against poaching is therefore a union priority. The board assigns one of its members to work on this task full time. "Customer poaching" is subject to a fine that can range from 6,000 to 12,000 CFA francs for cars and 24,000 to 50,000 CFA francs for buses.[33] The amount of the fine depends on the driver's attitude towards the union in the past and at the time he commits the offence. A portion of the fine is systematically given to the police officer. On the other hand, the board member in charge of combating poaching may sometimes keep some of the payment for himself. Although the police are civil servants, they are so completely subordinated to the union that, in the eyes of some motor park workers, they are perceived as full-fledged union employees.

Taxation and rubbish disposal in the motor parks

Collecting taxes and site cleaning offer further opportunities for the union to "make deals" – not with the police but with various municipal departments. The collection of municipal taxes on vehicles entering the park seems to depend largely on the goodwill of the union, to such an extent that when both entities have tax collection systems on the same site, the union system takes precedence. Queries made to the municipal tax collector concerning station management are first referred to the union board. From the municipal tax collector's viewpoint, the union is the real manager of the station. Municipal tax collectors are located at the entrance to the station. Each vehicle pays 100 CFA francs (about 0.15 Euro) to the municipality in exchange for a ticket. The municipal tax collector's post is not readily identifiable as such; it takes the form of a curtain hung at the motor park entry. The person collecting the tax is usually surrounded by two or three other people. The "auxiliaries"[34] are there to ensure the safety of the tax collector, who is at the mercy of all sorts of aggressors. The outward appearance of the municipal tax collection post contrasts sharply with that of the union office, a permanent construction in the centre of the station where the union collects its own taxes. Upon arrival, each driver has to go to the union office and pay 50 CFA francs (about 0.07 Euro) to the secretary general. Unlike in cities such as Abidjan, Accra, Ibadan, or Lagos, municipal tax collection in Dakar is not entirely delegated to the union. The two collection systems operate side by side on the same site.

In addition to the authorisation to collect taxes on motor park premises in the strict sense, taxes may also be collected outside the station walls. Many unofficial bus motor parks have sprung up throughout Dakar. These stations are set up by drivers and hauliers who object to the way departures are organised at the official motor park and seek to circumvent the unions' management systems. At the official parks, buses are forced to wait their turn – sometimes for several days – before they are allowed to leave. To avoid waiting, drivers board passengers at other sites. These stations are not recognised by the state, but their activities are nevertheless taxed by the union. Board members travel around Dakar and take a percentage of the revenue generated by these initiatives. The union even has a vehicle for this purpose. To enforce the tax, board members sometimes call upon professional wrestlers.

The union is also an indispensable contact in site cleaning operations. Although municipal authorities, particularly the Urban Development Department, send contract employees to collect rubbish, any large-scale action apparently involves the union. Motor park sites are regularly criticised for their squalor. Lack of space and cluttered conditions might lead drivers to avoid certain motor parks, resulting in revenue losses for the union. The union therefore negotiates with the municipality. It prevents municipal agents from collecting taxes if rubbish has not been collected, thereby depriving the municipal authorities of a steady source of income. To continue collecting taxes, the municipality is thus forced to undertake cleaning and waste disposal. The work is carried out by intermediaries of the union, which receives a certain sum of money for this purpose from the municipality. The union also has its own cleaning staff that sweep the litter to the exit where it is picked up by the rubbish collection company. When the rubbish concerns retail spaces inside the station, the delegation of authority may take yet another form in which the union once again plays a central role. The union members encourage food stalls for cleaning their own portion of sites, and the food stall owners may in turn delegate the task to a young *talibé* [child beggar].

The union is an indispensable entity in the areas of security, rubbish disposal and tax collection. Through its board, it operates as a real brokers' association. By introducing new institutions, transport reform called into question the role of institutional creation during the socialist era, but what the reform questioned was more than a mere institution; it was a whole set of daily interactions that have helped to shape the standards for public action in the transport sector.

Motor park reforms in the PDS era

At the turn of the twenty-first century, the reform of transport services in the Senegalese capital was more intense than the earlier reforms implemented under the structural adjustment programmes launched by Abdou Diouf in the early 1990s. President Abdoulaye Wade clearly took possession of transport reform, making it the symbol of his policy of change. He explicitly declared his intention on the front page of the pro-government newspaper *Le Soleil*: "I want to revolutionise urban transport".[35] The new president even announced: "We are going to buy back *cars rapides* to house fish and shrimp".[36] Though the idea to renew the bus fleet were designed and financed by the World Bank, they were taken over by the Senegalese state and various economic actors in the transport sector. The reform was introduced at the expense of the unions despite their support for the *Parti démocratique sénégalais* or PDS [Senegalese Democratic Party]. The contracts awarded at the time of motor park privatisation and vehicle fleet renovation gave the PDS government an opportunity to build itself a new network in the transport sector. The reform allows a kind of "spoils system[37]" or, in other words, the possibility of changing the "discharge" contractor. Proactive intervention by the state is possible only because it coincides with "circumstantial opportunities"[38] for a series of economic players. The reform serves the interests of a composite group that was previously kept out of the management of passenger boarding sites. In the various motor parks studied, which have undergone reform, union opposition to a change in "discharge" contractors has led to the coexistence of two modes of motor park management: a new mode resulting from liberalisation, headed by the hauliers through EIGs (economic interest groups), and the old mode, an outgrowth of the socialist era, embodied by union management of driver representatives.

Motor park privatisation

A new traffic plan for Dakar backed by the World Bank provided an opportunity for the government to privatize the management of motor parks in the municipality. The Senegalese Ministry of Finance decided to award car park management to private operators. Reassigning the sites was viewed as a possible solution to traffic congestion in the centre of the capital in the late 1990s. Through an opaque bidding process, newcomers succeeded in rising to positions of motor park leadership. Those who played the role of experts in preparing the call for tenders won the contracts.[39]

The municipality of Dakar issued the call for tenders. The high rates charged for parking in Dakar-Plateau were to accompany the installation of a hub allowing vehicles to park at the entrance to the city and use a shuttle service to the city centre. A private company known as *Société africaine de gestion des espaces de stationnement* or SAGES [African car park management company], already in charge of parking in Dakar-Plateau, took over the management of Petersen motor park. At the time, the company was made up of former members of the ruling Socialist Party's inner circle who had remained in government after the regime change. Some of them also worked as consultants in preparing the call for tenders. Petersen established a precedent for extending privatisation to other motor park like Colobane. In the latter case, station management was awarded to a private operator via a much less sophisticated bogus public procurement process. A simple "mutual agreement" between the municipality and the contract winner allowed the latter to claim the authority to manage the motor park. The governor, as the direct representative of the government, played the role of arbiter in settling conflicts between various claimants. He decided against the union.

The drivers' unions at both motor parks have systematically opposed privatisation. They mobilised station workers, claiming to act on their behalf, and succeeded in forcing the withdrawal of the designated takeover entities. In the case of Petersen station, the entity was SAGES and, in the case of Colobane, an individual entrepreneur. In the Petersen case, the union has managed to bypass the authority of SAGES. Tensions surface regularly between the union and the company in situations such as the payment of rent or collecting taxes on vehicles that use the station. The union refuses to allow a SAGES employee to collect taxes directly from drivers, so a union employee performs the task. The SAGES employee in charge of collecting taxes from drivers arriving and leaving the station can do so only indirectly through the union. This system allows the union to combine the tax collected in the name of SAGES with several other taxes intended for the CNTS, to which the union is attached, and for itself. The union collects the taxes and distributes locations to retail outlets operating outside the buildings put up during station renovation. A henchman has been mandated by the union to collect a tax from hawkers. To sell wares inside the station, vendors have to buy a ticket with the words "Motor park Management Committee" printed on it. The presence of these words creates confusion in the minds of many vendors who think they are paying a tax to the municipality. SAGES is thus caught between the union and city hall. Indeed, the mayor has challenged the legitimacy of the new management company, accusing it of failing to meet the lease contract specifications, notably with regard to site upkeep. The municipal employees normally in charge of upkeep sometimes seem to be adrift in the station. Some have been reduced to begging from shopkeepers, while others combine their official job with informal hawking inside the station. SAGES appears to be focused on its most remunerative activity – managing parking metres in the city centre – instead of investing in the motor park. Consequently, the company and its employees lack sufficient legitimacy in the eyes of both the municipality and users to collect taxes inside the station without going through the union.

In the case of Colobane motor park, the union president relied on his networks in the administration and the Mouride Brotherhood to cancel the public procurement procedure, which took place in 2008. After losing an initial call for tenders, the union was ejected from the installations built during station renovation. The union members then built their own installations next to the new ones, which were kept under lock and key. Subsequently, the president of the union denounced the terms of the call for tenders to the public contracts commission. Faced with what he saw as a "political scheme", the union president appealed in particular to a former Socialist Party Minister of Transport who sat on the commission. He also called upon a *marabout* in the Mouride Brotherhood to advocate on the union's behalf. A second call for tenders was issued; this time the union won and became the official manager of the bus motor park. Like the transport trade unions in Nigeria, the Colobane union played on its political and party relationships to maintain its control over the park.[40]

Renewal of the vehicle fleet

Fleet renewal fostered the arrival of new actors, some of whom had already been involved in the transport sector in the mid-1980s when the unions took control of the motor parks, while others had worked in different sectors until then. The renewal came in response to one of the main criticisms of transport in the capital: the outdated Mercedes buses that, in some cases, had been in use for more than thirty years. The state did not immediately find a partner to finance the reform in 1999, but, in 2002, the World Bank approved a loan of 11 billion CFA francs (about EUR 16.7 million) to revamp the bus fleet.[41] The financing was coupled with a requirement to "professionalise"[42] the sector. Indeed, the authorities intended to support the renewal by "formalising" the operation of transport vehicles.

The selection of the first hauliers to benefit from fleet renewal played a decisive role in the exclusion of the unions. To benefit from the hire-purchase financing mechanism and receive new vehicles, the hauliers had to group together. After rejecting the idea of a single federation of hauliers, they agreed to join together in an association, which was supposed to manage the financing agreements. The *Association de financement des transports urbains* (AFTU) [Urban transport financing association] acted as an intermediary between the owners and the state in the loan repayment process. The Association was a federation of fourteen EIGs comprising the various beneficiaries of the renewal. The AFTU president was once a haulier himself and a Lebou like the Minister of Transport at the time.[43] This shared experience made him a privileged contact person. One of the main managers of reform implementation was the neighbour of the president of one of the EIGs in the AFTU, also a former haulier. They played football together on weekends. More surprisingly, some members of the EIGs included in the AFTU were in the liberal professions or civil servants. In these specific instances, fleet renewal was not involved; the operation enabled individuals outside the transport world to invest in it. One of the first beneficiaries was the trade union leader of the CNTS-FC (*Confédération nationale des travailleurs sénégalais–Force du changement*) [National confederation of Senegalese workers–Force for change]. This confederation was the principal opponent of the Confédération Nationale des Travailleurs du Sénégal (CNTS), the longstanding ally of the Socialist Party prior to the regime change. The creation of the CNTS-FC was openly supported by the ruling presidential party.[44] Its creation in 2002 led to violent clashes with the unions, which had generally remained loyal to the CNTS. The confrontations took place in and around the motor parks and at the Labour Exchange, where the two opposing trade unions were forced to coexist.[45] The cause of the clashes was not directly political; after the regime change, the CNTS-affiliated unions also gave their support to the new ruling party. Their primary concern was control over the motor parks and the money generated from managing them.[46]

The changes brought about by the arrival of the new vehicle models allowed loan beneficiaries to impose their own personnel in the stations at the expense of the drivers' union members. Fearing violence would break out when the new buses arrived, the authorities reserved a special area for this personnel in the centre of the stations. The buses departed at fixed times instead of waiting until they were full. They no longer called upon coaxers to determine the order of arrivals and departures. Most coaxers saw themselves replaced by a "track chief" hired by the leaders of the EIGs. Changes in the structure of the new buses also affected the boarding process. For example, new vehicles no longer had a running board. Apprentices, who usually belonged to the driver's entourage, would perch on the running boards of the old vehicles. In the "modernised" transport operations, drivers were required to make specific stops and no longer needed apprentices to harangue potential passengers along the way or signal to the driver when he should stop. The apprentices were thus replaced by "ticket agents" recruited from outside the world of transport or by employees of the EIGs. The ticket agents sold tickets to passengers when they boarded the bus and stayed on board the vehicle, where a special seat was reserved for them.

The presence of these various employees at the motor park enabled certain EIGs to set up operations at the boarding sites. The EIG issued its own internal operating rules as well as those governing the motor park. Drivers – the rank and file of the unions and their main source of legitimacy – were no longer allowed to join CNTS-affiliated trade unions if they were employed by one of the EIGs of AFTU. The latter required their drivers to pay a tax at each departure and would "intervene" with the police on their behalf in the event of a problem related to "brokering" practices. These changes applied only in the areas reserved for new vehicles; the unions continued to control the rest of the stations.

Union opposition to attempts at integration

The unions denounced "unfair operating conditions and discrimination that are said to have accompanied the project from the start".[47] After initially opposing the creation of the AFTU, the unions tried to join the financing association: they too wanted to benefit from fleet renewal. However, they ran into opposition from the original members, who had de facto control over the AFTU and its various EIGs. The reversal of the union's position can be explained by the high profits to be derived from the project and the state's involvement in it.

The "new" vehicles of the "new" hauliers were far more profitable, because the hauliers controlled every aspect of the operation. The introduction of tickets made it possible to check the exact amount of revenue generated by the vehicles. Each haulier had to go in person to the AFTU offices to buy his tickets, and each batch of tickets was numbered, so that the haulier knew the number of tickets sold and, consequently, the amount due from the receiver. A different system was used in operating the old Mercedes vehicles. The apprentice controlled receipts during the journey and counted them up at the end, together with the driver. The driver had to pay an average of 15,000 CFA francs (about EUR 23) per day to the haulier, which a vehicle operating in the greater Dakar area could make in one return trip. The rest went to the driver and the apprentice. The new contractual relationship between drivers and hauliers, as well as between ticket sellers and hauliers, was equivalent to fixed wages. Haulier employees could no longer benefit from extra revenues, so drivers and receivers no longer had anything to gain by overloading or making erratic stops along the way to pick up every last passenger. Mechanical issues, sometimes a point of contention between drivers and hauliers, were no longer a problem either, as Tata vehicles were repaired at a directly affiliated garage (Senebus, the company that assembles buses in Senegal). Drivers and mechanics could no longer work out a deal to siphon off a margin from the repairs.

The most influential hauliers in the AFTU also promoted parallel initiatives. They founded a new mutual fund and a new savings institution. Every AFTU employee was required to contribute to these initiatives, which made it a profitable business. As a result, some AFTU hauliers were able to join with members of the government to invest in a taxi service. Given the multiplication of yellow taxis bearing the name of their company, it is safe to assume that the initiative has been highly profitable. State support and the involvement of certain members of government also seem to have motivated project participants. One of the beneficiaries of fleet renewal observed that "to have greater control, one should always be close to the manager. One should always be close to the President". This idea has been reinforced by the fact that the police check old vehicles more often than new ones. Similar reasoning has prompted the unions and their leaders to draw closer to the ruling party.[48]

This article does not claim to have explained every aspect of transport reform in Dakar, Senegal. We have not discussed, for example, the creation of the CETUD[49](*Comité exécutif des transports urbains dakarois*) [Executive committee of Dakar urban transport], which is also an important aspect of transport reform in the region. Our aim has been to illustrate the ongoing process through which relationships between the public and private sectors are formed, using the example of the implementation of two reform measures. So far, motor park privatisation and vehicle fleet renewal have left out the drivers' unions. The reform has called into question a whole series of daily interactions between the members of the "board", which exists for and through motor park management and the agents of the state and the municipality working at the boarding sites. It is not so much the state that has been called into question by the reform financed by the World Bank, but rather the role of union board members in the local and national administrative system. The Senegalese state has circumscribed their power by introducing new institutions. An analysis in terms of "discharge" offers a more detailed explanation of the renegotiations at work when the reform was introduced, revealing the bridges between the public and private sectors. It also emphasises the reform's logic of "diverting" and "cornering" revenues. Both the Senegalese state and the transport actors have invested and used the measures demanded by donors in accordance with their own reasoning. The success of the reform and the state's ability to keep representatives in the transport sector is the result of a combination of the will of the state and the successive interests of certain players in the sector.

Endnotes

1   In 2000, Senegal experienced its first changeover of political power after a forty-year socialist reign. The change brought Abdoulaye Wade to power for a period of twelve years.

2   X. Godard, "D comme Dakar, ou le bilan mitigé d'une ville-pilote", in X. Godard (ed.), *Les Transports et la ville en Afrique au sud du Sahara. Le Temps de la débrouille et du désordre inventif* Paris, Karthala/Inrets, 2002, pp. 57–73.

3   See the special issue under the direction of Béatrice Hibou on "L'État en voie de privatisation", *Politique africaine,* no. 73, March 1999; B. Hibou (ed.), *La Privatisation des États,* Paris, Karthala/Ceri, 1999.

4   The Pompiers motor park has since witnessed tremendous reforms, with the site moved to a new purpose-built location on the outskirts of the city.

5   S. Cissokho, *La Réforme d'un secteur informel: les transports à Dakar*, Master 2 thesis in African Studies, Université Paris I Panthéon-Sorbonne, 2010.

6   C. Vandermotten and C.O. Ba, "Les organisations de producteurs dans les politiques agricoles", in T. Dahou (ed.), *Libéralisation et politique agricole au Sénégal*, Paris, Crepos/Karthala/Enda Graf Diapol, 2008, pp. 25–47.

7   For further information on the transport sector in the capital during this period, see M. Coulibaly, *Les Transports urbains au Sénégal de 1945 à 1970: le cas de Dakar*, Master's thesis in history, Université Cheikh Anta Diop de Dakar, 1993.

8   J. Lombard and O. Ninot, "Impasses et défis dans le transport routier", in M.-C. Diop (ed.), *La Société sénégalaise entre le local et le global,* Paris, Karthala, 2002, pp. 109–62.

9   C. Boone, *Merchant Capital and the Roots of State Power in Senegal, 1930–1985*, Cambridge, Cambridge University Press, 1992, pp. 182–97.

10 Kenyan hauliers received similar recognition in the early 1970s after having been previously sidelined. See K. Mutongi, "Thugs or entrepreneurs? Perceptions of matutu operators in Nairobi, 1970 to the present", *Africa,* vol. 76, no. 4, 2006, pp. 549–68; F. Grignon, "Les pierrots du bidonville. Peintres de matatu à Nairobi, Kenya", *Autrepart,* no. 1, 1997, pp. 151–61.

11 For further details on these reforms, see I. Diouf, "C comme Car rapide ou les tentatives d'intégration du transport artisanal", in X. Godard (ed.), *Les Transports et la ville......,* op. cit., pp. 45–57.

12 We might mention the example of hauliers such as Lobatt Fall or Ndiaga Ndiaye (whose name was given to the famous vehicles). Both men became secretaries of prestigious *marabouts*.

13 J. Lombard and O. Ninot, "Impasses et défis......", op. cit.

14 M.-C. Diop et M. Diouf (eds.), *Le Sénégal sous Abdou Diouf: État et société*, Paris, Karthala, 1990, pp. 223–9.

15 *N'diguel* means "instruction" in Wolof. Like the English word "instruction", *n'diguel* can refer to different realities. Here we are talking specifically about political *n'diguel*, in other words, endorsements on which candidate(s) to vote for.

16 D.C. O'Brien, "Le Contrat social sénégalais à l'épreuve", *Politique africaine*, no. 45, March 1992, pp. 9–21.

17 M.-C. Diop and M. Diouf, "Enjeux et contraintes politiques de la gestion municipale au Sénégal", *Canadian Journal of African Studies*, vol. 26, no. 1, 1992, pp. 1–23.

18 G. Salem, "Crise urbaine et contrôle social à Pikine. Bornes-fontaines et clientélisme", *Politique africaine*, no. 45, October 1992, p. 31.

19 C. Lund, "Twilight Institution. Public Authority and Local Politics in Africa", *Development and Change,* vol. 37, no. 4, 2006, pp. 685–705.

20 G. Blundo, "Dealing with the Local State: The Informal Privatization of Street-Level Bureaucracies in Senegal", *Development and Change*, vol. 37, no. 4, 2006, pp. 799–819.

21 The project to move the station to Baux maraichers, a suburb of Dakar, and privatise its management, finally happened in 2014.

22 The notion of factionalism seems more appropriate than the notion of patronage to describe the internal operation of the unions. See T. Dahou, "Entre engagement et allégeance. Historicisation du politique au Sénégal", *Cahier d'études africaines*, no. 167, 2002, pp. 499–520.

23 The secretary general of the Pompiers union had previously worked at a market. In his view, "the same language" applies to markets and motor parks. This assertion and the ease with which the secretary general assumed his role suggest that a logic similar to the one existing in motor parks is at work in the organisation of markets. Source: Interview with the general secretary of the Pompiers union, Dakar, March 2010.

24 S. M. Seck, "Transport et territoires: les 'coxeurs' de Dakar, du bénévolat à la prestation de service", *Bulletin de la Société géographique de Liège*, no. 48, 2006, pp. 7–17.

25 Internal Union Rules, Dakar, 2010.

26 These offices were razed in 2011. The board members and police forces now cohabit in another space organised in a more rudimentary fashion.

27 J.-P. Olivier de Sardan and G. Blundo, "La corruption quotidienne en Afrique de l'Ouest", *Politique africaine*, no. 83, October 2001, pp. 8–37.

28 N. Bako-Arifari, "'Ce n'est pas les papiers qu'on mange!' La Corruption dans les transports, la douane et les corps de contrôle", in J.-P. Olivier de Sardan and G. Blundo (eds.), *État et corruption en Afrique. Une anthropologie comparative des relations entre fonctionnaires et usagers (Bénin, Niger, Sénégal)*, Paris: Apad/Karthala, 2007, pp. 179–225.

29 Ibid., p. 195.

30 A "roster" is equivalent to a "line" for a specific type of vehicle.

31 Internal Union Rules, Dakar, 2010.

32 Ibid.

33 CFA 6,000 correspond to slightly more than EUR 9; CFA 50,000 to more than EUR 75.

34 J.-P. Olivier de Sardan and G. Blundo, "La corruption quotidienne…", op. cit., p. 22.

35 I.K. Ndiaye, "Le Président Wade veut révolutionner le transport", *Le Soleil*, 6 September 2005.

36 Ibid.

37 F. Dreyfus, *L'invention de la bureaucratie*, Paris, La Découverte, 2000, p. 188–9. In the United States, during the second half of the nineteenth century, newly elected government systematically replaced the members of the previous administration with members of their own party to ensure their loyalty to the new administration. This operating method was called the "spoils system".

38 B. Hibou, *Anatomie politique de la domination*, Paris, La Découverte, 2011, p. 207.

39 See S. Bredeloup, S. Bertoncello and J. Lombard (eds.), *Abidjan, Dakar: des villes à vendre? La Privatisation "made in Africa" des services urbains*, Paris, L'Harmattan, 2008, p. 69.

40 See I.O. Albert, "Between the State and Transporter Unions: NURTW and the Politics of Managing Public Motor Parks in Ibadan and Lagos, Nigeria", in L. Fourchard (ed.), *Gouverner les villes d'Afrique. État, gouvernement local et acteurs privés*, Paris, Karthala, 2007, pp. 125–39.

41 "Renouvellement du parc des cars rapides, un crédit de 11 milliards de FCFA de la Banque mondiale", *L'Info*, 11 March 2002.

42 "CETUD rationalise l'exploitation des cars rapides", *L'Info*, 22 January 2002.

43 The Lebou people are historically the largest ethnic group in the Dakar region.

44 M.A. Yalli, "Congrès constitutif de la CNTS FC, le PDS dispose de sa centrale syndicale", *L'Info*, 14 January 2002.

45 O. Diouf, "Incident à la Bourse du Travail: le feu couvait depuis deux ans à la CNTS FC", *Le Soleil*, 22 March 2002.

46 The clashes were more explicitly political in nature in the cities of Ibadan and Lagos. See L. Fourchard, "Lagos, Koolhaas and Partisan Politics in Nigeria", *International Journal of Urban and Regional Research*, vol. 35, no. 1, 2011, pp. 40–56.

47 D. Mané, "Les nouveaux minibus en service dès lundi", *L'Info*, 25 November 2005.

48 The transport branch of the CNTS, for example, was introduced under the PDS label at the time of local elections in 2009 in Djender, in the Thiès department.

49 The CETUD coordinates transport policy for the Dakar region. Set up at the end of the 1990s, it was first marginalised after the political changeover before becoming one of the core elements of transport policy in the Dakar region.

5

✳

Macroeconomic Calculations and Modes of Government: The Cases of Mauritania and Burkina Faso

Boris Samuel

Introduction

A "macroeconomic framework" analyses a country's economic and financial situation. Since the structural adjustment era, this exercise, produced jointly by national administrations and international organisations, has provided the basis for macroeconomic policymaking in African countries. It has served to determine the now famous "conditionalities", played a central role in national decision-making processes (such as budget preparation) and established the template for official economic discourse.

"Frameworks" are interesting from a socio-political point of view because they are situated on the boundary between several worlds of meaning and logics of action. They assume a legal nature in that their forecasts are featured in voting on the national budget. They are developed by experts as instruments to act upon reality, using techniques borrowed from economics and statistics to "steer" the economy.[1] In a related way, they appear to be the products of a comprehensive normative language through their use of accounting standards and tools such as models. However, frameworks are also a way of regulating access to resources; they provide technocratic support in debates on state action.[2] In some instances, they are very crudely injected into accumulation strategies and power games as an unavoidable step in the competition for resources or as part of the interplay of actors within the administration.[3] Finally, they are also related to the methods of extraversion practised by states. Since the 1990s, macroeconomic assessments of the International Monetary Fund (IMF) have served as a signal to the donor community, determining whether or not a country is reputable and thus affecting its access to aid resources.

The inclusion of macroeconomic frameworks in these multiple roles at various levels offers an occasion to question the forms of power engendered by the use of macroeconomic techniques. This is what we aim to do here by exploring the cases of Mauritania and Burkina Faso

Between standardisation and trial and error

Before we look at the situations in Burkina Faso and Mauritania, two points of reference will be useful for grasping the socio-political influence of macroeconomic frameworks. On the one hand, framework procedures have the power to standardise and act as disciplinary measures over national administration practices. On the other hand, the work appears concretely to be based on trial and error, improvisation and negotiations rather than on the implementation of a rigid technique.

Normative and disciplinary power

Developing a macroeconomic framework takes precedence over other forms of economic analysis performed by administrations. It sets guidelines for the actors' behaviour.

To begin with, the methods impose a standardised form on macroeconomic discourse. The "financial programming" used by the IMF to produce a framework generates a series of statistical tables in which the same timeframes, choice of indicators, formats and topics are applied to every country and seldom vary over the years.[4] A good illustration is the Selected Economic Indicators table ritually featured at the beginning of every report issued by the World Bank and the IMF. It contains a limited range of indicators deemed necessary to sum up a national economy, its foreseeable evolutions and its government's commitments. The same is true of the "statistical appendices" included in IMF mission reports on its Article IV consultations, during which it fulfils its statutory function of member country "surveillance".[5] The fifty or so tables are always displayed in the same order and format using the same presentational devices to achieve the same effects. Developing a macroeconomic framework thus defines how an economic situation in Africa "should" be assessed and converted into figures.

The macroeconomics of international organisations therefore exercises its authority as much by determining how things are done as by assessing compliance with conditionalities or imposing measures. Monitoring consultations in IMF "program-countries" are conducted at least three times a year: at the beginning of the year for an economic assessment, in July to launch the budget process and in December for a detailed analysis of the budget bill. All of these dates are closely watched by the country's top economists and the "donor community"; they set the pace for the country's administrative life and frame the debates of the moment.

Moreover, the system is panoptic, so to speak. The government, along with the international officials, reviews all of the country's macroeconomic aspects, which are divided into "sectors": growth and the productive sector (the "real sector"), public finances, foreign trade, currency and banks. The assessment looks at whether previously set goals have been reached, analyses the current economic situation and gathers the information needed to determine the "short- and medium-term outlook". It examines in detail all the measures the government intends to take as well as ongoing "structural reforms" (regulatory measures, privatisations, etc.). This overview makes it possible to appraise and validate (or invalidate) the broad economic guidelines as well as rule on technical details (the method for calculating an indicator, for instance). Preparing for these consultations involves all the economic and financial administrations, requiring them to gather information, review and update their files, coordinate, etc. As a result, the framework unquestionably occupies a central and dominant position in the country's economic management. The IMF allows frameworks to play this role, for it is convinced that by using such an approach it can "reveal" to national administrations what they do not know about their own economies.[6]

Some of the technical devices involved will then play a major part in the disciplinary process. International accounting conventions have become a key element of the international economic and financial structure, and their application ensures, for example, that a country's indicators are "standardised" and can be integrated into international databases and comparisons.[7] Complying with these standards is an "imperative" of globalisation. Nevertheless, many economic and financial administrations in Africa produce their indicators using old methods and formats that are not explicitly defined and may not be consistent with those of other administrations. Producing a consistent image of the economy is therefore one of the major contributions of the thorough review produced in conjunction with IMF teams. The resulting figures are considered the only consistent, reliable statistical source, so much so that the work accomplished with the IMF often becomes an indispensable piece of the puzzle of national administrative procedures.

Models also play a critical role. In addition to standardising the figures, models help formulate macroeconomic reality within the context of certain problems and give legitimacy and status to certain interpretations of the economy. The model used by the World Bank, for example, which has inspired the work of most forecasting departments in African countries, makes growth automatically dependent on foreign investment.[8] Hence, a country's attractiveness to investors and its need for outside financing become pivotal factors in any discussion about which policies should be implemented (thereby justifying the Bank's actions). The analytic approach used by the IMF relies on a causal connection between monetary creation and trade deficits, making the adoption of strict monetary policies the only way to contain imbalances.[9] The macroeconomic debate is therefore focused on repertories of orthodox practices through concrete economic modelling.

Macroeconomic frameworks produced through trial and error and arrangements

The concrete practices of macroeconomics can be better described as processes of negotiation and trial and error. As Richard Harper has shown, producing figures is like peeling an onion.[10] Every indicator is dissected, each component is analysed, every source is assessed and discussed, etc. This work is especially fastidious in the African context because, when the quality of a country's data is poor, the smallest bit of information is potentially useful, and producing an overall picture of the economy requires collecting a great deal of disparate, uncertain data in a kind of giant puzzle.[11] This means that the entire IMF intervention methodology is rooted in a very pragmatic approach to macroeconomics. The delegations of experts shuttling between luxury hotels and the offices of finance ministries are full of people who tinker with numbers; their mission in a country is not complete until a sufficiently complete picture of the economic situation has somehow or other been concocted. They hold endless meetings with national administrations. They cover every square inch of the city seeking information. World Bank economists even make fun of their IMF counterparts, who spend months at a time on the menial task of filling out spreadsheets to produce economic tables.[12] The core mission for these highly qualified university graduates is, in fact, to fill in the empty boxes of huge computerised tables with whatever pieces of information they are able to gather, resorting to all sorts of tricks and recipes.[13]

The socio-political scope of these practices is broad, making it possible to resolve certain internal contradictions. The Bretton Woods institutions are often criticised for their methods and models, which are seen as ill suited, ideologically biased or based on outmoded economic views.[14] There are grounds for this criticism, but it never pertains to the actual practices themselves or takes into account the conditions under which the methods are employed. Yet the financial institutions justify their approach with the same argument: the models are never used for their inherent explanatory power but rather for the practical logic of dialogue and negotiation they generate and into which they are then incorporated.[15] The fact that they are unsatisfactory from a theoretical standpoint or even based on "false" relationships matters little. Although such arguments fail to appease rebel economists, as evidenced by the regular attacks launched by "insiders" like Joseph Stiglitz and William Easterly against the development community, they are nevertheless highly significant in our own socio-political approach. First, they acknowledge that the use of faulty models, pulled chaotically in one direction or another, is at the core of the quantifying and analytical approach employed by international organisations.[16] Second, the normative, disciplinary role of the framework is based on the use of unrealistic models. In an apparent paradox, the rigour of the framework process we are describing relies, in fact, on the use of highly questionable tools.[17]

These criticisms are at the core of our analysis of macroeconomic work in Burkina Faso and Mauritania. For both these countries, the question is: How is power actually exercised between the implementation of normative rules and the little arrangements that make up the economic narrative?

Indeed, both countries are reputed to have been "model pupils" that scrupulously complied with aid-related specifications. Their political regimes thus obtained funding and benefited from diplomatic and even military support. But they also have a reputation for displaying fig-leaf images of themselves. In 2005, the Mauritanian government admitted to lying for fifteen years about its macroeconomic data, while Burkina Faso is known to have built a façade of good management over the years, while making widespread use of informal procedures to circumvent the constraints of complying with the rules.

Mauritania: the emergence of macroeconomic fiction

In Mauritania, bogus macroeconomic numbers are usually seen (in the national press, international reports, etc.) as the result of a process deliberately designed to create a "façade". The procedures are said to be instrumentalised to promote patronage-based modes of regulation; in the late 1990s and early 2000s, the race to control rents and the logic of profit were pillars of Maaouya Ould Taya's regime.[18] This analysis does not account for the way macroeconomic discourse operates. A fictional macroeconomic narrative emerges as much from the implementation of management procedures as from circumvention and falsification.

Converting a largely indistinguishable economic reality into figures

First, there is one observation that cannot be disputed: macroeconomic figures are determined in a context of widespread uncertainty due to dissimulated misappropriation as well as to the failure of statistical tools. The statistical tools allow enormous margins of appreciation. This is evident in the example of economic growth.[19] GDP is calculated on the basis of sector-specific estimates that prove to be quite fragile and subjective.[20] For instance, growth in livestock, a major economic activity in Mauritania, was calculated in the mid-2000s by extrapolating from livestock data dating back to the early 1990s and calling on unverifiable "expert opinions" to estimate the breeding and slaughtering volumes in the interim. In the construction sector, calculations are based on vague indicators for cement sales with none of the necessary data on the price of construction materials. Estimates on the fishing industry are based on (officially registered) landings in Mauritanian ports, when in reality a significant share of the catch is not landed in Mauritania.

There are many other examples. Estimates for transport are based on fuel imports and those for telecommunications on the number of new telephone lines with no consideration of investment costs, etc. As a result, the country's growth indicators appear to be relatively unreliable fabrications opening the door to negotiations. Aside from possible manipulation of the figures, the methods for converting information to numbers seem arbitrary and contingent.

To what extent are the numbers manipulated? Price measurement gives us some indication. Inflation was largely falsified during the years of statistical deceit, especially between 2000 and 2003.[21] At the time, underestimating inflation had its advantages. It presented an image of economic stability and elided ongoing depreciation of the national currency (the ouguiya), a key IMF variable when official and informal currency markets represented high stakes and sources of graft and corruption.[22] Despite these incentives, the role of statistical uncertainty in turning out false figures cannot be overlooked. Until a new "standardised" price index was established in 2003–2004, inflation was measured with an index using a base dating back to 1983.[23] This index was based on a 1980s consumer basket devoid of many products, including mobile telephones, computer-related products and even milk in cartons and frozen food. It was no longer relevant, but the ensuing uncertainty made manipulation possible because, from an economist's point of view, there was insufficient benchmark data to declare that the numbers were wrong. Starting in late 2003, for example, although the price index produced by l'Office national de la statistique (ONS) [the national statistics bureau] had not budged, the media continually reported soaring prices and currency depreciation.[24] This led many observers to denounce the ONS for producing false data. However, for national and international economists, the unreliability of the index was a possible cause of the fact that the numbers were obscure; there was no way of discerning the actual figures and, for want of something better, the index served to ground official national and international reports, with no questions asked.[25] It was not until the end of 2004, with inflation still spiralling upwards, that the facts "spoke volumes" and the institutions, notably the IMF, had to face what was really happening. Falsification had thus been possible, among other reasons, because the methodology was vague and could be manipulated. In fact, as soon as a new method was established in late 2003 under the watchful eye of international experts, the manipulations stopped.[26]

This discussion is useful for questioning state expenditures. Here, uncertainties and possible discrepancies take on special meaning. Figures can be used to "conceal" transactions such as misappropriation or unauthorised discretionary expenditures. Falsified numbers then appear to reflect profiteering strategies, but the reality is much fuzzier and more ambivalent. In the early 2000s in Mauritania, procedures were so vague that it was difficult to distinguish misappropriations from ordinary state transactions. For one thing, there was massive dissimulation of irregular transactions, especially extra-budgetary expenses that were paid by the Ministry of Finance or the Central Bank without legal authorisation. They included major off-budget spending programmes such as the 2003 emergency food plan and huge military programmes.[27] As the Taya regime deployed its patronage strategy to the full, sections of the economic elite plundered public institutions, in particular by way of the Central Bank.[28] Official total expenditure or money creation meant very little at the time; in terms of expenditure, for instance, omissions amounted to more than 40 percent in 2003.[29] And yet the "fiction" in the figures was lost in the widespread informality of public finance management and was not seen as clear-cut "instrumentalisation" of resources. The Budget Department authorised much of the routine expenditure by circumventing the control systems and making no reference to a budget line (itemised as "automatic debit notes" or "requests for immediate payment" procedures).[30] Fast-track procedures were used for purposes of simplicity and speed, to purchase office paper or organise a meal, etc., but they also increased the fuzziness of state action.[31] The same fuzziness prevailed at the Central Bank. The President's office, for instance, raised funds without informing the Ministry of Finance. This was totally illegal, but no one kept a serious record of credit lines, whether regular or not.[32] In the figures, there was no way to distinguish misappropriation from the most routine transactions. Statistical "fiction" was thus not only synonymous with dissimulation. It governed the actions of the state. The anarchy in financial management was actually a weapon in the hands of the Taya regime, which stayed in power by maintaining patronage relationships and sharing out resources according to the "tribal equation".[33] It was widely known that formal procedures were ambivalent.

"Converting to figures"

Despite this fractious context, the work on macroeconomic steering went on. Tables with numbers and batches of indicators were produced, collected and published in international reports. In the early 2000s, Mauritania enjoyed the status of a "model pupil", and the country received IMF missions to conduct macroeconomic surveillance on a regular basis. How then should the production of these aggregates be interpreted? Where did the "quantitative imperative" lead?

Let us take the example of public expenditure. The government's financial transactions table (*Tableau des opérations financières de l'État* – TOFE) was issued as required by the international organisations. In addition, it more or less matched the minimum presentation standards.[34] Yet the TOFE data was by no means complete, given that a whole section of state transactions and extra-budgetary expenses were left out. Nonetheless, the data was not entirely disconnected from reality and could even be used at some of the stages of social negotiations. For instance, the TOFE took into account the official salaries of government employees and was occasionally used to negotiate an "index point" increase with the IMF. This happened in 2004 when Taya first increased wages in anticipation of a supposed influx of oil revenues (which never really took place). The work done under the Medium Term Expenditure Framework (MTEF) testifies to the fact that negotiations on real measures could rely on completely false numbers.[35] Macroeconomic measurement can be performed, even when it is disconnected from reality.[36]

The case of Mauritanian foreign trade casts a harsher light on how figures are obtained. Up until 2005, Mauritanian customs "recorded" trade flows in terms of volume instead of ad valorem. The containers reaching port were neither opened nor inspected; they were taxed at either a flat rate or per cubic metre, so vegetables were registered in the same way as computer chips, used clothing or bags of rice. This "taxation" procedure actually concealed a series of multiple power relationships. Being able to negotiate taxes with customs officials was a critical factor for importers needing to compete in the domestic market. It was also a way of regulating access to positions of power.[37] Producing statistics on foreign trade thus became very risky; import data provided in cubic metres was neither reliable nor meaningful. It reflected a "blackout" on the figures more than a description of the actual flow of goods.[38] The conversion into figures was therefore highly subjective, but this did not keep the quantification procedures from being implemented. The IMF reports presented price indices and import volumes in the usual format, as if nothing were amiss, in order to evaluate variations in the "terms of trade".[39] The figures in this case were disconnected from the real transactions, and no attempt was made in the quantification process to overcome these deficiencies with "rough" estimates. The absence of reliability and the omissions in the budget mentioned earlier led to a situation in which numbers were produced (committed, one should say) that were known to have absolutely no descriptive value. The figures were nevertheless presented as legitimate, even official, in the international literature, which was deemed preferable to having an empty box in a spreadsheet.[40] "Conversion to figures" took on a value of its own, and numbers became a fetish.[41] Macroeconomic "measurement" was accomplished through lack of transparency, not in spite of it, as one would expect in a functionalist interpretation.[42]

Formal procedures as socio-political reality

Having examined the meaning of macroeconomic variables, we must now ask how the quantification procedures are concretely implemented. What we find is this: the quantifying process conducted by the IMF together with national governments is not only a social process, as Richard Harper has shown,[43] but also involves power relations, bringing different forms of dominance into play. The example of foreign trade is telling. The procedures are standardised; the software used for customs statistics – "Sydonia", the international benchmark – was introduced with support from the French Cooperation Agency. Nevertheless, the quantification process can only be understood when reconstructed in the Mauritanian context. Under Taya, Sydonia software was managed by Sid'El Mokhtar, a civil servant reputed to be one of the key figures in blocking information and a keeper of the flame where extracting rents in the Ministry of Finance was concerned.[44] He was the one who published the scant information intended for the ONS or the IMF, who oversaw the upgrading of statistical methods and who laid down the law for national economists by protecting the customs bastion with a policy of opacity. Statistical data were considered state secrets, and Sid'El Mokhtar kept the hard disks containing it with him at all times.[45] Positioned within the system of rent management, he was the right-hand man of Colonel N'Diaga Dieng, then Director General of the customs administration, who was very close to the president and protected because, among other reasons, he was the token black-mauritanian in an essentially Moorish regime accused of segregation. This did not prevent Sid'El Mokhtar from playing up the technical dimension of his work or from claiming the need to perform it according to standards. Prior to 2005, for example, he used the excuse that the system had not yet been completely brought up to standard to drastically restrict access to data, thus covering up opaque customs procedures with a technical narrative.[46] He justified his virtually systematic refusal to send data to national and international institutions by arguing that he had been unable to finalise the needed changes in nomenclature. Standards were therefore at the core of "conversion into figures" while also serving as an excuse to withhold information. Standardisation was used as grounds for state informality, with procedures casting a veil over the administration's power relations and predatory activity. Macroeconomic calculations were also the result of the overlapping positions of expert assessment, power and accumulation. The methods for calculating any single aggregate thus reveal the full complexity of social relationships and domination.[47]

Macroeconomic fiction and modes of government

Converting to figures in Mauritania therefore appears ambivalent. The figures produced were unrealistic and false, but the formal procedures were real and rooted in social reality. One might even go so far as to say that the fiction of the numbers produced in conjunction with the IMF concealed a genuine mode of government.

The activities related to developing macroeconomic frameworks and steering the economy were embodied in relationships within the administration. Administrations aligned themselves with the technical work carried out with the IMF, considering the figures produced to be official and preferring them to the ones produced by their colleagues. The Budget Department, for instance, used IMF inflation and growth forecasts to prepare the budget. These were more reliable and better informed, more "official", to the point where the department had "no need" for other frameworks than those developed by the IMF.[48] Many inter-administration relationships were thus structured by macroeconomic monitoring, sometimes implicitly. Extreme compartmentalisation prevailed, and withholding information was commonplace. Since none of the data was reliable, suspicion of one's peers was the rule. Even within the ONS, data did not circulate among the offices. Details on prices, which were often manipulated, were not readily available to manage national accounts or the current economic situation. Conversion to figures took place above all for purposes of discussion with the IMF. Unofficial systems could then be used to circumvent the difficulties created by compartmentalisation; administrations with privileged contacts could help each other out by sharing the information they had collected, and civil servants made use of personal friendships or group solidarity, which took precedence over institutional relationships. The Ministry of Economic Affairs and Development, which had easier access than the ONS to data on mining or customs, could transmit the figures it obtained. Thus, a constellation of relationships formed around the macroeconomic surveillance exercises and framework development conducted with the IMF.[49] The process of producing false figures helped shape the configuration of social relationships within the ramifications of the "rhizome state".[50]

This intertwining also explains why the Mauritanian authorities always sought to make sure IMF missions were maintained. After Mauritania came to dispose of oil resources in 2006, and no longer required financing, the country asked to have an IMF Staff Monitored Programme set up (involving no loans), mainly to ensure administrative continuity and extended IMF surveillance, which was grafted, so to speak, onto national administrative activity.

Macroeconomic fiction thus appears to be a broad social process. A narrative is constructed, closely tied to the IMF, with ongoing references to standards, and bogus numbers are produced via the formal logic of statistical calculations. Though extremely unrealistic, the macroeconomic narrative nevertheless emerges because standards are implemented, rather than by overlooking small discrepancies and circumventing the rules. Instead, it reflects the impossibility of distinguishing between true and false, which underpins power relationships.

How to reconcile orthodox procedures with discretionary resource management in Burkina Faso

The difficulty of separating the respect of statistical standards from the elaboration of a fictional narrative about the economy may help to explain the seeming contradictions of Burkina Faso, another "model pupil". First, procedures in Burkina Faso are much more structured and sophisticated technically than in Mauritania, and the country is often cited for its "best practices". Second, since the mid-1990s, analysts of the regime have noted that it has carefully constructed a reformist façade. This façade is said to enable informal manipulation of the procedures, down to the smallest details, to benefit the patronage system managed by the President and his entourage.[51] Examining the country's macroeconomic procedures sheds an interesting light on power practices in Burkina Faso. The macroeconomic aspect of the regime's façade appears to stem from the intertwining of multiple dynamics more than from deliberate manipulation.[52]

Macroeconomic calculations: between expertise, "bureaucratic anarchy" and discretionary authority

Administrations in Burkina Faso monitor the economy regularly, have modelling tools at their disposal and produce macroeconomic scenarios. Since the structural adjustment era,[53] the work has been coordinated by a technical "secretariat".[54] This ad hoc structure reports directly to the Minister of the Economy and Finance and falls outside the control of the ministry's organisational hierarchy. It even has its own independent budget. The secretariat is perceived as a unit of high-level expertise producing what, for want of "capacities", the other administrations cannot achieve. As the privileged contact on economic and financial matters for international and European financial institutions, it is also seen as the interface between the administration and donors. This position raises questions about the social and power relationships hidden behind its actions.

How can "bureaucratic anarchy" be reconciled with high-level technical expertise?

There is no denying the secretariat's expertise or its role in overseeing macroeconomic work. It produces sophisticated reports and can call upon high-level expertise due, in particular, to support from international donors and the privileges granted by the Burkinabe government (its members are paid by the state on a par with those in international organisations). Since the adjustment period, the secretariat has been systematically put in charge of the most influential macroeconomic calculations. For a long time, it housed the national macroeconomic model, the *Instrument automatisé de prévision* (IAP), set up in the 1990s with support from the GTZ (*Deutsche Gesellschaft für Technische Zusammenarbeit*, the German technical co-operation agency).[55] The model was notably used to negotiate financial programmes with the IMF and to prepare the budget. In the early 2000s, the secretariat took over the MTEF – the post-adjustment aid solution designed to serve as a framework for future spending policies.[56] It is also responsible for preparing the highly strategic TOFE. All of its work has benefited from sizeable technical investment, sophisticated models and the ongoing presence of foreign technical assistants.

The secretariat's actions cannot be described solely in terms of technical considerations, however. Its dominant position reflects power relationships within the administration. First of all, it overlaps with the missions of several administrations, leading to work duplication. Under the Ministry of the Economy and Finance, the economic planning directorate (*Direction générale de l'économie et de la planification* – DGEP), the studies and planning department (*Direction des études et de la planification* – DEP) and the national statistics and demographics bureau (*Institut national de la statistique et de la démographie* – INSD) are supposed to carry out macroeconomic analyses and forecasting.[57] These agencies are hard-pressed to produce regular, reliable results, as shown by INSD's delay in producing national accounts (in 1999, the most recent available accounts were those issued in 1993).[58] The secretariat succeeded in taking over, offering to marshal its full efficiency to meet the "macroeconomic imperative".

However, a narrative in terms of efficiency does not convey the whole picture. In fact, a sort of "bureaucratic anarchy" holds sway, in which macroeconomic work is a medium for power relationships involving the secretariat.[59] At the end of the 1990s, despite its limited resources, the INSD sought to develop a macroeconomic model of its own, different from the one housed in the secretariat. It failed, but the attempt generated considerable envy towards the secretariat, which was seen as illegitimate and unduly privileged. The statistics bureau also came under repeated attacks from the Central Bank. With plenty of resources at its disposal, the Banque centrale des États d'Afrique de l'Ouest or BCEAO [Central Bank of West African States] conducted the same quarterly surveys of the "economic environment" as those carried out by the INSD, even though no one was interested in them.[60] It also expressed a desire to produce the national accounts, which was the INSD's responsibility. There have thus been numerous clashes between economic and financial administrations, with technical reports as their battlefield. Old rivalries between members of the administrative corps were dragged up, among other issues.[61] Conflictual relationships built up, leading to a fragmentation of macroeconomic monitoring tasks. The DEP, for instance, managed to keep a "niche" for itself: tax revenue projections.[62] In 2002, the DGEP recovered the responsibility for managing the macroeconomic model against a backdrop of intense struggle linked to the split of the Ministry of the Economy and Finance into separate ministries, but strategic issues now belong to the domain of public finances and the MTEF, which still reports to the secretariat. Hence, activities have been reconfigured and fragmented, mixing technical and organisational considerations with power struggles among administrations, individuals and rival corps. Amid this jousting and relative anarchy, the secretariat has positioned itself by capitalising on the urgent need to meet outside demands, hence assuming a "maverick" role backed by extraversion ploys.[63]

Modelling as "formatting" in macroeconomic language

In macroeconomic steering, technical work is inextricably linked to the game of negotiating with the international financial institutions. The secretariat's role thus appears extremely ambivalent, because it implies, above all, mastering the use of "formatting" logic in the macroeconomic language expected by outside institutions.[64]

The MTEF production method can be interpreted in this way. Burkina Faso's MTEF is intended to meet the demands of donors, who want to see public expenditure gradually redirected towards social sectors. The Burkinabe MTEF generates a sort of escalation of good practices, using allocation keys to ensure that every available CFA franc in the budget will be automatically earmarked for social action.[65] This goes beyond the donors' expectations, and the MTEF is therefore considered very sophisticated. At the same time, it is also largely fictional, because in Burkina Faso the budget is substantially revised and reallocated in the course of the fiscal year.[66] Thus, "formatting" logic takes precedence over the management objective.

Macroeconomic modelling and growth calculations can help us grasp the scope of macroeconomic "formatting". At the end of the 1990s, with no national accounting data made available by the INSD, practical solutions had to be found to produce GDP figures. The unit in charge of managing the IAP model, under the direction of Rolf Meier, a German technical aide, used the projection model to provide estimates of past growth. This calculation exceeded the model's capabilities and produced only very rough numbers. The situation nevertheless offered advantages because the model was capable of cobbling something together with the IMF teams. Although different from IMF tools, it was a "quasi-accounting" model, and its flexibility made it possible to combine calculation methods and negotiations, which turned out to be highly useful. Indeed, it was not unusual for the IMF to want to display favourable numbers or to impose its data, as the research work of Rolf Meier and Marc Raffinot and of Richard Harper has shown.[67] Despite the model's limited reliability, the fact that it was easy to manipulate allowed it to produce the figures while simultaneously negotiating with the IMF and thus to vertically integrate the tasks.

This was to have far-reaching consequences, as one episode reveals. The agricultural season in 1997–1998 was very poor, and it became necessary to subject the final production figures to several major revisions. As the data were gradually fine-tuned, the drop in production grew to almost 20 percent, whereas the initial estimate had shown a decline of less than 10 percent. As a result, the growth calculation for the previous year also had to be revised. The IMF stubbornly refused to revise the data, because the numbers were considered official. The Burkinabe economists had no choice but to accept the decision and use the now incorrect figure, with serious repercussions as a result. The data for agriculture cannot be isolated from the rest of the economy; for example, the figure for agricultural production has corresponding figures in household income and food imports. Faced with the IMF's demand, there were only two possibilities open to the unit economists: either to integrate the incorrect number into the model and preserve economic coherence by adjusting all the other numbers – but then the entire economy would be misrepresented – or to tinker with the model to "disconnect" the imposed figure from the rest of the model, violating accounting rules, if necessary, and finding a way to "twist" the model in order to keep a free hand despite IMF requirements. They chose the second option, which is hardly surprising, as the use of such methods is commonplace in an "interface" like the secretariat. Forecasting often consists in acting "as if" the IMF figures were the ones produced by the model or consistent with them, even if this is not true. A considerable part of the economists' work is thus devoted to dressing up the negotiations with accounting and economic formatting.

The resulting exercise is paradoxical. It is technically complex and can only be accomplished by economists, but its usefulness for economic analysis is limited. Expertise, on the one hand, and tinkering, manipulation and sometimes dissimulation on the other, are two sides of the same coin. Although some authors have testified to the role of negotiation in macroeconomic work, its implied effects on the practices used in formulating the economic narrative go beyond their observations.[68] Indeed, the end results of negotiations and arrangements bear the hallmark of technical expertise and standards, and the models blur the boundary lines between negotiation and the technical approach using calculations. Manipulation appears to be such an integral part of macroeconomic calculation techniques that the two are ultimately indistinguishable. In line with Michael Power's observations regarding audits, opacity is seen here as an essential matrix of the relationships between the IMF and the country and cannot be dissociated from the combined use of technical language and the logic of negotiations.[69] This is in no way unique to Burkina Faso; it reflects, above all, relationships between a lender and a borrower, like the auditor and the audited in Michael Power's work.

From expert legitimacy to discretionary action

The secretariat's work can only be undertaken by teams invested in the social process of negotiation who, at the same time, have a command of the technical aspects of macroeconomic language. It combines a technocratic ethos with the positioning strategies of government dignitaries in a process characterised by an overlap between expertise and positions of power.

On the one hand, the secretariat makes ample use of expert profiles. All the foreign advisors working at the secretariat possessed a high level of expertise and occupied key positions of responsibility. Rolf Meier directed the unit in charge of managing the IAP model for ten years, just as Ali Achour managed the TOFE (as a technical assistant, first for the European Union, then for France). In contrast to the foreigners, a number of Burkinabe executives followed a more administrative path. Eugénie Malgoubri, for example, for many years the economist in charge of the IAP model, was a very "legalistic" technician. Recognised for her competence, she was promoted after leaving the secretariat but continued to work on the same type of reports. She was responsible in particular for managing the Poverty Reduction Strategy Paper, a task involving both technical skill and keeping up appearances.[70] The permanent secretary, François Zoundi, who remained in his position from the 1990s to 2010 (when he was named Deputy Minister in charge of Budget), was also known for his competence and had even become personally involved in the most complex technical work. However, his technocratic approach was associated with a discretionary, even instrumental, logic of power. François Zoundi was part of the small circle of former BCEAO officials appointed by Prime Minister Kadré Désiré Ouédraogo in the mid-1990s to head public finances in Burkina Faso.[71] These men formed one of the core groups in the Compaorist elite. François Zoundi, in particular, was very close to a former director of the Treasury who had recently been Minister of the Economy and Finance (Lucien Marie-Noël Bembamba) and who was Blaise Compaoré's son-in-law. Thus, the secretariat should also be perceived as representing the dominant group in the Compaoré regime.

The secretariat's methods are a good example of the logic of discretionary power, by the way. It is believed that, behind a façade of best practices, the MTEF is used to set aside a portion of yearly budget margins for the country's leaders, from ministers to the president. In 2008, we were told those sums amounted to approximately EUR 40 million a year or 20 percent of total annual budget margins.[72]

Thus, the secretariat inextricably intertwines various technical repertories, which at the same time bear the stamp of power plays. It is the symbol of a certain style of government at the intersection of technocracy, extraversion, and discretionary, patronage-based control over access to resources.

Burkinabe macroeconomic fiction at the intersection of multiple dynamics

At this point, let us widen our scope and look at how the macroeconomic narrative fits into public management. The "Compaorist" management style is usually represented as manipulating appearances to produce the illusion of good management while maintaining control over access to resources. Macroeconomic work in Burkina Faso shows that the modes of dominance used in the country can, indeed, be instrumentalised, but the fictional narrative is the combined result of far more heterogeneous, complex and, in some ways, unintentional dynamics.

To prepare the state budget, the macroeconomic approach begins by esti-mating the total amount to be allocated. As soon as the framework scenarios are prepared, disagreements arise within the Ministry of Finance. With re-gard to tax revenues, for instance, the revenue collection departments (cus-toms and taxes) seek low projections, barely higher than in previous years, to give them plenty of leeway, even if this means achieving 120 percent of the initial objective.[73] The DEP is charged with coordinating the departments to come up with initial revenue projections for the framework. It wants to boost tax collection but lacks the power to influence the collection depart-ment's proposal.[74] The initial framework is discussed with the IMF, and low revenues and expenditures are forecast, giving the framework an aura of orthodoxy.

During the preparation of the budget bill, a different reality takes over. Little by little, the original macroeconomic scenario is "extended" by multi-ple changes introduced by other players. First, the Minister of the Economy and Finance raises the forecast in order to present a proactive budget likely to fund as many "priority projects" as possible. The Minister is eager to help transform Burkina Faso into an "emerging country" but s/he probably wants to make patronage-style promises. However, s/he is not alone; when the budget is examined, parliamentarians exert further pressure to increase it so as to maximise the amounts redirected to their respective constituencies. In other words, between the commitments contained in the initial formal framework and the budget preparation process, successive efforts to push projections upward come into play.[75] The initial "orthodoxy" puts on a good show, but it is followed by other frameworks seeking to legitimise proac-tive intervention; the Poverty Reduction Strategy Paper, for instance, uses much higher forecasts. In the end, successive, contradictory frameworks pile up and work their way through the annual administrative cycle. The frame-work thus turns out to be a foundation for heterogeneous dynamics and repertories.

These number games have a crucial influence on resource management. The budget that is finally adopted is unrealistic, with revenue objectives about 10 percent higher than actual future revenues.[76] Readjustments therefore have to be made during the year, and budget implementation triggers "scar-city management" as ministries fail to receive the appropriations they had planned on. These redeployments open up broad margins for discretionary allocation.[77] A second series of negotiations ensues on the subjects of budget regulations and Finance Act amendments, and completely different hands are dealt based on cuts. Now power plays are organised around the Budget Department. The budget director, known for the refusal to compromise, then assumes the role of an unofficial minister, not to say unofficial Prime Minister, for part of the year, because s/he holds the keys to reallocation.[78]

In this case, the macroeconomic framework and its transformations generate leeway for discretionary reallocation, but this situation does not reflect a single, perfectly controlled and deliberate strategy. Burkinabe macroeconomic and budgetary management is a game with fluctuating stakes and heterogeneous players, and hence contingent. Between the framework and the revised budget appropriations, there is a succession of "moments" in which various protagonists and their divergent interests come into play. There are frequent conflicts, for instance, between the secretariat, which confirms the orthodox direction of the initial framework in its MTEF, the budget director, who controls funding appropriation, and the Minister of Finance, who is both the guardian of orthodoxy and responsible for development policies. The budget director, a dreaded corps member but not from the same group as the one made up of former BCEAO officials (to which François Zoundi and his minister both belong), often stands up to the Minister. By comparison, the permanent secretary is nothing more than the "donors' lackey". In reality, everyone has a window of opportunity in the steering process, and the framework appears to be swallowed up in a bureaucratic anarchy in which the idea of macroeconomic policy is lost in a maze of procedures and power plays. The framework is by no means a disciplinary process enabling precise control of state action. It allows a certain amount of leeway, but it is not a symbol of a full, final control. Rather, it is a technical process with multiple meanings, the embodiment of a variety of practices ranging from predation to the promotion of orthodoxy or proactive intervention. In this way, the Burkinabe state shows its capacity to play with competing and apparently contradictory repertories.

Conclusion

The analyses we have presented of Burkina Faso and Mauritania testify, above all, to the fact that macroeconomic procedures are a fertile ground for analysing power practices, provided they are seen as "signs" of social relationships and struggles for dominance and, at the same time, as a source of govern-ment techniques.[79] The calculation procedures and bureaucratic activities of the Ministry of the Economy and the Ministry of Finance, often viewed as politically neutral, are also ways of governing state action, avenues for implementing international recommendations and standards and a means to establish the relationships of dominance in which they are embedded.

In Taya's Mauritania, the fact that figures were fabricated reveals the ex-tent to which rules and standards, at once violated and implemented, work in osmosis with the multiple facets of relationships of power and dominance. Behind the fictional narrative, the conversion into numbers takes place by including and omitting information, showing a concern for rigour as well as wilful misrepresentation or concealment. This results in infinite combinations of the licit and illicit, the formal and informal, straddling the vague bound-ary lines between them and helping to redefine them. Macroeconomics and its standards are thus a fundamental place for understanding how power is exercised, revealing the socio-political depth of the "interface" between com-prehensive technical objects and historically constituted social relationships. The formal languages of economics, often neglected by analysts, seem to play an ambiguous – or at least never neutral – role in developing practices of dominance.

The Burkinabe case confirms the importance of the "macroeconomic in-terface" in forming relationships of dominance. The formal procedures for macroeconomic steering embody conflicts within the Burkinabe government apparatus, structuring the competition among individuals, groups and state administrative bodies for access to resources. Moreover, macroeconomics offers room for the exercise of discretionary power, which is deployed in the interstices of formal procedures and around their implementation. The "interface" is thus at the core of the regime's power mechanisms. At a deeper level, the analysis of macroeconomic techniques in Burkina Faso reveals the importance of "formatting" logic in the language of international standards. International recommendations are followed zealously, thereby helping to establish the legitimacy of the regime's management methods. However, these processes end up producing fragile, unstable fictions that are continu-ally challenged and renegotiated, fuelling conflicts or even anarchy within the state apparatus. And although "compliance with standards" is achieved, it becomes a source of uncertainty and contingency in the management of power.

The Mauritanian situation confirms the fact that macroeconomic "formatting" logic generates instability. The country's fictional macroeconomic narrative, decried by the IMF and acknowledged by the Mauritanian state, was finally given the status of a lie in late 2004 after prevailing in state action for 15 years. The fall of the Taya regime in 2005 coincided with the collapse of Mauritania's macroeconomic fictional narrative and the de-legitimisation of its macroeconomic conversion into figures, which went hand in hand with that of the regime.

Endnotes

1   On forecasting, see A. Desrosières, "Historiciser l'action publique: l'État, le marché et les statistiques" in P. Laborier and D. Trom (eds.), *Historicités de l'action publique*, Paris: PUF, 2003, pp. 207–21 and "Naissance d'un nouveau langage statistique entre 1940 et 1960", in *Gouverner par les nombres. L'argument statistique II,* Paris: Presses de l'École des Mines, 2008, pp. 61–78; F. Fourquet, *Les Comptes de la puissance. Histoire de la comptabilité nationale et du plan*, Paris: Encres, 1980; A. Terray, *Des francs-tireurs aux experts. L'organisation de la prévision économique au ministère des Finances, 1948–1968*, Paris: Comité pour l'histoire économique et financière de la France, 2002; A. Vanoli, *Une histoire de la comptabilité nationale*, Paris: La Découverte, 2002.

2   On the role of statistics in the public debate, see W. N. Espeland, *The Struggle for Water. Politics, Rationality, and Identity in the American Southwest*, Chicago: University of Chicago Press, 1998; T. Porter, *Trust in Numbers. The Pursuit of Objectivity in Science and Public Life*, Princeton: Princeton University Press, 1995. On macroeconomic aspects, see A. Desrosières, "Du réalisme des objets de la comptabilité nationale", in *Gouverner par les nombres*, op. cit., pp. 257–70.

3   On these themes, see B. Hibou, *L'Afrique est-elle protectionniste? Les chemins buissonniers de la libéralisation extérieure*, Paris: Karthala, 1996; *Anatomie politique de la domination*, Paris: La Découverte, 2011; "Économie politique du discours de la Banque mondiale en Afrique subsaharienne: du catéchisme économique au fait (et méfait) missionnaire", *Les Études du CERI,* no. 39, 1998, pp. 1–46.

4   See R. Daumont, M. de Zamaróczy, Ph. Callier and B. Ziller, *Programmation financière. Méthodes et application à la Tunisie*, Washington: Institut du Fonds monétaire international, 1999. On IMF methods, see M. Mussa and M. Savastano, "The IMF approach to economic stabilization", *IMF Working Paper*, No. 104, 1999, pp. 1–42.

5   Article IV of IMF bylaws requires every member state to disclose all the information needed for the assessment of its economic situation.

6   See R.H.R. Harper, *Inside the IMF. An Ethnography of Documents, Technology and Organisational Action*, San Diego: Academic Press, 1998.

7   See M. Capron (ed.), *Les Normes comptables internationales, instruments du capitalisme financier*, Paris, La Découverte, 2005. On national accounting, see A. Vanoli, *Une histoire de la comptabilité nationale*, op. cit.

8   The World Bank model is called the RMSM (Revised Minimum Standard Model).

9   This is the "Polak" model, named after its author. See J. J. Polak, "The IMF monetary model. A hardy perennial", *Finance & Development*, Vol. 34, No. 4, 1997, pp. 16–19; R. Daumont, M. de Zamaróczy, Ph. Callier and B. Ziller, *Programmation financière*, op. cit.

10 See R. H. R. Harper, *Inside the IMF*, op. cit., p. 195.

11 See M. Séruzier, "Une discipline spécifique. La mesure en macroéconomie", *Statéco*, No. 90–91, 1998, pp. 19–30.

12 Conversations with World Bank officials, Nouakchott and Washington, 2004.

13 Derived from the Tunisian case. See R. Daumont, M. de Zamaróczy, Ph. Callier and B. Ziller, *Programmation financière*, op. cit.

14 See the tracts by J. Stiglitz, *La Grande Désillusion*, Paris: Fayard, 2002 and W. Easterly, *Les Pays pauvres sont-ils condamnés à le rester?*, Paris: Éditions d'Organisation, 2006. On models, see W. Easterly, "The Ghost of Financing Gap. How the Harrod-Domar Growth Model still haunts development economics", *World Bank Policy Research Working Paper*, No. 1807, 1997, pp. 1-30; A. Berg, P. Karam and D. Laxton, "A Practical Model-Based Approach to Monetary Policy Analysis. Overview", *IMF Working Paper*, No. 06/80, 2006, pp. 1–43.

15 On the World Bank, see T. Ranaweera, "Foreign Aid, Conditionality and Ghost of the Financing Gap: A Forgotten Aspect of the Aid Debate", *World Bank Policy Research Working Paper*, No. 3019, 2003, pp. 1–29. On the IMF, see the seminal article by M. Mussa and M. Savastano, "The IMF Approach to Economic Stabilization", op. cit.; J. J. Polak, "The IMF Monetary Model", op. cit.; International Monetary Fund, *Policy Formulation, Analytical Frameworks, and Program Design*, Washington, 2004.

16 They are indeed "false" models. The World Bank model, for instance, projects future growth based on the amount of investment during the current year, even though the connection between the two has been clearly refuted by empirical observations of past behaviour. Moreover, the IMF acknowledges that its forecasts in Africa are systematically biased (overestimated growth and underestimated inflation). See, for instance, International Monetary Fund, *Policy Formulation*, op. cit.

17 P. Macherey, *La Force des normes. De Canguilhem à Foucault*, Paris: La Fabrique, 2008.

18 See A.W. Ould Cheikh, "Les habits neufs du sultan. Sur le pouvoir and ses (res) sources en Mauritanie", *Maghreb-Machrek* No. 189, 2006, pp. 29–52; Z. Ould Ahmed Salem, "'Tcheb-tchib' et compagnie. Lexique de la survie et figures de la réussite en Mauritanie", *Politique africaine*, no. 82, juin 2001, pp. 78–100; B. Samuel,

"Trajectoire technocratique and instabilité politique en Mauritanie, 2003–2011", *Les Études du CERI* No. 178, 2011. On oil, see B. Augé, "Les Enjeux du pétrole en Mauritanie", *L'Année du Maghreb*, Vol. III, 2007, pp. 349–67.

19 The analyses concerning Mauritania in this article are based, in particular, on my own participation in research work between 2003 and 2007.

20 For a description of the methods mentioned in this paragraph, see Ministère des Affaires économiques and du développement, *Estimation de la croissance en 2005*, Nouakchott, 2005. See also the "metadata" published on the IMF website, <dsbb.imf.org>.

21 See République islamique de Mauritanie, *Rapport sur la révision des données macroéconomiques, 1992–2004*, Nouakchott, 2006.

22 This was a central theme in the public debate. See, for instance, B. Ould Ghoulam, "L'euro à 407 UM, le dollar à 3336 UM. La dévaluation a-t-elle eu lieu?", *Nouakchott Info*, 9 May 2004, or the interview of Ahmed Ould Hamza, "Crise des devises. 'La Plupart des entreprises perdent de l'argent actuellement'", *Nouakchott Info*, 4 April 2004.

23 See Office national de la statistique, *Argumentaire pour le passage à l'Indice harmonisé des prix à la consommation (IHPC) en Mauritanie*, Nouakchott, 2003; République islamique de Mauritanie, *Rapport sur la révision des données*, op. cit., pp. 17–8.

24 See, for instance, B. Gueye, "Flambée des prix. Le Panier de la ménagère soumis à rude épreuve", *Nouakchott Info*, 23 February 2004; F. Mint Bilal "Mais où est passé l'État ?", *L'Authentique*, 13 January 2004.

25 See, for instance, Table 22 in International Monetary Fund, *Islamic Republic of Mauritania: Statistical Appendix, Country report No.03/16*, Washington, 2003, p. 24; International Monetary Fund, *Staff Report for the 2003 Article IV Consultation, Country report No.03/314*, Washington, 2003, pp. 18–19, 31 and 33.

26 The new index was not officially adopted and published until early 2004, but it had been calculated since April 2003, and comparison with the former index for 2003 showed very distinct disparities. The new index immediately revealed price increases that the former had left out.

27 See République islamique de Mauritanie, *Rapport sur la révision des données*, op. cit.

28 See for instance B. Cherif, "Scandale de la Banque centrale de Mauritanie: pourquoi Ould Nagi a-t-il été arrêté ?", *Le Quotidien de Nouakchott*, 17 November 2009.

29 Conversations with various senior officials at the Ministry of Finance at the time. On these elements, see, in addition, République islamique de Mauritanie, *Rapport sur la révision des données*, op. cit., p. 22.

30 These two so-called "fast-track" procedures, provided for by law, made it possible to avoid the usual controls over expenditure commitments and disbursements. They were theoretically intended to be used exceptionally, but their use had in fact become routine.

31 Conversations with senior officials at the Ministry of Finance, 2005. The report on data review specifies that, in 2004, more than 15 percent of state expenditure on goods and services was based on automatic debit notes (p. 23).

32 Conversations with a World Bank official at the time, Nouakchott, April 2011.

33 On tribal mechanisms in the Mauritanian political system, see P. Marchesin, *Tribus, ethnies et pouvoirs en Mauritanie*, Paris: Karthala, 2010 [1992].

34 See World Bank and International Monetary Fund, *Public Expenditure Management: Country Assessment and Action Plan, Mauritania, 2004*, Washington, 2004, p. 14. Nevertheless, the IMF regularly requested that it be improved.

35 See République islamique de Mauritanie, *Cadre de dépenses à moyen terme 2004–2006*, Nouakchott, 2003, p. 22. Other important increases took place in 2006 and 2007.

36 In a sense, this happens all the time, because "measurement" is a very vague notion in macroeconomics. See M. Séruzier, "Une discipline spécifique", op. cit.; A. Desrosières, "Du réalisme des objets", op. cit.

37 Conversations with businessmen, Nouakchott, 2011. On power games surrounding customs, see B. Hibou, *L'Afrique est-elle protectionniste?*, op. cit. On tradesmen, see P. Bonte, "Faire fortune au Sahara. Permanences et ruptures", *Autrepart*, No. 16, 2000, pp. 49–65. On customs, see Z. Ould Ahmed Salem, *Fraude and piratage halieutique en Mauritanie. Étude pour le ministère de la Défense et le CERI*, Paris, CERI, 2000.

38 Personal experience in the national statistics bureau.

39 See for example Table 46 in International Monetary Fund, *Islamic Republic of Mauritania: Statistical Appendix*, op. cit., p. 48.

40 See R.H.R. Harper, *Inside the IMF*, op. cit., Chapter 6.

41 On the fetishism surrounding numbers, see J. Guyer, *Marginal Gains: Monetary Transactions in Atlantic Africa*, Chicago: University of Chicago Press, 2004; B. Samuel, "Le cadre stratégique de lutte contre la pauvreté et les trajectoires de la planification au Burkina Faso", *Sociétés politiques comparées*, No. 16, 2009, pp. 1-76 and *Statistiques, action publique et dialogue social. Une économie politique du chiffre dans le conflit social de 2009 en Guadeloupe*. Étude réalisée pour le Fonds d'analyse des sociétés politiques et l'Agence française de développement, 2012. On the social value of figures, see A. Ogien, "La volonté de quantifier. Conceptions de la mesure de l'activité médicale", *Annales. Histoire, sciences sociales*, Vol. 55, no. 2, 2000, pp. 283–312.

42 On opacity, see M. Power, *La Société de l'audit. L'Obsession du contrôle*, Paris: La Découverte, 2005.

43 R.H.R. Harper, *Inside the IMF*, op. cit.

44 On Sydonia, see the work of T. Cantens, "La réforme de la douane camerounaise à l'aide d'un logiciel des Nations unies ou l'appropriation d'un outil de finances publiques", *Afrique contemporaine*, No. 223–4, 2007, pp. 289–307.

45 This was how customs statistics were saved during the attempted coup on 8 June 2003, when the customs facilities were ransacked.

46 Conversations at the customs agency, Nouakchott, November 2004. See also, P. Couaillac, *Rapport de mission en Mauritanie*, Bamako, Afristat, 2004.

47 On bureaucratic procedures as embodiments of social relationships, see A. Riles (ed.), *Documents, Artifacts of Modern Knowledge*, Ann Arbor: University of Michigan Press, 2006.

48 Conversations with the Budget Deputy Director, Nouakchott, May 2005. See also G. de Monchy, *Compte rendu de mission en Mauritanie*, Paris: Ministère de l'Économie et des Finances, 2005.

49 B. Samuel, "Trajectoire technocratique", op. cit.

50 See J.-F. Bayart, *L'État en Afrique. La Politique du ventre*, Paris: Fayard, 1989, p. 270 ff.

51 On the "façade", see M. Hilgers and J. Mazzochetti, "L'après-Zongo. Entre ouverture politique et fermeture des possibles", *Politique africaine*, No. 101, March 2006, pp. 5–18; A. Loada "L'élection présidentielle du 13 novembre 2005. Un Plébiscite par défaut", *Politique africaine*, No. 101, March 2006, pp. 19–41. See also M. Hilgers and J. Mazzochetti (eds.), *Révoltes et oppositions dans un régime semi-autoritaire. Le cas du Burkina Faso*, Paris: Karthala, 2010.

52 This case study is based on my personal participation in the work of the Burkinabe economic administrations in the late 1990s at the national statistics bureau, as well as on information gathered during stays in 2008 and 2009.

53 The first adjustment programme agreed upon with international financial institutions was introduced in 1991, whereas the country entered the era of the "fight against poverty" in 2000.

54 The Permanent Technical Secretariat for structural adjustment programmes (STP-PAS), which became the Technical Secretariat for Economic Development and Social Policy Coordination (STC-PDES) in 1998, and later the Permanent Secretariat for Financial and Policy Programmes after the Ministry of the Economy and Finance was split in 2002.

55 See Ministère de l'Économie and des Finances/GTZ, *Une maquette macro-économique pour gérer l'économie du Burkina Faso: l'instrument automatisé de prévision version 1.3. Tome 1: présentation détaillée, relations and modes de recalcul*, Ouagadougou, 1997.

56 See B. Samuel, "Le cadre stratégique de lutte contre la pauvreté", op. cit.

57 On the history of Burkinabe economic and financial administrations, see the seminal book by P. Zagre, *Les Politiques économiques du Burkina Faso: une tradition d'ajustement structurel*, Paris: Karthala, 1994. See also, B. Samuel, "Le cadre stratégique de lutte contre la pauvreté", op. cit.

58 Personal experience at the INSD.

59 By "bureaucratic anarchy" we are referring here to the way in which the quantity, disorder and accumulation of technical works has become the core characteristic of administrative work, leading to constant renegotiation of social and power

relationships within the government apparatus. See A. Blum and M. Mespoulet, *L'Anarchie bureaucratique. Statistique et pouvoir sous Staline*, Paris: La Découverte, 2003.

60 These are surveys on the morale of business leaders formulated in quarterly reports on the economic situation published by INSD and BCEAO, respectively.

61 In Burkina Faso, the cultures of government corps and rivalries between them are quite intense, particularly between administrators of Ministry of Finance management bodies (including the secretariat) and planners (economists and statisticians) working under the Ministry of the Economy. The central bank constitutes another hub. On these corps, see P. Zagre, *Les Politiques économiques du Burkina Faso*, op. cit.; B. Samuel, "Le cadre stratégique de lutte contre la pauvreté", op. cit.

62 See ibid., p. 64. See also, B. Samuel and J.-B. Gros, *Analyse des procédures de planification, programmation and budgétisation au Burkina Faso*, Dakar, Programme des Nations unies pour le développement, Pôle régional d'appui aux CSLP, 2008, pp. 29–30 and 38–40.

63 We are referring to the expression used by A. Terray in *Des francs-tireurs aux experts*, op. cit.

64 We are of course thinking of the extraversion grammar of J.-F. Bayart, "L'Afrique dans le monde. Une histoire d'extraversion", *Critique internationale*, no. 5, 1999, pp. 97–120.

65 See Ministère de l'Économie and des Finances, *Rapport du Cadre de dépenses à moyen terme 2008–2010*, Ouagadougou, 2007; Linpico, "Mesure de la performance de la gestion des finances publiques au Burkina Faso selon la méthodologie PEFA, Ouagadougou, 2007", *Indicator* No. 12, pp. 61–4.

66 See ibid., *Indicator* No. 2, pp. 30–1.

67 R. Meier and M. Raffinot, "S'approprier les politiques de développement. Nouvelle mode ou vieille rengaine? Une analyse à partir des expériences du Burkina Faso et du Rwanda", *Revue Tiers Monde*, Vol. 46, No. 183, 2005, pp. 625–49. See R.H.R. Harper, *Inside the IMF*, op. cit.

68 See R. Meier and M. Raffinot, "S'approprier les politiques de développement", op. cit.; R. H. R. Harper, *Inside the IMF*, op. cit.

69 See M. Power, *La Société de l'audit*, op. cit.

70 See B. Samuel, "Le cadre stratégique de lutte contre la pauvreté", op. cit.

71 Conversations, Ouagadougou, December 2008.

72 Same as above and B. Samuel, "Le cadre stratégique de lutte contre la pauvreté", op. cit., p. 37.

73 See Linpico, "Mesure de la performance", op. cit. Generally, on tax revenue forecasts in Burkina Faso, see M. Raffinot "'Motiver' et 'chicoter': l'économie politique de la pression fiscale en Afrique subsaharienne", *Autrepart*, No. 20, 2001, pp. 91–106.

74 Conversations, Ouagadougou, April 2008. The tax burden is very low in Burkina Faso (12 percent in 2006).

75 See Linpico, "Mesure de la performance," op. cit., *Indicator* No. 3, pp. 32–33.

76 Ibid.

77 See B. Samuel, "Le cadre stratégique de lutte contre la pauvreté", op. cit.

78 Interviews, Ouagadougou, December 2008.

79 See P. Lascoumes and P. Le Galès, "Introduction: l'action publique saisie par ses instruments", in P. Lascoumes and P. Le Galès (eds.), *Gouverner par les instruments*, Paris: Presses de Sciences Po, 2005, pp. 11–44.

6

✳

The Temporary Electrification of the Carrières Centrales Casablanca Slums: Aspects and limitations of grassroots transformation of public policy

Lamia Zaki

Introduction

For a long time, the state resisted formalising the electrification of the Casablanca slums, even though it was likely to improve the quality of life of residents.[1] The plan was not given serious consideration until the Lyonnaise des Eaux de Casablanca (Lydec) replaced the state-owned utility[2] in 1997. Since the late 1980s, the Moroccan authorities had gradually allowed slum dwellers to divert electricity under certain conditions, within limits and always on a case-by-case basis. They preferred to turn a blind eye to the expansion of these practices rather than officially connect the slums to the grid. Their priority was to ensure social stability at minimal political cost, i.e. without formally implementing any land use that could be interpreted as recognition of the slums' right to exist. The government strategy was also an effective way of keeping pressure on the residents by maintaining their illegal status.

Lydec opposed electricity hijacking, highlighting the need for economic profitability, and instead supported officially connecting the slums. The practice of hijacking electric current evolved into more organised and violent forms of theft, eventually forcing the authorities to accept the principle of legal – though temporary – electrification of the area's slums. Authorisation was given to launch a pilot project in February 1998, but the global agreement in principle did not put an end to hijacking. On the contrary, it increased in the slums that were not yet connected. The electrification process was slow; it was carried out only on a case-by-case basis at the request of local officials and subject to specific authorisation from the governor of the prefecture[3] in which the slum was located. It was not until 2004 that most of the urban slums of Casablanca (30,000 households in all) were fully electrified.

To bring out the dynamic relationship between public policies and patterns of popular mobilisation in Morocco, I will analyse the transformation of electricity hijacking practices in one Casablanca slum that was electrified in 2002. Carrières centrales has long been one of the largest slums in Morocco. It is also one of the oldest, originating in 1939 when the Protectorate merged several slums outside the city limits[4]. By 2005, it was occupied by over 6,000 households comprising nearly 40,000 residents. Renowned as a hotbed of resistance during the country's struggle for independence, Carrières centrales was the focal point of several unsuccessful resettlement projects in the late 1950s, the 1970s and, finally, in the 1990s. In late 2007, a new relocation project[5] for the people living on the outskirts of Casablanca was officially developed and is currently being implemented.

In this case study, I will examine the contradictory styles used by the various actors to legitimise or oppose power hijacking. I am not seeking to demonstrate a direct causal link between context and action. Instead, I aim to show the importance of the interpretive styles developed by the players, particularly the ability of slum residents to reappropriate for their own purposes the constraints and resources of political and economic liberalisation introduced by the regime in the 1990s.[6] Furthermore, the widespread hijacking also shows that the resistance strategies employed by slum residents are not always "fragmented" and "silent"[7] but can also be collective and more openly adopted to counteract the prohibitions imposed by the authorities. Therefore, this study comes in the wake of other research that challenge the opposition between resistance strategies and survival strategies and that question how individual actions are linked to collective protest.[8]

The increase in hijacking practices in Casablanca following the arrival of Lydec raises questions about the complexity and ambiguity of the relationships between slum residents, a private operator, local officials and regional authorities and shows how these interactions affected the way the project evolved.[9] Finally, I will come back to the difficulties faced by the private operator in dealing with slum-dwelling consumers whose customer status was never fully recognised. The relative failure of the attempted electrification over the medium term – the operator had a great deal of difficulty collecting the price of power consumption in Carrières centrales – partly explains why electrification operations were frozen in 2005. It also reveals the challenges confronting a private operator attempting to set up a large-scale social project without government management. Lydec has since radically redefined its efforts to give disadvantaged people access to services. It now focuses on programmes jointly determined with the public authorities prior to implementation and in line with clearly identified public policies.

Proliferation of legitimising discourse in a context of authoritarian liberalisation

Basic infrastructures are of crucial importance in disadvantaged areas, where they raise a number of political, economic and human challenges. Their strategic importance can be grasped by analysing the opposing discourses – legitimising or denunciatory – developed by the various actors to justify their positions and practices regarding slum electrification. The protagonists use specific, normative repertories to invoke conflicting definitions of reality. Although each repertory makes sense in itself, they are mutually exclusive and excluding, thus ruling out any competing arguments.

From accepting illegal connections to resisting institutionalised electrification

In a country where territorial control is a key aspect of management, and authority is implemented through urban policies (usually with security aims in mind),[10] the Moroccan government has adopted an ambiguous position with regard to slums, oscillating between prohibition and tolerance. In these neighbourhoods, the state exercises its power negatively; it neglects the public service roles it performs (or delegates) in legal urban neighbourhoods (such as providing utilities and security) and generally prohibits slum

residents from taking action to acquire infrastructure, although it may sometimes overlook such initiatives to keep the peace. Thus, the securitarian approach is not strictly antithetical to *laissez-faire* policies, and political control is not necessarily reduced to systematic repression or insurmountable
prohibition.[11] It has more to do with keeping the population in a state of
uncertainty by playing on the inherently revocable nature of their informal
settlements while, at the same time, tolerating certain adjustments in line
with the local configuration and balance of power.

Since the early 1990s, with the opening (albeit relative) of electoral competition to new entrants, slum dwellers have gradually improved their living conditions (for example, by introducing sewage systems), often with the
support of elected officials. In such cases, slum "politics" thwarted slum "policies". Indeed, residents discovered they were in a position to demand new
services in exchange for their votes. To get elected, candidates for parliamentary and local offices were induced to defy (to some extent) government
prohibitions, thereby changing the status quo on land use by slum dwellers.[12]

The new services were introduced informally. Municipalities[13] often
posted the related costs as "extraordinary expenses" in their budgets. While
the need for electrification had been officially recognised since 1998, the
public authorities required the governors of Casablanca's eight *arrondissement*
prefectures to treat the operation in slum areas as a temporary solution,
pending implementation of (often hypothetical) resettlement programmes.
In its temporary electrification contracts, Lydec agreed to dismantle its electrical installations within a few days if requested by governors.

Caught between market forces and "civic commitment"

The state justified its refusal to include slums in the municipal power grid by
invoking the need to respect private property and comply with city planning
laws and regulations[14]. Lydec, on the other hand, demanded that electricity
hijacking be stopped in the name of market rules and economic efficiency.
The utility operator wrote numerous letters to the governors stressing the
hazards of hijacking both for slum dwellers and for its own agents who had
to dismantle illegal connections and decrying its widespread negative effects
on service provision to surrounding neighbourhoods. In these letters, Lydec
invoked respect for private property and underscored the responsibility of
the "authorities" to guarantee it.

It seems that, prior to the arrival of Lydec, electricity hijacking was viewed as a marginal phenomenon by the former state-owned utility. However, the private operator's assessment of the losses generated by the practice substantially changed the perception of hijacking in the slums. In a special section of the company activity report for September 1998 to September 1999 entitled "Disadvantaged Neighbourhoods", Lydec evaluated the total losses for the year at roughly 12 million dirhams (EUR 1 million) and subsequent dismantling work to offset the dysfunction at nearly 1.2 million dirhams (about EUR 100,000). The report's recommendation was "to find a solution within an institutional framework to make the slum dwellers pay".[15] The evolution of the company's official discourse also shows that slum electrification was becoming a goal in itself for Lydec, which set up a special "Disadvantaged Neighbourhoods" unit in late 1998. Thanks to the dedication of a staff often strongly committed to their social mission, the operator sought to show that, contrary to its image as a foreign company coming to do business in Casablanca, "the mission to serve the public is at the heart of its corporate culture".[16]

From human rights to slum dwellers' rights

Slum residents experienced life without electricity as being materially and symbolically discredited, whereas they considered hijacking electricity, on the contrary, to be a legitimate form of appropriation. This made sense, in that it shifted the blame to the state and its agents for the failure to provide legal(ised) housing for slum dwellers, despite presenting slum eradication as a public policy objective ever since Independence and after several aborted projects to relocate the Carrières centrales neighbourhood. However illegitimate the slum might be, this did not justify, in the eyes of the residents, the way they had been treated over the years.

To justify hijacking electricity – and their broader social demands – slum residents invoked their *rights* rather than the law.[17] They opted for a universalist discourse and appealed to values that transcended the standards they had violated, thereby lending legitimacy to their aspirations and to specific demands such as access to electricity:

> For years we have been living like animals. We have waited and waited, but nothing ever happens – no housing, no jobs, always the same contempt for us. The state does nothing. Nothing but promises, while we continue to suffer. With

electricity, we are laying claim to our rights; at least the children can do their homework at night, life is a little better".[18]

The rights argument proved an effective mobilising tool. It appropriated the vocabulary used since the 1990s by the central government, which had tried to neutralise the demands of human rights associations by turning them into an issue for consensus decision-making.[19] Furthermore, when the alternating government[20] was set up after the 1997 legislative elections, the public policies implemented in slums came under serious scrutiny. After a series of evaluations, the housing ministry declared that social factors should be taken into account as a major component in devising policies for action in the slums,[21] although the subsequent guidelines for policy action remained unchanged.[22] By taking over the vocabularies of human rights and "social" discourse, slum residents positioned themselves as dissidents; they advocated a system of authority based on human rights principles and justified resistance to existing authority as a way of compelling the application of these principles.[23]

The liberalised political context encouraged protestors to address their demands to the authorities, but it also imposed limits on their actions, limits which they accepted while interpreting them to suit their own purposes. In a speech in August 2001, King Mohammed VI made social housing a national priority. The speech was surprising in its stated determination to implement an uncompromising policy of imposing sanctions on the civil servants, elected officials and inhabitants responsible for the proliferation of illegal installations in informal settlements. Slum dwellers nevertheless hailed the speech as evidence of the king's sensitivity to their situation. In their comments on the speech, slum residents reinterpreted a rather repressive speech, turning it into an argument for the legitimacy of hijacking. Perceived reality was thus shaped collectively:

> We are doing what *Sidna* (the king) would want for us. He is the king of the poor![24] He wants us to live, he wants what is good for us, because he knows we are citizens, he said so in his speech. If the state did what *Sidna* wants, we would all live in dignity and peace, with water and electricity and real houses.[25]

The slums thus produced "built-in"[26] advocacy resources by imbuing their personal experience with insights drawn not only from the media but also directly from the political discourse of the king himself. We can gauge the importance of those resources not only from the context but also from the representations and meanings constructed when resistance to the imposed order crystallised. We will see that the process of widespread hijacking also revealed the fluid link between individual and collective action.

From individual to collective electric power diversion: professionalising hijacking

When the phenomenon of hijacking electricity first appeared in the 1980s, it was carried out by isolated individuals via makeshift connections to the streetlight system. Wires were connected only at night, so as not to draw the attention of the authorities. The connections were rudimentary, and power quality was often poor. Hijacking expanded initially through imitation, by capillarity. At that point, it was less a collective mobilisation than a series of incremental individual or inter-individual initiatives; wires were "shared" between neighbours or "given" to friends and relatives whose shanties were not too far away.

The concept of the free rider does not apply in the case of diverting electric power, or at least not in the same way as in a conventional struggle to obtain a public good, in which individuals may try to take advantage of the positive impact of a mobilisation without participating in it. The immediate enjoyment of the coveted good provided by hijacking is a direct incentive to slum residents to take part in the action. However, there is a false contradiction here, which James Scott has pointed out, between seeking an immediate good and performing an act of resistance.[27] From the outset, hijacking took a political turn in the sense that its first practitioners saw it as defiance against an unjust system. Testimonials collected in 2003 from five slum dwellers who claimed to have been among the initiators of hijacking at Carrières centrales are significant in this respect. The five were all friends and neighbours and presented themselves as former supporters of the far left. They said their decision to take action was influenced by an activist friend belonging to the Moroccan Human Rights Association (known for its refusal to deal with the authorities), who did not live in their neighbourhood but in a different slum nearby. The ability to harness an argument based on social justice to implement and legitimise illegal power diversion was decisive in adopting this practice.

The spread of hijacking swiftly accelerated in the 1990s. In this case, the collective pressure of numbers was exerted and objectivated differently than in more traditional protest actions such as demonstrations or marches. There were no individuals making themselves visible, no bodies or voices occupying space to demonstrate their strength (in numbers). Instead, there were cables marking the boundary lines within which slum residents could exercise and assert their power. The more consumers there were, the smaller the risk of individual repression, and collective punishment was usually limited to dismantling illegal connections.

As hijacking became generalised, it also turned into a more technical and commercial business. It was organised under the impetus of professional electricians who streamlined the illegal connections to improve the distribution of current and reduce the hazards. However, when Lydec upgraded the power grid, the amateur connections came to an end, and henceforth the cables were protected by shields, as well as coded to prevent the hijackers from identifying them. Unlike the movement's initiators, the professional hijackers had no qualms about occasionally bribing central government representatives at the local level (*moqaddems*) to avoid repressive measures, although an institutionalised market was never established between the two types of actors, at least in the case of Carrières centrales. The professionals were thus assured of a monopoly on the hijacking market, and they developed real commercial relationships with slum residents.

As a result, the vast majority of households already had electricity before authority for the service was delegated to Lydec.[28] In 2001, at least one full-time chief electrician officiated in each of the six sections of Carrières centrales, along with one or two apprentices. Every night and during the weekends, hijacking technicians to whom residents could turn when a problem arose were on call. Other slum dwellers were responsible for collecting fees. Each household had to pay a fixed price of 40–100 dirhams (EUR 4–9) on average every month, in addition to the initial connection fee, to cover the cost of maintaining the network and paying the hijackers.

The power to install illegal connections became concentrated in the hands of a small minority with decisive technical resources, creating a sort of oligarchy of hijackers in Carrières centrales. The system worked, partly due to ties between neighbours that ensured some payment flexibility (which shows that the mobilisation was not only a matter of logistics but also relied on social networks) and partly to the immediate sanctions that hijackers could impose on residents. For example, electricity was cut off during football matches that attracted large audiences, and anyone who wanted to watch or listen to the game had to pay an additional fee. In addition to the gains realised by the hijackers from their captive customers, this provision made it possible to regulate power consumption to avoid potential problems arising from overconsumption on undersized networks.

Play of alliances and radicalisation of hijacking

Under the supervisory authority granted to the ministry of the interior over utilities and service concessions, the former public utility company had been more likely to operate according to a logic of politics and patronage. A private operator like Lydec, on the other hand, was forced to obey a logic of efficiency and profitability. The arrival of the company contributed to the radicalisation of hijacking, prompting the governors to allow formal electrification of the Casablanca slums on a case-by-case basis. However, the relative failure of the temporary electrification system after the first few years revealed the diverging interests and objectives of the various actors involved.

Lydec: a vector for crystallising the struggle for power

When Lydec arrived in Carrières centrales, hijacking, already well organised, gave rise to new forms of action that betrayed certain underlying tensions. In the final analysis, what was being called into question was the public policy of limiting community-owned infrastructure in the slum. Nevertheless, the protest hardened, and collective cohesion crystallised into a confrontation with the private operator that concealed the opposition to the state:

> The arrival of Lydec changed people's behaviour. Whereas it had been unthinkable to oppose agents of the RAD [Autonomous Power Distribution], there was a significant increase in verbal and physical violence against Lydec agents during its campaigns[29] – to such an extent that it can no longer operate in some of these areas.[30]

The radicalised protest action can also be explained by the plan, introduced by Lydec after the first pilot electrification experiment in Ben M'sik in 1998, to dismantle the illegal connections. The disconnections took place while awaiting authorisations for electrification of the other slums, which were granted on a case-by-case basis by the governors of the prefectures. The scale of certain power cuts revealed the full extent of the hijacking. Lydec agents dismantled connections in Carrières centrales on 16 December 2000 on ten points of fraud in one section; in the Thomas section, two tons of cables and seven poles were removed on 22 March 2001.[31]

The dismantling campaigns were implemented with the support of the public authorities. Lydec succeeded in convincing the governors to send police into the slums to ensure the safety of its staff. Despite the involvement of law enforcement, the hijacking organisers reacted with reprisals and intimidation. The company records contain accounts of numerous attacks on Lydec agents, notably with knives, and there were other incidents. For example, steel cables several metres long were thrown onto power lines serving feeder stations, causing significant power outages in several towns and forcing the private operator to isolate certain high voltage antennas from the network. Near one slum, hijackers padlocked a feeder station after connecting their cables directly to the main switchboard. The commando style of the actions was accentuated by its hazardousness; agents were only allowed to enter the stations, where the current reached 22,000 volts, wearing special protective gear and after receiving appropriate training. To put a stop to recurring retaliatory practices, Lydec posted round-the-clock security guards at the slum's power supply points, using police officers paid by the company.

Along with these styles of violent action, the entire slum population resorted to more peaceful forms of mobilisation, including multiple marches and sit-ins in front of the prefecture to protest the Lydec power cuts. The protesters demanded the "restoration of public lighting in the streets".[32] In fact, slum residents had never had public streetlights, but they knew this demand would appear more legitimate to the general public than claiming a right to free electricity. Here again, the slum residents showed their ability to reinterpret a situation in order to legitimise their actions. Another common mode of action was to organise gatherings of women in front of power supply points to prevent Lydec agents from cutting off electricity; gendered resistance designed to minimise the risk of violent repression is a well-known repertory of slum protest action. The power cut campaigns may not have been effective in preventing illegal connections, but they were also intended to put financial pressure on slum residents (twisted cables are expensive) to persuade them they would be better off in the end paying for a regular supply of good quality electricity than maintaining the practice of hijacking. The dramatic confrontation between Lydec and the slum dwellers was also a forceful argument to make the governors speed up the process of granting permits to electrify the various slums. The logic of economic efficiency defended by Lydec lent support to the collective demand for improved infrastructure.

Ambiguous role of local officials

Local elected officials also played a key role in the ongoing tug-of-war with governors to make them accept formal slum electrification on a case-by-case basis. Acting as intermediaries between the state, the private operator and the slum residents, the officials were eager to reconcile these divergent interests, striving to appear as good representatives in the eyes of their constituents while maintaining good relations with the representatives of the state. Nevertheless, the vital nature of the struggle over electricity in the slums often drove the municipal councillors to object directly to the government, thus helping to change the status quo on land use.

In order to electrify a slum, Lydec first had to receive a request for electrification from the president of the municipal council (the district council starting in 2003) as well as an authorisation from the governor. Thus, in some cases, electrification became an important object of transaction used by local elected officials or campaigning candidates to attract and ensure voter support. The issue of connecting the slums to the city's power grid has also been used by the decentralised authority to promote the re-election of municipal council presidents, their election to parliament or, on the contrary, to undermine their legitimacy and damage their political careers.

Following the Lydec dismantling operations, some municipal council presidents went ahead and used local resources to reinstate illegal connections for their constituents. One council president of a municipality north of Casablanca metropolitan area, interviewed in March 2002, offered this explanation:

> Here [a slum in his constituency], the relocation project failed. These people [the slum residents] are going to be here for years to come. I am here to help them, and in my view we cannot ignore the problem. That is why I allowed them to take electricity from the town.

According to Lydec agents, the elected official himself sent electricians employed by the municipality to connect slum residents to the public power grid. Several connection points were made from utility poles but also directly from a transformer station (the electricity consumed in this case was paid for by Lydec). In another slum within the same prefecture, Lydec agents discovered that, the day after a dismantling operation conducted in the presence of the local authority and a police brigade in March 2001, the slum residents were reconnected by the municipal team using a bucket truck, in the presence of the slum's elected representative, who claimed to have an authorisation from the governor. We are not arguing that local officials should be seen as instrumental in destabilising or subverting the political system. Their actions nevertheless helped crystallise new patterns of mobilisation in the slums and encouraged the shift from individualised, fragmented action to collective action that ultimately turned into open, head-on resistance. Thus, the existence of vertical ties does not systematically hinder collective mobilisation; it can even give it a boost.

Redeployment of hijackers in formal electrification

The subversive power of professional hijackers was finally neutralised by integrating them into the formal electrification system organised by Lydec. Indeed, many of the orchestrators of electric power diversion became mediating agents between slum dwellers and the private operator. Given the illegal use of land by these customers, the company installed a collective meter for each "block" consisting of twenty to fifty households. Subscription contracts were signed only with block "representatives" (umanâ', literally "guarantors"), who were fully responsible for payment of collective invoices, coordinating infrastructure work and maintaining the "secondary network" (a private network connecting the "head meter" at the top of the street to the individual household meters in the block). The head meter was serviced by Lydec, but the company was not responsible for any malfunction in the secondary network.[33] The representatives were the only customers recognised by Lydec, and they were in charge of recovering the amounts due from each consumer household.

According to the contract proposed by Lydec, the representatives were to be designated by the residents. In fact, organising genuine consultations proved too problematic, and the representatives were appointed by the municipality based on recommendations made by local elected representatives. The local officials often proposed former hijacking leaders for the job, first because they already had authority and influence over the population and, second, to keep them from organising resistance to the formal electrification process out of fear of losing their livelihood. Even so, the decision to redeploy former hijackers, which was not lost on state authorities or the private operator, did not prevent serious problems later on, particularly with regard to payment for electricity consumption.

Limitations of the system in the medium term

The relative failure of the Lydec system after a few years (especially since 2006) reflects the difference between the interests of the private operator and those of the slum dwellers. It also highlights the lack of political support for the operation.

A difficult-to-secure condominial network

Technical innovations were introduced to minimise costs and adapt standards,[34] accompanied by a new business management approach mainly involving the "delegation" of condominium-type[35] final network distribution to a community representative. Both types of innovation contributed decisively to the policy compromise reached with the authorities. At the same time, they were a key factor in crystallising tensions between Lydec, the community representatives and residents in the years following slum electrification, particularly after 2004.

Numerous technical problems were reported on the private networks managed by the representatives. The networks soon proved too small to meet the slum residents' actual consumption needs, partly due to pressure from commercial activities that had not been taken into account. The policy consensus reached with the authorities limited electrification solely to household consumption (the public authorities had no intention of stimulating the informal economy). To avoid repeated outages due to overloaded collective meters, slum dwellers increasingly made their own direct connections to the main grid upstream from circuit breakers, whereas most of the ground connections installed by Lydec gradually disappeared (they were made of copper and thus had significant market value). The danger of these makeshift installations was confirmed by an increase in fires. No accidents or fires had been reported in electrified slum neighbourhoods prior to 2004,[36] but at least three fires were recorded between May 2009 and March 2010 in the Carrrières centrales slum alone.

Thus, after several years, although electrification led to a perceptible improvement in the residents' quality of life, Lydec was not always able to honour its commitment to secure electrical installations, notably in large slums where amateur tampering with the private networks managed by community representatives was especially widespread.

Collection problems related to the shared management system

Furthermore, the principle of self-managed payment established by the temporary electrification contracts has not always worked over time. While the recovery rate on electricity bills was still 96 percent in early 2005, by 31 March 2010, the total amount of payments due for Casablanca slums stood at over 40 million dirhams (EUR 3.6 million),[37] compared to annual revenue from slum electrification of approximately 24 million dirhams (EUR 2 million) in 2005.[38] In Carrières centrales, the problem reached an unprecedented level, with nearly 10 million dirhams (EUR 900,000) in delinquent payments in early 2010 (already more than 8 million in July 2009), equivalent to approximately 80 percent of the unpaid bills for the entire prefecture of Ain Sebaa Hay Mohammadi.

The increased failure of households to keep up with their electricity bills stemmed primarily from the solidarity system imposed *de facto* on the population, above all in large slums, which was impossible to enforce. Many community representatives gradually refused to pay the company the full amount collected from residents. The representatives did not receive a fixed salary but rather a small profit on electricity consumption. They were theoretically entitled to a maximum 20 percent margin between the price per kWh they had to pay Lydec and the price they charged consumers, but, in reality, the margin seldom exceeded 10 percent,[39] and the representatives often felt poorly compensated for their workload and responsibilities.[40] Thus, although slum dwellers actually paid more for their electricity than low-consuming families in the rest of the city – 1 dirham on average (EUR 0.09) compared with 0.89 dirham (EUR 0.08) per kWh – the compensation system failed in the long run.

At the same time, it was extremely difficult for the company to determine how much of the unpaid amount was attributable to the community representatives and how much to the slum dwellers. Resident collectives repeatedly came to Lydec's various prefectoral delegations asking to pay their bills individually, but their requests were rejected by the governors. Lacking legal status, slum households were not recognised as full-fledged customers, which added to their sense of disempowerment. The community representatives, in turn, had little leeway to enforce payment on the private networks they managed. Social pressure made it very difficult to disconnect the poorest families, and there was also a major technical constraint; people could illegally reconnect to the network if their electricity was cut off. The problem of controlling free riders, rendered particularly difficult by the electrification system, was compounded when the payment issue became politicised in certain slums, among them Carrières centrales. It appears that the topic of longstanding free electricity for slum residents[41] sometimes became an important issue in electoral campaigns.

Finally, it is essential to grasp the changing political context to understand why the system was eventually discontinued. Following the bombings on 16 May 2003,[42] the public authorities introduced an ambitious public policy to "eradicate" all slums in Morocco by 2012. After launching the "Cities Without Slums" programme" in 2004 and finally abandoning the option to restructure certain slums in 2006, relocation and resettlement became the only instruments available to policymakers to remove the slums from the urban landscape. After ten years of relative tolerance for solutions cobbled together to improve living conditions in the slums, this about-face had an undeniable influence on the calculations and expectations of slum dwellers. A Lydec consultant discovered that the announcement of the slum resettlement project in 2007 coincided with an explosion of payment delinquency in Carrières centrales (even when some bills dated as far back as 2003, they had hitherto been relatively contained). Knowing they were about to be expelled, the residents had less incentive to pay for their electricity, especially since the authorities did not take any effective measures to support the private operator.

Lack of strong political backing

Theoretically, Lydec had the right to suspend the supply of electricity to any block that was not fully paid up (Article 10 of the temporary electrification contract). However, partly owing to pressure put on the company by the authorities, removal procedures were by no means systematically conducted. The company claims that local officials "repeatedly asked Lydec to suspend power cuts until solutions could be found, with the help of the *arrondissement* councils, for payment of arrears and invoices".[43] It should be noted that today, although almost half of Carrières centrales has been resettled, the payment problem is still unresolved.

To be sure, the governors of the various prefectures continued to back Lydec's planned dismantling by dispatching police officers, just as they did prior to electrification, but they also repeatedly invoked the security issue to postpone outages. In the slums, the authorities feared a resurgence of crime if streetlights were cut. More broadly, at the prefecture or even at city level, public authorities were worried that power cuts would lead to uncontrolled protest demonstrations. Lydec's civic commitment in the slums was widely acknowledged after the 2003 bombings, and, for several months, feedback meetings took place between the company's "Disadvantaged Neighbourhoods" unit and the Social Development Agency team,[44] which was working on the concrete implementation of the concept of public project contracting (now called social support to reduce substandard housing). Nevertheless, in a certain way, by asserting its leadership in introducing a public service for disadvantaged populations, the company found itself trapped in the political and social management of the slum and forced to assume part of the cost.

Conclusion

In Casablanca, the liberalisation of utilities and the delegation of electric power distribution to a private company led to the official electrification of three quarters of the slums in the metropolitan area between 2001 and 2004. Analysis of the slum residents' struggle to obtain electricity shows that top-down institutional reforms do not always achieve the local results attributed to them at the national level and are always ambiguous. To some extent, they were beyond the control even of an authoritarian government, often due to inconsistencies in stated and/or implemented public policies. In the slums, public land management, plagued by lack of planning, lack of utilities and so on, was at odds with the imperatives of political and economic liberalisation – including the principle of delegating public services – adopted by the authorities since the 1990s.

The arrival of Lydec upset the fluid balance among the various players at the local level. It became a catalyst for more open resistance from slum dwellers to the government veto on infrastructure development in these informal settlements. During the early years of its implementation, the temporary electrification system appeared to be a success and was promoted for its flexibility and lower cost. In the medium term, however, the system proved unsustainable due to both the impossibility of managing the collective, solidarity-based system and the government's failure to support the operation. Formal electrification clearly changed the status quo between public authorities and slum residents, making access to electric light a legitimate service. However, it did not fundamentally transform the political management of slums by the authorities. To maintain social stability, local officials continued to ignore certain practices, particularly electricity hijacking, which resurfaced in other forms after Lydec's electrification campaign, leading the company to bear the cost of a social policy it had initiated itself.

After the National Human Development Initiative (INDH) was launched in 2005, Lydec officially brought slum electrification to a halt. INDH was an ambitious public project, backed by the king and with a 10-billion-dirham budget (EUR 900 million) for the period 2006–2010, to connect the populations in neighbourhoods with unsanitary housing to infrastructure and basic social services. To achieve this goal on a citywide scale in Morocco's economic capital, Lydec signed a framework agreement in September 2005 with the *wilaya*[45] of Greater Casablanca to undertake a major project called INMAE (literally "development" in Arabic). It aimed to provide electricity, water and sanitation services to 85,000 households (500,000 people) living in illegal housing "whom the authorities decided would remain on site".[46] Lydec was put in charge of connecting" unauthorised neighbourhoods", slums and "outlying suburban *douars*"[47] to the drinking water network, whereas Idmaj Sakane, a semi-public company under the direct supervision of the *wali* of Greater Casablanca, was responsible for connecting the urban slums.[48]

In this new division of labour to install utilities, the public authorities appear to be increasingly standardising the work performed by Lydec. The private company operates only in priority areas identified by the state as part of the INDH project, which are intended to be gradually brought in line with the law. It is actively involved in upstream negotiations with the governors to ensure that the authorities are committed to taking action in the areas concerned, particularly by drawing up lists of names of beneficiaries whose land ownership situations are expected to be eventually legalised. Through the INMAE project, Lydec also installs standardised connections similar to those proposed in other areas of Casablanca but at lower rates. Rather than position itself as the initiator of social programmes and risk being overtaken by events beyond its control, the company now strives to support public action with guidance and a firm commitment from the public authorities.

The disappointing experience of temporary slum electrification in Casablanca brought out the adjustments and the interplay of actors resulting from the liberalisation of utilities in Morocco. It illustrates the theoretical argument that economic liberalisation does not mean the withdrawal of the state but rather its redeployment.[49] The Lydec initiative also helped to expand the range of possibilities in the slums and to transform patterns of popular action. Protest, which had traditionally been fragmented and silent, became more open and collective during the period from 1990 to 2000.[50]

Endnotes

1   This article is based on data collected from residents of the Carrières centrales slum between 2000 and 2003 during fieldwork for my thesis. I conducted fifteen interviews with people directly involved in electric power diversion and/or the representatives in charge of the private power networks set up under the supervision of the Lyonnaise des Eaux de Casablanca (Lydec). In September 2003, I participated in the activities of Lydec's "Disadvantaged Neighbourhoods" unit for three weeks as an informal trainee. See L. Zaki, *Pratiques politiques au bidonville. Casablanca (2000–2005)*, doctoral thesis in political science, Institut d'études politiques de Paris, 2005. I later updated the data by interviewing managers of the Lydec electrification contract and the INDH (*Initiative nationale pour le développement humain* – National Human Development Initiative)-Inmae project during the summer of 2010.

2   Lydec, the Moroccan subsidiary of Suez Environnement was then awarded, by decision of the Board of the Urban Community of Casablanca, the delegated management of the distribution of electricity, drinking water and liquid sanitation services in Casablanca and Mohammedia.

3   The prefecture is a key level of territorial control devolved to local authorities. The Greater Casablanca region is composed of eight prefectures headed by governors appointed by the king. District councils are also elected by universal suffrage in each district, which is the territorial jurisdiction of a prefecture.

4 Between 1912 and 1956, most of Morocco was a French Protectorate, while north-ern and southern zones of the country formed a Spanish Protectorate.

5 In Moroccan administrative jargon, the word "relocation" refers to giving slum resi-dents plots of land already equipped with infrastructure on which they must build their own housing in accordance with certain rules. Resettlement, on the other hand, generally means moving people from slum areas into apartments.

6 The process, initiated by Hassan II and continued by Mohammed VI, has been far from linear. For one of the many studies on the limits of analysing the regime in terms of democratisation, see J.-N Ferrié and J.-C. Santucci (eds.), *Dispositifs de dé-mocratisation et dispositifs autoritaires en Afrique du Nord*, Paris: CNRS Éditions, 2006.

7 The vocabulary here is borrowed from A. Bayat, *Street Politics. Poor People's Movements in Iran*, New York: Columbia University Press, 1997.

8 On the need for an analysis in terms of a continuum between "hidden channels" and "open challenge" (including a fresh look at the work of J.C. Scott, A.O. Hirschman, A. Bayat and J.-F Bayart) see O. Fillieule and M. Bennani-Chraïbi, "Exit, voice, loy-alty and among many others…," in M. Bennani-Chraïbi and O. Fillieule (eds.), *Résistances et protestations dans les sociétés musulmanes*, Paris: Presses de Sciences Po, 2003, pp. 58–74..

9 On the issues surrounding the analysis of mobilisations from a dynamic perspective, see O. Fillieule, "Requiem pour un concept. Vie et mort de la notion de structure des opportunités", in G. Dorronsoro (ed.), *La Turquie conteste*, Paris: CNRS Éditions, 2005, p. 210.

10 See, among many other publications, H. Rachik, *Ville et pouvoirs au Maroc*, Casablanca: Éditions Afrique-Orient, 1995.

11 Several studies highlight the logic of political patronage behind the creation of in-formal neighbourhoods, and the relationships between public figures, local officials and local representatives of the central state. See, in particular, A. El Maoula El Iraki, *Des notables du Makhzen à l'épreuve de la 'gouvernance'. Élites locales, gestion ur-baine et développement au Maroc*, Paris: L'Harmattan, 2003; A. Abouhani, *Pouvoirs, villes et notabilités locales. Quand les notables font les villes*, Rabat: Inau/Urbama, 1989.

12 L. Zaki, "Le clientélisme, vecteur de politisation en régime autoritaire?" in M. Camau, V. Geisser and G. Massardier (eds.), *Autoritarismes démocratiques, démocraties autoritaires. Convergences NordSud,* Paris, La Découverte, 2008, pp. 157–80.

13 It should be noted that in 2003 Casablanca's 27 municipalities were merged into a single municipality through the implementation of a new municipal charter. The ar-rondissements that replaced them at the local level no longer operate on their own budgets. See M. Catusse and L. Zaki, "Gestion communale et clientélisme moral au Maroc. Les Politiques du Parti de la justice et du développement", *Critique internationale*, no. 42, 2009, pp. 73–91.

14 Whereas special dispensations have, in fact, been a characteristic feature of Moroccan city planning, including in the creation of legal neighbourhoods.

15 Lydec, *Rapport d'activité 1998–1999*, Casablanca, 2000, section "Quartiers Défavorisés".

16 R. Massé, *Etude d'impact du programme d'électrification dans les bidonvilles de Casablanca* [study commissioned by EDF], Paris: Groupe de recherche et d'échanges technologiques, 2005, pp. 47–9.

17 Partha Chatterjee has conceptualised a similar phenomenon of politicising "the governed" through rights in India. See P. Chatterjee, *Politique des gouvernés. Réflexions sur la politque populaire dans la majeure partie du monde*, Paris: Éditions Amsterdam, 2009.

18 Interview with Zoubida, Carrières centrales, 7 July 2001.

19 See F. Vairel, "Le Maroc des années de plomb. Equité et réconciliation", *Politique africaine,* no. 96, December 2004, pp. 181–95.

20 The expression refers to the return to government of parties confined to the opposition for several decades, in particular the *Union socialiste des forces populaire* [Socialist Federation of Popular Forces], which led the first alternating government set up in 1998.

21 F. Navez-Bouchanine, "Évolution de la prise en compte de la dimension sociale dans les interventions en bidonville sous le gouvernement d'alternance", *Critique économique*, no. 8, 2002, pp. 285–304.

22 L. Zaki, "L'action publique au bidonville. L'État entre gestion par le manque, 'éradication' des *kariens* et accompagnement social des habitants", *L'Année du Mahgreb*, no. 2005–2006, pp. 303–20.

23 M. David-Jougneau, *Le Dissident et l'institution, ou Alice au pays des normes,* Paris: L'Harmattan, 1989.

24 This expression was commonly used, especially in the early years of the reign of Mohammed VI, due to his highly publicised commitment to help disadvantaged populations.

25 Interview with Khaled, Carrières centrales, 9 September 2001.

26 W.A. Gamson, *Talking Politics*, Cambridge: Cambridge University Press, 1992.

27 J.C. Scott, *Weapons of the Weak. Everyday Forms of Peasant Resistance*, New Haven: Yale University Press, 1985.

28 R. Massé, *Étude d'impact du programme d'électrification...*, op. cit., p. 19.

29 The delegated management contract required Lydec to take over the entire RAD staff. The agents of the private operator were therefore essentially the same as the public ones.

30 Lydec, *Rapport d'activité, 1998–1999*, op. cit.

31 Lydec, *Rapport d'activité, February–March 2001,* Casablanca, section "Quartiers défavorisés".

32 *El Ahdath*, no. 828, 24 April 2001.

33 In some slum neighbourhoods, the authorities agreed to temporary electrification, but without authorising Lydec to work in the slum. In such cases, the company's action was limited to installing one or more "temporary meters" known as "fraud heads" outside the neighbourhood, to which one or more private networks were connected using the same principle described above.

34 A. Merceron, "Électrification des bidonvilles à Casablanca", *Liaison Énergie-Francophonie*, no. 63, 2004, pp. 60–61.

35 In a "condominial" system, a local network is connected to the main grid through a collective connection that can serve an entire block of houses.

36 Ibid., p. 64.

37 To grasp these amounts in relation to the company's overall business, it should be noted that revenue from the supply of electric power to private households in Casablanca stood at 228 million dirhams, including tax (EUR 20 million), for the month of January 2010 alone.

38 S. Botton, "L'accès à l'eau et à l'électricité dans les pays en développement. Comment penser la demande?", *Idées pour le débat*, no. 9, 2006, p. 57.

39 A. Merceron, "Électrification des bidonvilles…", op. cit., p. 63.

40 According to the estimates of Lydec agents, representatives in charge of several blocks could earn from 2,000 to 2,500 dirhams per month (EUR 180–220), the equivalent of the minimum wage.

41 A topic linked to that of free water, traditionally distributed at fire hydrants and paid for by the towns.

42 The attacks, carried out by young terrorists mostly from the same slum in the outskirts of Casablanca, increased the stigma attached to slum dwellers (already treated like potential criminals) by equating slums and poverty with terrorism and Islamism. For an analysis that challenges this equation, see L. Zaki, *Pratiques politiques au bidonville…*, op. cit., pp. 78–124.

43 Lydec, Direction des opérations, "Note relative au programme d'électrification provisoire des quartiers bidonvilles", Casablanca, 4 June 2010.

44 A public body set up in 1999.

45 Equivalent to a regional prefecture in France.

46 Lydec, *Rapport annuel*, Casablanca, 2010, p. 31.

47 Unlike slum dwellers, the residents of unauthorised neighbourhoods owned their land but built their housing without a permit. In theory, the term *douar* refers to a village in a rural environment.

48 For further details, see C. de Miras, "Initiative nationale pour le développement humain et économie solidaire au Maroc. Pour un accès élargi à l'eau et à l'assainissement", *Revue Tiers Monde*, no. 190, 2007, pp. 357–78.

49 See in particular B. Hibou (ed.), *La Privatisation des États*, Paris: Karthala, 1999; M. Catusse, *Le Temps des entrepreneurs ? Politique et transformations du capitalisme au Maroc*, Paris: Maisonneuve et Larose, 2008.

50 Cf. L. Zaki, *Pratiques politiques au bidonville...*, op. cit.

7

✳

Neoliberal Reforms, Patronage and Protest Movements in an Authoritarian Context: The case of the Gafsa mining region in Tunisia

Amin Allal

Introduction

For almost six months in 2008, the Gafsa region in southwest Tunisia was engulfed in a large-scale protest movement in response to changes at the Gafsa Phosphate Company, a major state-owned mining company in the region. The rise and decline of the protests had multiple causes: the company's diminishing impact on the regional economy, the accompanying erosion of patronage practices, the resurgence of the widespread image of Gafsa as a "rebel region" and the organisation of the protest movement and its fluctuating interactions with the state, particularly the security apparatus, and with various political organisations.

In 2008, Tunisia experienced the longest and largest protests the country had seen in decades.[1] The trouble began on 6 January 2008, after the Compagnie des Phosphates de Gafsa (CPG) [Gafsa Phosphate Company][2] announced the results of a competitive recruitment examination. Over the next six months, the residents of the main towns and villages in the mining centres of the Gafsa region engaged in a series of massive protests that resulted in hundreds of detentions and left three people dead and dozens injured.[3]

Since the late nineteenth century, the history of the Gafsa region has co-incided with that of the CPG. The company, originally a colonial enterprise until it was "Tunisiafied," has always been at the core of this impoverished outlying area of southern Tunisia. When the country achieved independence, the major state-owned mining company, considered an eldorado for work-ers, became a symbol of nation building and the focal point of enormous expectations.[4] Since the mid-1980s, however, the company's restructuring in line with neoliberal principles[5] led to the decline of its activities in the re-gion. The CPG, one of the largest producers of phosphate in the world (eight million tonnes in 2007),[6] virtually stopped hiring. Since then, 10,000 jobs have been eliminated, intensifying unemployment, especially among young people, in the region, where the CPG is one of the few opportunities for jobseekers.

It was in this context that the 2008 protests broke out, revealing the con-siderable social, political and economic discontent of the local population, latent since the 1980s. To understand the movement, it is necessary to ana-lyse the underlying factors that fuelled it: a feeling of despair among many of the unemployed, particularly young jobseekers at the forefront of the pro-tests, rejection of the local patronage system resulting from CPG restructur-ing, which was perceived as unfair, the resurgence of a traditional collec-tive imagination that inspired hopes of a favourable outcome and, finally, the very dynamics of the protests and their subsequent repression, with tactical moves by local potentates competing with one another to tap into public discontent, the organisation of the movement around local union leaders and unemployed graduates and widespread repression.[7]

We will begin by analysing these dynamics, the chronology of events and the key players. Next we will examine why the CPG lies at the heart of the problems in this impoverished mining region and how it generated a local patronage system during its "neo-liberal moment", which was challenged by many unemployed youths in the region. Finally, we will take a close look at an aspect of the protest specific to this region: the representation of Gafsa as a "rebel region" in the collective Tunisian imagination.[8]

The dynamics behind the 2008 protests: struggle, coercion and negotiations

The protests that began in early 2008 were unparalleled in the Tunisia of President Ben Ali. On 7 November 2007, the authoritarian political regime had celebrated the twentieth anniversary of Ben Ali's accession to power as the president of "change" in a political landscape marked by repression of political opposition, strict control over "civil society", a justice system kept in check and a muzzled media.[9] The Rassemblement constitutionnel démocratique (RDC) [Constitutional Democratic Rally], the hegemonic presidential party, engineered tight political control through multiple district committees, cells and other coordinating bodies. The political police, along with "social development" agencies such as the Tunisian Solidarity Bank (TSB), maintained a balance between repression, fear and patronage, which characterised the Tunisian regime and guaranteed its "stability".[10]

In this context, popular expectations of the state were high, and the tension was palpable in the region. In 2007, roadblocks were set up by the unemployed in M'dhila (located 20 kilometres southwest of Gafsa) to stop buses of workers and trucks carrying phosphate. In Gafsa, the jobless went on hunger strikes, and outbursts of violence increased at stadiums during football matches between regional teams. The 2008 protests started when the results of the CPG recruitment examination were announced.

The spark and early mobilisations

When the company announced on 5 January 2008 that only 380 workers and managers would be hired out of more than a thousand applicants, the region's large unemployed population felt betrayed. Protest actions began on 6 January, first in Redeyef (population: 26,000) and then in Oum El Araies (population: 24,500), M'dhila (population: 12,500) and Metlaoui (population: 37,000). Tents were set up to block rail and truck traffic between quarries and factories, thus paralyzing all phosphate-related activity. Occasional riots took place, especially in M'dhila, targeting the symbols of local authority and the CPG. Sit-ins were organised outside government headquarters, hunger strikes were launched and demonstrations took place.

Denunciation of the CPG's nepotistic method of allocating positions provided the pretext for a huge rally of the unemployed as well as their families and, sometimes, CPG staff — in short, ad hoc "activists" from all sides.[11] As the days went by, the protests grew. Unemployed university graduates organised, especially in Redeyef where they joined forces with local trade union leaders, most of whom came out of the grassroots primary school teachers' union. In Oum El Araies, the local committee of unemployed graduates[12] coordinated the protests. Sit-ins were staged in addition to demonstrations by laid-off workers and protests by mothers whose sons had been imprisoned following the early demonstrations. The discontent spread as teachers, high school pupils and university students joined in supporting the strike.

"The company is our fate. It has always made us suffer; still we have no other choice but to go back to it". These were the words of one unemployed graduate, who was seated in front of the tent he put up alongside those of dozens of other demonstrators on the railway tracks connecting the nearby quarry to the phosphate processing plants.[13] It was early February in Oum El Araies. Similar scenes were taking place in the nearby mining towns. The young demonstrator from Oum El Araies hung three portraits on his tent. Pointing to the first photo, he explained: "My grandfather was recruited at the mine by the French when he was 13. He died of cancer at age 42, as poor as when he started". The second picture was a portrait of his father. The small sign stated, not without irony, that thanks to the country's independence, he spent a little time in school before entering the mine at the age of 17 and, in turn, dying from lung cancer at age 45. The third portrait was a photo of himself. His comment was scathing:

> I earned a Master's degree in history in Tunis. I don't have enough connections to obtain a teaching position, so I have to go back to the company. I am 35 years old. Hurry up, hurry up – I only have ten years left to live.[14]

Unemployed youths, like this demonstrator from Oum El Araies, formed the core of the protest movement. In fact, during the first two months of mobilisation, political organisations, "civil society" and the trade union federation kept a distance from the protesters. At that point, the opposition parties, which have no significant presence outside Tunis, were more concerned with preparations for the presidential election in October 2009. A case can be made for the fact that being "under-politicised" in the early period actually helped the movement take off, since seemingly poorly coordinated mobilisations were able to expand despite police control in Tunisia.

The growing strength of the movement can also be explained by the power structure in the region. This local configuration is characterised by competition between RCD executives and regional leaders of the trade union federation. The fact that executives from the Union générale tunisienne du travail (UGTT) [Tunisian General Labour Union] were among the few CPG hires aroused jealousy. Local competitors, who were officials of the party in power, seized the opportunity to channel early expressions of discontent more or less directly against certain regional trade union leaders.[15] The latter were accused of using dubious methods to award jobs. The regional secretary of the UGTT in Gafsa, a target of such criticism, openly opposed the protests and threatened to take disciplinary action against union members who joined in them.[16] The local competitors from the RCD took comfort in the idea that "they're targeting the union, not us". This refrain, which sounded more like a plea not to panic than genuine reassurance, also helped the protest movement take off.

During the first three months of 2008, the authorities were careful to keep the protests from unifying and spreading. They relied primarily on law enforcement but occasionally entered into negotiations with protesters here and there. Their efforts to break up the movement involved a strategy of containment, with the police encircling the cities and conducting roadside checks as well as engaging in talks with small groups of protesters.[17]

Those who took part in the protests and those who did not

Though the UGTT refrained from taking part in the protests, a few of its disillusioned members did join the ranks of the demonstrators. They were mostly marginal union leaders at the regional level from the non-workers' unions of Redeyef. Two charismatic figures emerged, Adnane Hajji, secretary general of basic education in Redeyef, and Bashir Laabidi, also a unionised teacher. There were also numerous unemployed graduates among the protestors. While these participants were difficult to coordinate, a few dozen activists had already been carrying out actions in the region for several years. In Gafsa, they tried to gather at the UGTT headquarters, where they were often denied entry, and led marches as well as a sit-in in front of the Redeyef delegation (sub-prefecture). The embryonic movement of unemployed graduates[18] was joined by activists close to the Tunisian Workers' Communist Party (PCOT in French, an illegal party). One of them, an activist who went into hiding after being sentenced to six years in jail, covered the demonstrations for the opposition satellite TV station El Hiwar Ettounsi. The presence of individuals from communist circles – there were only a few dozen among the activists in 2008 – was a reminder that a number of towns in the region, including M'dhila and Redeyef, had once been communist bastions. The opposition parties gradually began supporting the protests,[19] often from Tunis with a few trips to the Gafsa region. "Civil society" organisations also spoke up, including the Association tunisienne des femmes démocrates (AFTD) [Tunisian Association of Democratic Women] and the Tunisian Human Rights League (LTDH). Operating from France, the Fédération des Tunisiens pour une citoyenneté des deux rives (FTCR) [Federation of Tunisians for a Citizenship of the Two Banks], an association founded by Tunisian immigrants in France, published press releases and organised demonstrations, for which its president, Mouhieddine Cherbib, was sentenced in abstentia to two years in prison. Finally, the National Support Committee for the Residents of the Gafsa Mining Basin, whose spokesperson is in charge of the LTDH in Kairouan, comprised activists, opponents and trade unionists from different regions of Tunisia. It published press releases and organised meetings in Tunis. Its members sometimes joined demonstrations, especially in Redeyef, when the police did not prevent them from doing so. All the same, the situation deteriorated, despite the organisation of the movement and the negotiations between national authorities and trade union leaders at the head of the movement in Redeyef.[20]

Escalation

Up until the month of April, the authorities maintained a police cordon to curb protests in Redeyef, where the mobilisation was strongest. On the morning of 7 April, a sudden reversal of strategy prompted the often violent arrest of more than twenty prominent members of the protest movement in Redeyef. They were released a few days later, under pressure from local trade unions in Redeyef and with significant backing from the population. The denunciation and media coverage of the arrests were organised inside Tunisia by the Support Committee for the Residents of the Mining Basin and in France by the FTCR (with demonstrations in Nantes and Paris).

The repression continued to escalate during the months of May and June. On 5 May, Hichem Ben Jeddou El Aleimi, a 24-year-old unemployed youth, died from electrocution after a brutal police intervention with tear gas and beatings. The police were seeking to dislodge a small group of protestors occupying the site of a generator supplying electricity for CPG workshops in the village of Tabbedit, between Oum El Araies and Redeyef. Dozens of outraged residents pretended to leave the city that very afternoon with their suitcases to "abandon Redeyef to the police."[21] On 29 May, the first trial was held in a packed courtroom at the district court of Gafsa. Eleven defendants, all from Redeyef except one individual from M'dhila, appeared before the court facing multiple charges: violence and threats to public officials, stabbing, carrying knives, public indecency, public drunkenness and disturbing the peace. One of the accused doused himself with gasoline and threatened to set himself on fire. The court handed down prison sentences of three to four months, which in some cases were suspended. In June, the death toll worsened. On 2 June, Nabil Chagra was run over by a National Guard vehicle pursuing demonstrators and died. On 6 June, the police fired live bullets at demonstrators in Redeyef, perforating the lungs of a 25-year-old man, Hifnawi al Maghazoui, who was killed instantly. Over two dozen protesters and security forces were injured.[22] On 7 June, the army was sent out to surround and occupy Redeyef on orders from the president.

Apart from the short-term dynamics specific to these events, the protests stemmed from local socio-economic factors and the political management of CPG resources.

The decline of the CPG at the heart of an impoverished mining region

The Gafsa region, an almost six-hour drive southwest of Tunis, is far-removed from the more prosperous Tunisian coastline. It is the reverse side of the Tunisian "economic miracle"[23] praised for its sustained growth (5% annual growth according to official figures) based on a service economy and SMEs. Gafsa is a mining region where agriculture has been devastated, mainly due to aridity, inadequate rainfall and the monopolisation of the local water supply by CPG washing stations.[24] Most of its economic activity depends on the phosphate mines. Poverty is widespread in the villages, particularly in the eastern part of the region, as well as in the mining towns.[25] The unemployment rate in the governorate of Gafsa is among the highest in the country, almost twice the national rate according to figures in Tunisia's closely-"monitored" national statistics.[26]

The mining industry, the main source of employment, is declining. The four mining towns of Redeyef, Oum El Araies, M'dhila and Metlaoui were created *ex nihilo* by and for phosphate. Until 1975, the CPG provided full employment for men in the area. The company supplied grocery stores, pharmacies, health centres, schools, transportation, football clubs, etc., and substantially supported social and economic life. Between 1975 and 1985, the distribution and sale of drinking water and electricity were transferred, along with shops and banks, to various public and private national operators: the Tunisian Electricity and Gas Company, the National Water Utility, the *Magasin général* (a chain of supermarkets), etc. Until the mid-1980s, the CPG needed manpower for these four mining towns as well as administrative staff for its offices, especially in Gafsa. However, in 1985, the company undertook a "modernisation" process resulting in staff cuts. Nearly 10,000 jobs were eliminated, and today only 5,200 employees still work for the CPG. The strategic plan to reform the company was financed by the World Bank as part of the "improvement" of the Tunisian economy through which World Bank loans fuelled the Fonds de restructuration des entreprises publiques (FREP) [Fund for the Restructuring of State-Owned Companies].[27] The first credit tranche, initiated in July 1986, was devoted to the reform of the CPG.

The CPG's socio-economic impact on the region went into decline just as phosphate prices worldwide rose abruptly in 2004, thus increasing the industry's profits.[28] In fact, the phosphate industry has never really benefited the region other than through employment.[29] From the very first concession contracts granted in the late nineteenth century during the French protectorate, the regional impact of the production system lay essentially in its large workforce units. The work, particularly hard at the time,[30] the concentration of workers from diverse backgrounds (Souafas and Kabyles from Algeria, Libyans and Moroccans, with Italians and French in management positions) and the experience of the first strikes, brutally quelled on 2 March 1937, highlighted the importance of trade union action in the minds of CPG personnel.[31]

As the centrepiece of a pauperised working-class region, the CPG has created its own specific balance of patronage over the past twenty years. Like other impoverished areas in the country, the region is structured by conventional patronage and control mechanisms typical of Tunisia's political economy.[32] As part of the "conversion" of the company, this system was maintained by the *Fonds de réorientation et de développement de centres miniers* (FRDCM) [Mining Centre Conversion and Development Fund] modelled on *Charbonnages de France* [French Coal Board]. The fund, a venture capital company founded in 1991, was set up to finance small business startups to offset job losses. Until 2008, such business activities remained marginal, with 1,500 beneficiaries at most. Small entrepreneurs generally received loans as gifts to fund non-viable economic activities. These "secured loans"[33] were granted via local patronage networks, mainly in non-mining areas of the region, contrary to the fund's stated purpose. Another redistribution mechanism commonly used in the region was developed over the last twenty years within the framework of CPG "modernisation". The regional management of the UGTT, by mutual agreement with the CPG, takes part in selecting the candidates to be hired, whereas only 20 percent of early retirees are replaced. Initially, local residents were to be given priority in the hiring process on the basis of "social" criteria, e.g. children of maimed employees of the company, families of workers killed in work-related accidents, etc. Gradually, however, this scarce resource, concentrated in the hands of a few executives holding various positions within the trade union federation, became the chief bargaining chip in a restricted political and economic patronage system that, above all, benefited the regional secretary of the UGTT, who is an RCD parliamentary representative and runs subcontracting companies of the CPG. This *big man* embodies and symbolises the local configuration of power. The corruption of the trade union's "acquired right" thus provided a pretext for the 2008 mobilisation.

With the drop in CPG employment and no job creation in the public service, young people, whether graduates or not, often have no choice but to fall back on "odd jobs" generated by informal trade, involving commuting back and forth between Libya and neighbouring regions of Algeria. This is by no means easy. The security measures are so tight that travelling between Tunisia and Algeria is practically impossible for most young people under age 25. Those who manage to do so earn a living smuggling and reselling petrol, mobile phones and other consumer products made in China. For the vast majority, such "jobs" do not significantly improve their living standards. Then there is the option of exile. Leaving the country can be a promising alternative to unemployment in regions of Tunisia where emigration networks sometimes lead to more prosperous horizons. For youth in the Gafsa region, however, migration is seldom advantageous; nowadays, these journeys often end in impoverished districts on the outskirts of Tunis.[34]

In the heart of an impoverished, working-class region, the declining impact of CPG activity, the resulting economic problems and local power configurations help to explain the 2008 protests. The revival of collective representations of the Gafsa region in the past also formed the backdrop for these mobilisations.

Gafsa, the "rebel region"

Statements like the following were repeatedly made in the interviews we conducted:

> Though we fought in the resistance, we were pushed aside after Independence and even more so after 1963. We were punished for the courage of our ancestors who were feared by Bourguiba and his successors.

> Our region only serves to provide a workforce to enrich the rest of Tunisia, but nothing is done here to help our children.

> The people of Gafsa have never given up in the face of injustice and never will.[35]

Both before and after the events of January 2008, local residents frequently mentioned the mythologised history of Gafsa and its conflict-ridden relationship with the country's central political authorities. The interviewees included a broad cross-section of the population: CPG workers and managers, farmers, shopkeepers, rich and poor, women and men, young people, illiterates, academics, trade unionists, members of the political opposition, activists in development associations and RCD officials. The story of dissent in the Gafsa region, the injustices it has endured, the rebellion of its people and their disenchantment with "Tunis" came up every time, at some point, in more or less assertive, specific or scholarly terms.

It is quite difficult to reconstruct the sources of this "collective awareness" and how it is (re)produced. "Gafsa the Rebellious Region" is a paradoxical concept combining an indigenous critique of regional pauperisation with a culturalist view of the "hot-blooded, hard-headed people of Gafsa" as a security threat, propagated especially by national and regional government officials."[36] In numerous interviews, government officials in Tunis or local administrative officials assigned to the Gafsa region claimed that "southerners and especially people from Gafsa are unruly by nature or that Gafsa culture "is a tribal culture; add to that the mining culture and you get violent people." In one instance, an official of the Gafsa *wilaya* [province] stated bluntly that "the only language they understand is the stick".

While many people spoke of Gafsa as a proud and frustrated region, this image was conveyed with varying degrees of intensity that gave no indication of the future actions of the speakers themselves. Yet in a country where the price of protest is very high, the possibility of rebellion was never ruled out in any of these accounts.[37] For the 2008 protestors, the perception of what could be achieved was rooted in the memory of all the previous struggles in Gafsa. The history of the region is full of such events, which fuel the narrative of Gafsa dissidence. The fight for independence, trade unions struggles and the revolts of the late 1970s and early 1980s were often evoked in interviews and observations:

> Who was the leader of the Mujahidin?[38] Who set the real tone for the struggle for Independence?

Through such provocative questions about the history of the CPG, a retired executive of the company was led to evoke the name of Lazhar Chraiti,[39] a native of the Gafsa region and leader of the guerrillas in the fight for independence. To demonstrate the courage of the Gafsa people in the face of colonial tyranny, the heroic exploits of these combatants – nearly half of whom were from the region according to the interviewee – were often recalled.

The story typically ends with a reference to Habib Bourguiba's ingratitude towards the region, which is believed to have been the reason behind the armed conspiracy against the president at the time. Indeed, in December 1962, many participants in the coup against Bourguiba came from Gafsa. Thereafter, the former president never showed anything but contempt for the region – home to a large number of supporters of Salah Ben Youssef (Bourguiba's opponent) – and the feeling was mutual.

Another common narrative pertains to trade unionism and its early leaders, recalling the first major strikes in the area under the French protectorate (such as the March 1937 strikes) and above all the outstanding figures in the history of the struggle. Ahmed Tlili, who came from the Gafsa region and was Secretary General of the UGTT from 1956 to 1963, has a special place in the hall of fame of local heroes. The general strike of 1978 and the powerful support it garnered throughout the region were emphasised to further illustrate the strength of the union struggle in Gafsa. Interviewees frequently brought up the "Gafsa events" of 1980, a reference to the group that sought to use the city as the starting point of an armed insurrection.[40] The "bread riots" of 1983–1984, which began in late December in the south, mainly in Gafsa, before spreading to Tunis in January, and their importance in the region were often mentioned as well.

Narratives about "Gafsa the rebel region" and its struggle against "central political authority" are sometimes presented in scholarly accounts of historical events dating back to the Roman period. In some interviews, teachers, academics or ordinary history buffs explained that Capsa (the name of the city founded by the Romans in the second century BCE, which gave its name to Gafsa today) was the setting of the first Christian schism brought about by the Donatists. The area was also a hotbed of *Kharijism* (one of the earliest schisms within Islam) and later on became the capital of a small independent state with its own currency, the Beni Rand, in the twelfth century. The region is also said to have witnessed several uprisings against the central authority of the Hafsid dynasty at the end of the thirteenth century.[41]

These narratives, which we have only partially summarised here, have continued to circulate and produce a collective awareness that permeates the region to this day. They spurred the audacity of young protestors and, in the eyes of the authorities, served to justify repressive policing of the population. They formed the backdrop of the 2008 protests, helping to give meaning to the feeling of deadlock experienced by thousands of unemployed youths in the region, which they expressed through concrete forms of protest.[42]

Endgame?

In June 2008, the main leaders of the protest movement were arrested, imprisoned and given harsh prison sentences.[43] On 16 July, President Ben Ali summoned the members of the Gafsa Regional Council to a special session at the presidential palace in Carthage to settle the problems in the mining area once and for all. During the meeting, the president highlighted for the first time the "irregularities committed by officials of the Gafsa Phosphate Company in the course of the recruitment process and the resulting disillusionment and disappointment for the youths involved in the process".[44] The axe fell, and scapegoats were designated. The Chairman and CEO of the CPG was dismissed,[45] the *Wali* of the Gafsa governorate was replaced (without being discredited – he received a diplomatic assignment) and the delegate (sub-prefect) of Redeyef was removed. A presidential decree ordered the Gafsa Municipal Council to be dissolved. The powerful RCD representative, who was simultaneously the regional secretary of the UGTT in Gafsa, was the only one who remained in place after this political reconfiguration.

Multiple measures were announced and, as always after an intervention by the president of Tunisia, laudatory comments came pouring in from all sides.[46] The decisions were presented as a "Marshall Plan" for the Gafsa region,[47] with a total investment of 944 million dinars (EUR 499 million), which, according to its promoters, would create 9,000 permanent jobs. The financial crisis cast doubt, however, on the government's ability to meet its promises. While the plan championed by the Minister of Industry was unprecedented in scale, it was to be funded through "incentives" such as tax cuts, a method that had already revealed its limitations in an area often viewed as unattractive by major investors.[48]

Apart from media coverage in favour of the "regional development" of Gafsa, there were few public statements in Tunis about the "events in the South", as with anything else that might crack the official veneer of a stable, prosperous Tunisia.[49] The few media that dared to cover the protests, such as the weekly opposition party newspapers *Al Maoukif* and *Attariq Al Jadid*, the *Kalima* radio station and the *El Hiwar Ettounsi* television channel, were subjected to even stronger repression than usual (seizure of issues, trials, curtailing the free movement of journalists, etc.).

With no visible opposition, the regime of "change" seemed more than ever to be enjoying long-term "healthy stability". As we have shown, this situation could only be maintained through a system of mobilisation and coercion authorised by tight territorial control. For twenty years, the status quo had been kept in place by various official and unofficial agencies that controlled citizens through disciplinary measures and patronage as well as political and economic means[50] and the support of powerful foreign partners.[51] In addition to the characteristics of contemporary Tunisian politics, it should be noted that the UGTT leadership was increasingly viewed as corrupt. The trade union federation proved to be more and more out of step with the struggles under way and unable to harness and channel grassroots demands.

In this political context, the aspirations for a better life and the frustration of a certain fringe of the Tunisian population rarely come out into the open. The exceptional protest movement in Gafsa forced us to revise our position with regard to two commonly accepted ideas about Tunisia: first, that its economy was a success and, in particular, able to guarantee social protection to its citizens; second, that the Tunisian population was incapable of speaking out, notably in the form of protest. Either repression made public demonstrations too risky or the redistribution system, deemed effective, undermined any attempt to protest. The pauperised mining region of Gafsa unveiled what Tunisia's "economic miracle" and its apologists had been concealing: the existence of huge regional disparities.

The case of Gafsa also revealed that government repression, even when severe, cannot silence all of the people all of the time. Moreover, the patronage systems that functioned as "redistribution" mechanisms were vulnerable in this region, where there was so little to "redistribute", notably job-wise. In this environment, the large numbers of unemployed in the Gafsa region deemed their living conditions intolerable and unjust. In response, the revived a collective memory that opened up the possibility of struggle and persuaded significant parts of the population who were not afraid of repression to follow them.

Endnotes

1   The two major revolts that occurred in Tunisia since its independence were the January 1978 strike and the "bread riots" of January 1984. See M. Rollinde, "Les émeutes en Tunisie: un défi à l'État?" in D. Le Saout, M. Rollinde (eds.), *Émeutes et mouvements sociaux au Maghreb*, Paris: Karthala, 1999, pp. 113–26; O. Lamloum, "Janvier 84 en Tunisie ou le symbole d'une transition", in D. Le Saout and M. Rollinde (eds.), ibid., pp. 231–41. This list should also include the armed rebellion that took place in January 1980, during which a commando of Tunisian opposition forces trained in Libya and Algeria took over the city of Gafsa for nine days and tried unsuccessfully to launch a national uprising.

2   The CPG is the state-owned company in charge of Gafsa's phosphate industry. It merged in 1994 with one of the leading industrial groups in Tunisia, the Group Chimique Tunisien [Tunisian Chemicals Group], which is also state-owned.

3   These figures are of major political significance but difficult to establish with any certainty. The number of prisoners is particularly hard to estimate because most of the protesters were quickly released without charge after their arrest or were charged with assault or drunk and disorderly conduct. The leaders of the movement, on the other hand, received long prison sentences (see below). *Attariq Al Jadid* and *El Maoukif*, the weekly magazines put out by the opposition, were among the

few Tunisian media to cover the events. See in particular, the archives available at
<http://www.attariq.org>.

4   See M. Camau, "*Tarajjî ya dawla* ou la force de l'espérance. Propos sur le désengage-
ment de l'État en Tunisie", *Bulletin du Cedej*, no. 23, 1988, p. 81–108.

5   In 1985, a strategic reform plan entitled "CPG rehabilitation plan" was set up by the
Tunisian government. Financed by loans, first, from the World Bank and, later, from
the African Development Bank, the plan included mechanising production, reducing expenses and operating costs, and downsizing (for more details, see reports
available on the website of the African Development Bank: <www.afdb.org>).

6   See CPG's website: <www.gct.com.tn>.

7   In addition to interviews conducted in Tunis with government officials, CPG executives and union and party organisations, this article has relied on several survey
trips in the region since the spring of 2006. It is based, in particular, on interviews
and observations gathered in 2008 during five one-week stays in Gafsa and other
large towns and villages nearby: Redeyef Oum El Araïes, Métlaoui, M'dhila and El
Guettar. We wish to thank the many people who agreed to receive us with such
great hospitality. Their willingness to freely share their experiences, despite their
difficult living conditions and the risk of repression, is, in itself, a way of challenging
the deplorable situation in the region.

8   This collective imagination has been handed down through generations and sometimes revived by various individuals and groups for mobilisation purposes. Its origins are difficult to reconstruct, because it is the result of a long process of gestation
involving various purports and actors. In this article, we will simply examine some
of the ways it has been used within the protest movement.

9   For studies on the political regime in Tunisia, see M. Camau and V. Geisser, *Le
Syndrome autoritaire. Politique en Tunisie de Bourguiba à Ben Ali*, Paris, Presses de
Sciences Po, 2003; S. Khiari, *Tunisie, le délitement de la cité. Coercition, consentement,
résistance*, Paris, Karthala, 2003. For a more recent analysis, see V. Geisser, É. Gobe,
"Un si long règne… Le régime de Ben Ali vingt ans après", *L'Année du Maghreb*, no.
4, 2008, pp. 347–81.

10 For more information, see B. Hibou, *La Force de l'obéissance. Économie politique de la
répression en Tunisie*, Paris: La Découverte, 2006. For a discussion of "stability", see
also S. Elbaz, "'Stabilité' et développement: critique d'une vision 'partagée' par la
Tunisie et ses bailleurs de fonds", presented at the conference entitled "Les mots
du développement. Genèse, usages et trajectories", Paris, November 2009.

11 Portraits of Ben Ali could be seen alongside slogans (rather rare) caricaturing the
president's campaign slogan "Ben Ali for 2009" by turning it into "Ben Ali for 2999".

12 In the last two decades, the term "unemployed graduate" has almost become a social
category in the Maghreb. It is the target of public policies and has become a category
for mobilisation. In the case of Morocco, see M. Emperador Badimon, "Diplômés

chômeurs au Maroc: Dynamiques de pérennisation d'une action collective plurielle", *L'Année du Maghreb*, no. 3, 2007, p. 297–314.

13 Interviews and on-site observations (February 2008).

14 These remarks refer to a longstanding complaint one still hears in the region about the effects on people's living conditions of pollution from the mines. Health problems attributed to cadmium from mining, which causes multiple diseases, were often mentioned during interviews.

15 However, the opposition between UGTT executives and RCD executives is by no means consistent, since some individuals and groups belong to both entities. For instance, the powerful regional secretary of the UGTT in Gafsa is also a RCD member of parliament. The local configuration of power is also characterised by the important role of various tribal groups.

16 In general, the gap between the UGTT leadership and its base can be explained by increasingly tight control over and within the trade union federation. Anti-subversion efforts carried out at the political and law enforcement level were strengthened under President Ben Ali's regime, resulting in increased "internal" control of the UGTT by its head. Indeed, since the 1989 congress, and even more since the 1993 congress, control over the trade union federation had become increasingly centralised in the hands of the Secretary General. The latter put in place a selection process for union officials. The most vocal officials within the federation were marginalised through patronage and censorshipp. For studies on the relationship between politics and trade unionism in Tunisia, see S. Khiari, "Reclassements et recompositions au sein de la bureaucratie syndicale depuis l'Indépendance. La place de l'UGTT dans le système politique tunisien", web publication of CERI, 2000, available at <www.ceri-sciences-po.org>; S. Hamzaoui, "Champ politique et syndicalisme en Tunisie", *Annuaire de l'Afrique du Nord*, vol. 38, 1999, p. 369–80.

17 For instance, the group of "widows of Oum El Araies", made up of wives of CPG workers who died from work-related accidents. They pitched their tents and demanded that their children be hired but took them down in February after receiving assurances that the children would indeed be hired.

18 These groups have been active primarily in Tunis and Gafsa since 2006, led by the Union of Unemployed Graduates, an association that has not been recognised by the authorities.

19 We might mention *Ettajdid* (an outgrowth of the Communist Party), the Parti démocrate progressiste (PDP) [Progressive Democratic Party] and the Forum démocratique pour le travail et les libertés (FDTL) [Democratic Forum for Labour and Liberties], whose activist member Zakia Dhifaoui was sentenced to a lengthy prison term, as well as the Parti socialiste de gauche [Socialist Left Party], an illegal party, which denounced the imprisonment of one of its activists in the movement's leadership.

20 In the "Lettre de prison de Adnane Hajji" published in the opposition weekly in Arabic *El Maoukif* (no. 461, 18 July 2008, p 6), the author expressed his surprise at being arrested: "During the five months of peaceful protests, we strove [...] to prevent possible excesses. And we had talks with local, regional and national authorities to find solutions to problems. We met several times with the authorities [...]. We continued discussions with the authorities, including the Ministry of the Interior and Health, right up until the day of our arrest."

21 Face-to-face interviews, Redeyef, August 2008.

22 AFP report, "Tunisie : un mort et plusieurs blessés lors d'accrochages à Redeyef", 6 June 2008.

23 Many studies have rightly criticised the operating mode of the Tunisian economy, in particular its relationship with the authoritarian political regime. For an analysis of political economy studies on Tunisia, see M. Camau, "Tunisie: vingt ans après. De quoi Ben Ali est-il le nom?", *L'Année du Maghreb*, n° 4, 2008, pp. 507–27. On the slowing of this system in the neoliberal context, see S. Khiari, *Tunisie, le délitement de la cité...*, op. cit.

24 In the nineteenth century, there was significant production of oil, dates and fruit, as well as livestock farming, in the region. Since then, agriculture has steadily declined. See M. Tlili, *La Vie communautaire dans la ville de Gafsa et les villages oasiens environnants, du début du XVIIIᵉ siècle à 1881*, doctoral thesis in history, Faculty of Humanities and Social Sciences of Tunis (Arabic), 2002.

25 Poverty has evolved in opposite directions. In the mining towns, the situation has deteriorated very quickly since the 1990s, whereas in the eastern agricultural area near Sened, deemed very poor, the situation has gradually improved, thanks to the agricultural policies of the early 1990s, particularly incentives to use greenhouses, which are less affected by extreme weather variations.

26 The unemployment rates reported by Tunisia's National Statistics Institute, based on the 2004 census, are as follows: 38.5 percent in Oum El Araies, 20.9 percent in Métlaoui, 27.9 percent in M'dhila and 27 percent in Redeyef, compared with a 14 percent rate nationwide. See <www.ins.nat.tn>.

27 Several laws have been passed within the framework of the privatisation programs undertaken by the Tunisian state since the 1980s. Article 79 of Law No. 85–109 of 31 December 1985 concerned "the creation of a special Treasury fund, the *Fonds de restructuration des entreprises publiques* (FREP) [Fund for the Restructuring of State-owned Companies], to restructure the state's stake in the capital of state-owned companies and possibly help finance a turnaround of state-owned companies."

28 There was an exceptional fourfold increase in phosphate prices in 2007–2008 (interviews with CPG executives, Tunis, 2008).

29 Already in "Gafsa comme enjeu", *Annuaire de l'Afrique du Nord*, vol. 19, 1980, pp. 485–511, Pierre-Robert Baduel questioned whether the mining industry was not

in fact "sterilizing" the region after the armed uprising in 1980 in Gafsa. He noted: "(…) the nationalisation of the mines did not change the typically capitalist logic behind phosphate mining. Indeed, the economic growth generated by the mining company was not accompanied by local development. The city of Gafsa is 'just a corridor where nothing ever stops' (…) The Gafsa–Sfax railway line is to phosphate what a pipeline is to oil: a remote system for sucking up the resources of Gafsa" (p. 501). His observation remains valid despite the arrival of other industrial units in the region since then.

30 Several studies reported this. See A. Bouhdiba, "Les conditions de vie des mineurs de la région de Gafsa", *Études de sociologie tunisienne*, vol. 1, 1968, pp. 165–233. He refers to the "daily proximity with death" (p. 171). N. Douggi talks about "the phosphate prison" and "military mining discipline". See N. Douggi, *Histoire d'une grande entreprise coloniale. La Compagnie des phosphates et du chemin de fer de Gafsa, 1897–1930*, Tunis, Publications de la Faculté des Arts de Manouba, 1995, p. 291 et seq.

31 On this event, see the divergent interpretations of S. Hamzaoui, *Conditions et genèse de la conscience ouvrière en milieu rural: cas des mineurs du sud de la Tunisie*, graduate thesis in sociology, École pratique des hautes études, 1970, and of M. Kraiem, "Les événements de Métlaoui et de M'dhila de mars 1937", *Revue d'histoire maghrébine*, no. 23–24, 1981, pp. 221–42.

32 As illustrated in particular by the role of the Tunisian Solidarity Bank (TSB) and presidential funds (2121 and 2626). Both institutions promote what Béatrice Hibou calls the "security pact". Hibou notes: "The bank, as part of the security pact set-up, is both an institution that grants protection and security and an institution that creates dependence, control and surveillance". See B. Hibou, *La Force de l'obéissance…*, op. cit., p. 404. See also K. Zamiti, "Le Fonds de solidarité nationale. Pour une approche sociologique du politique", *Annuaire de l'Afrique du Nord*, vol. 35, 1996, pp. 705–12; D. Chakerli, "Lutte contre la pauvreté et solidarité nationale", web publication of the CERI, 2000, available on <www.ceri-sciencespo.com>.

33 The phrase is from Béatrice Hibou's description of the TSB's role. The same type of relationship was established under the FRDCM. The loan was, in fact, granted without collateral based on an interview with the beneficiary and information gathered from party cells, neighbourhood committees and the social worker or *omda* (the representative of the "sector", i.e. the smallest administrative echelon of the Ministry of the Interior), or directly from police reports (personal observations and interviews, Gafsa, 2006–2007).

34 All the same, we should mention the example of the Nantes "network," composed of migrants from Redeyef who actively supported the protesters. There are also industries offering jobs in masonry in the coastal region of the Sahel and in the hotel trade in Djerba.

35 Excerpts from interviews, Gafsa region, 2006–2008.

36 The quotations here are excerpts from interviews conducted between 2006 and 2008 with government officials in Tunis, notably from the Ministry of the Interior and Local Development and the Ministry of Development and International Cooperation.

37 For an analysis of protest movements in Tunisia, especially in recent times, see M.-B. Ayari, *S'engager en régime autoritaire. Gauchistes et islamistes dans la Tunisie indé-pendante*, doctoral thesis in political science, l'Université d'Aix-Marseille III, 2009. For an analysis covering the "Arab world" as a whole, see V. Geisser, K. Karam et F. Vairel, "Espaces du politique. Mobilisations et protestations", in E. Picard (ed.), *La Politique dans le monde arabe,* Paris, Armand Colin, 2006, pp. 193–213; M. Bennani-Chraïbi and O. Filleule (eds.), *Résistances et protestations dans les sociétés musulmanes*, Paris, Presses de Sciences Po, 2003.

38 In the region, the terms *Thewar* or *Moujahidine* refer to the armed resistance: the guerrillas. The term *Fellaga*, more commonly used in Tunisia, France and elsewhere, is considered an insult.

39 Lazhar Chraiti was the leader of the guerrilla struggle against French occupation until Independence in 1956. He was sentenced to death and executed in 1963 after the attempted coup against President Bourguiba in 1962.

40 "*Houna Idaat Gafsa*" ["This is Radio Gafsa"]: the radio announcement by members of the 1980 commando is still often repeated as a joke or in protest, recalling the unprecedented moment in contemporary Tunisian history when an area occupied by a group of armed dissidents "broke away" from the country for a few hours.

41 Many of these elements relating to the military and political history of the region can be found in a book by P. Bodereau (based on a thesis and written in the typical style of a colonial monograph): *La Capsa ancienne. La Gafsa moderne*, Paris, Augustin Challamel Publisher, 1907.

42 Traces of these "awareness-generating devices" (primarily concerning the disparities in how the Sahel and Gafsa regions are treated by "Tunis") can be found in reports available on the website of the *PCOT* <www.albadil.org>. For more information on this aspect, which is often ignored in political science analysis, see J. Siméant and C. Traïni, "Pourquoi et comment sensibiliser à la cause?", in C. Traïni (ed.), *Émotions… Mobilisation !*, Paris, Presses de Sciences Po, 2009, pp. 11–34.

43 The main leaders risked 20 years in prison for some of charges, namely "gang membership; conspiracy to prepare and commit assault against property and persons, and rebellion by more than ten people with the use of weapons." After several new developments and tumultuous court sessions, the Gafsa Court of Appeal in February 2009 handed down sentences for the 38 defendants ranging from two-year suspended sentences to eight years in prison.

44 Excerpts from the "Statement from the President" available at <www.carthage.tn>.

45 In an initial gesture to calm things down, President Ben Ali announced the Governor of Gafsa and the Chairman and CEO of the CPG would be replaced in March, but replacement of the latter did not take effect until July 2008.

46 Thus, in addition to the press releases put out by "client" opposition parties (political parties that depend directly on the presidency, also called "rump parties" by M. Camau and V. Geisser, *Le Syndrome autoritaire…*, op. cit. pp. 238–40), such as the PUP and the PSL or the Regional Council of Gafsa, many articles were published expressing a similar point of view, such as the one available on the website <www.webmanagercenter.com> on 10 February, 2009 entitled "Gafsa: the new deal!": "With hundreds of billions to be poured into Gafsa […], a New Deal is in sight […] with everything that implies in terms of indirect development to breathe new life into the region and make it more attractive… you'd better get on board now!"

47 Economist Ben Romdhane offered a much more nuanced, even critical, analysis of the socio-economic, demographic and ecological situation in the area and the first measures that were announced. See the special report "Le bassin minier de Gafsa, problèmes et perspectives" published in *Attariq Al Jadid*, no. 90, 26 July–1 August 2008.

48 In interviews conducted in Tunis, major entrepreneurs called to invest in the Gafsa region often declared that state interventionism distorts the "economic game". While such clichés are commonplace in the business world (and have not kept these same entrepreneurs from benefiting from multiple state subsidies), they do seem to indicate greater "fear" of investing in the Gafsa region than anywhere else. For instance, Hedi Jilani, head of the Tunisian Union for Industry, Commerce and Handicrafts, who was sent to the region for the "Day of Partnership and Promotion of Private Investment" held on 11 November 2009, said: "As we know, the people of Gafsa are highly politicised, which can be an advantage, but it must not jeopardise the stability of the region or scare away developers who need to be reassured that the future of their investments is secure" (statement taken from the economic information website <webmanagercenter.com> in an article dated 13 November 2008). For a study of Tunisian business community and its relationship to politics, see B. Hibou, " 'Nous ne prendrons jamais le maquis'. Entrepreneurs et politique en Tunisie", *Politix*, no. 84, 2008, p. 115–41.

49 Televisions and newspapers are strictly controlled. The same is true of the Internet, which is overseen by *Aam Mkass* ("Uncle Scissors") strikes. This cartoon character refers to the censorship that cracked down on numerous websites (including "major ones" such as Youtube, Dailymotion, etc.). Nevertheless, the censors are unable to control everything: several videos of the Gafsa protests could be viewed on websites accessible in Tunisia. On these issues, see the work of L. Chouikha: "Autoritarisme étatique et débrouillardise individuelle. Arts de faire, paraboles, Internet, comme formes de résistance voire de contestation" in O. Lamloum and B. Ravenel (eds.),

La Tunisie de Ben Ali. La société contre le régime, Paris, L'Harmattan, 2002; R. Lecomte, *Réflexion sur la cyberdissidence et la sphère publique*, graduate thesis in political science, Université libre de Bruxelles, Université catholique de Louvain and Facultés universitaires de Saint-Louis, 2007.

50 The harsh prosecution of the leaders of the protest movement in Redeyef followed the same logic. The system will not tolerate the emergence of local leadership outside the party.

51 During a visit to Tunisia in April 2008, when the protest movement in the Gafsa region was in full swing and journalists were on hunger strike, French President Nicolas Sarkozy declared: "The scope of freedom is widening [in Tunisia] today" (speech delivered on 28 April 2008, available on <diplomatie.gouv.fr>).

8

✳

"Discharge", the New Interventionism

Béatrice Hibou

Introduction

In 1996, Revenue Management Associates Ltd., a subsidiary of the Lazard Frères Bank, signed a contract to manage and collect indirect taxes in Cameroon. In 1994, South African black empowerment was delegated to large private consortiums through the stock exchange. All structural adjustment programmes now include a component to privatize public companies and public service concessions, and starting in the late 1980s, inspection, verification, testing and certification companies (such as SGS or Veritas) took over customs valuation, sometimes extending the scope of their services to collecting customs duties. Every day, donor institutions encourage "civil society" to assume greater responsibility for development, and in the press, there are daily reports on the expanding role of private security and mercenary firms.

Is there any consistent feature in these events currently taking place in Africa? At first glance, all these processes appear to call into question the role of the state and of public action, a conclusion reinforced by the growing number of doctoral dissertations on the "retreat", "impotence" or decline of the state. While such an appraisal has become quite common, it nevertheless poses a problem insofar as it is expressed negatively in terms of decrease, loss, reduction and disintegration. These analyses are implicitly based on normative references that are both dated and incidental, reflecting the developmentalist ideology first articulated in the 1950s and a so-called Weberian conception of the state as a rational-legal bureaucracy permanently engaging in direct, institutionalised interventions. Confining the scope of state action to such well-defined limits prevents us from thinking about the possibility of transformations in the nature of interventionism; we see any change in the form of public action as a sign of the state's destruction, disappearance, retreat or loss of control. In contrast, the analysis presented here – and in other papers soon to be or only recently published[1] – proposes to refine our understanding of the state and of public action from the perspective of "privatising the state". I have deliberately chosen this paradoxical expression to reveal the ambivalence of the situations in Africa today. On the one hand, the expression evokes the rise of private actors, intermediaries, networks and markets as well as the increased role of economic and financial logic. On the other hand, it indicates the state's continuous formation, which constantly renegotiates the relationship between the "public" and "private" spheres and engages in processes of delegation and control *ex post facto*. I show how the state deals with privatisation, and even more, how privatising the state introduces a new challenge in the exercise of power and produces new relationships and spaces of power.

What we are witnessing is *not* the destruction of the state or a challenge to its existence or a loss of its legitimacy and sovereignty, but the ongoing formation or reconfiguration of the state in a context of increasing constraints as well as international opportunities. I am not suggesting that nothing is shifting or that profound transformations are not under way, merely that modes of governing are changing in the direction of ever-greater delegation. The state today has not relinquished its prerogatives, but it intervenes less and less directly, and its ability to control and regulate has been altered. Government is predominantly exercised through indirect interventions and private actors. In this context, the term "discharge" (from the German terms *Verpachtung* and *Uberweisung*)[2] as used by Max Weber with regard to feudal societies is particularly enlightening. "Discharge" in this sense characterised non-bureaucratized societies that received little or no support from a management apparatus and was a way of exercising power without having to pay for a sizeable administrative structure. The use of intermediaries and indirect government is also typical of the mode of government that prevails in the contemporary world. The present-day shift to "discharge" has modified the relationship between "public" and "private" and between the "political" and "economic" spheres. It has modified the logic of extraction and redistribution that give politics its legitimacy as well as the relative importance of values, norms and rules and the relationship between them – in other words, it has modified subjectivities. Privatising has less to do with making the economic sphere autonomous and separate from the political sphere than with reshaping the ways of being and acting in both the economic and political spheres.

A look at method

This critique is useful in that it allows us to explain our choice of method. All the research work emphasising the state's loss of sovereignty or legitimacy, or even its retreat, has implicitly adopted the same substantialist, normative view of the state. Such a view was rejected by analyses in the historical sociology of the state (P. Anderson, C. Tilly, T. Skopol) and the historicity of the state (J.-F. Bayart), which do not take the state for granted or define it in advance. Similarly, what I want to capture are the continuities and especially the breaks in history, the changes in the configuration of the political and economic spheres rather than the recurring patterns in political and economic systems. These theoretical positions correspond to a specific methodological approach in which politics or the state is not defined *a priori*. The approach we have chosen thus avoids eliminating aspects considered *a priori* as outside the scope of the state. It also avoids postulating *a priori* a clear-cut distinction between the economic and the non-economic, the political and the non-political or the public and the private.

Obviously, this approach raises legitimate concerns about the fuzziness of the concepts employed, notably the confusion between the state, power and elites. In answer, I would first point out that the state cannot be grasped and truly understood apart from power or ruling elites. In other words, to understand the state, we must understand the people in power as well as their games, strategies and longstanding practices. This mutual interdependence is what gives the state its specific shape: it is impossible to separate the economy from politics, private interests from public interests, the particular from the general. The political role of private interests and the monopoly on wealth held by elites or ruling cliques do not necessarily go against the state, inasmuch as the private players are also public and state actors. In Africa, it is impossible to comprehend how the state is formed without taking into account the processes of negotiation between the elites and other actors, including foreign players. Such negotiations take many forms, notably war and conflict, and over time, "belly politics" (which involves much more than corruption) has become a way of managing the public.[3]

Second, to understand the transformations now under way, it helps to differentiate among the various attributes and functions of the state. In particular, it is useful to distinguish state authority from sovereignty and the state's ability to exercise its power from its ability to control a regulatory authority – in concrete terms, to control a country's economic policy, wealth, the economic productivity of the population or even the population itself. This distinction shows how the state's regulatory capabilities can erode without affecting its power, which remains intact and is merely directed elsewhere. It also highlights how new methods of resource appropriation, which may sometimes involve privatisation, can be compatible with modes of state intervention without necessarily undermining the foundations of state authority.[4] It is because the state is defined, for example, in terms of sovereignty or by its monopoly on legitimate violence and taxation that we conclude it is in decline or is being challenged by new sovereign powers (such as transnational networks, "mafias" or major multinational consulting and assessment firms). On the other hand, if we accept that state action can extend beyond institutions and that sovereignty is a separate issue from state authority, the emergence of these actors, flows and powers seemingly in competition with the state can be understood as places of its intervention, whether they are new or not. In short, by freeing ourselves from incidental, normative and reductive definitions of the state, I am seeking first and foremost to observe original processes of exercising power and governing.

Transformations of the ties between public and private and political and economic spheres

The privatising approach at least has the advantage of rethinking the relationship between the public and the private, their fluidity and how they overlap. First, it allows us to go beyond deterritorialisation processes to discover the various practices and processes that reconfigure state territory. What determines new places of state intervention and changes the way the state appears in space is the use of intermediaries, the entry of new actors forcing states

— sometimes without their realising it — to modify the places where they intervene, and the emergence of new demands on the part of society.[5]

Second, the emphasis placed on negotiations, fluidity and unstable economic, political and social standards and relationships argues against the thesis of the disappearance of the state due to war and conflicts. The logic of war does not rule out the existence of other logics governing the reconfiguration of power and negotiating partners, nor does it exclude exchange and patronage processes[6]. These other logics are compatible with centralised, consolidated state power, even when this results from heightened conflict, loss of legitimacy and the spread of violence.

Such situations of war or intense conflict demonstrate that, no matter what new forms it may take, politics in Africa is still based on negotiations.[7] In keeping with recent studies in economic history[8] and the political anthropology of violence,[9] when we grasp changes in modes of government in terms of delegation and privatisation, we see that war, extraction and wealth accumulation, often private, unintentionally interact to shape African states. As the work of Ferdinand Braudel and Charles Tilly showed long ago, the phenomena of banditry, plunder, piracy, gang rivalries and war lie on a single continuum and can all play a part in shaping the state.[10] The "reappearance" of war and violence in Africa cannot be understood as the end of the state; the monopoly on legitimate violence has seldom been a characteristic of states on the African continent, and situations of war and conflict are recurrent ways of organising the region.[11]

Third, by giving importance to indirect methods of state intervention and delegation processes, states can keep their loss of control over economic, fiscal and financial activities to a minimum. For example, the mix of financial practices in Nigeria reveals alliances between civilian politicians and profiteering soldiers.[12] In general, privatising financial management (debt, taxation) does more than merely indicate the state's inability to conduct public affairs; it may be a strategy of structural adjustment or, conversely, a way of freeing the state from such exterior constraints. Just as so-called informal, illegal practices such as fraud, smuggling and criminal activities have been shown to enter into the formation of trade policy,[13] certain social and economic functions (education, health care, basic infrastructure) can be delegated to other actors without disengaging state power. Evergetism[14] corresponds both to practices that compete with those of the state and to practices that support them, as such expenditures revert to the "public". In the context of Africa, it is a "new" mode of patronage-based social management. It reflects a shift in state power away from the institutions at the centre (thereby contributing to deinstitutionalisation) that actually strengthens and consolidates the power held by the state.

In opposing an overly functionalist, proactive interpretation, privatisation should not be viewed as a deliberate strategy on the part of one or more states. Admittedly, the use of intermediaries, particularly outsourcing to the private sector, may correspond to a gap between rising demand and the state's limited ability to meet it in a formal, institutionalised way, as delegating functions to private companies and various public service concession operations suggest. It can also serve as a politics of survival and "dirty tricks" typical of fragmented societies,[15] illustrated by the expanded use of mercenaries. However, at a more basic level, the privatising of the state is the combined result of a number of sometimes contradictory strategies that most notably reveal a lack of confidence in state institutions and the priority given to loyalty over functional relationships.

In fact, privatising the state is not so much the fruit of the state's own strategy to survive or to consolidate itself as it is the fruit of numerous actors and logics of action, for example, the logic governing the relationship between the state and society (or rather between different segments of society), the logic that defines the political relationships within the group in power, war strategies, the administrative, financial and missionary strategies of aid donors and, similarly, the logic of resistance to aid donors, the logics of enrichment, patronage, extraversion, etc. Although, in the end, these various factors may not necessarily weaken the state, they are a clear sign of its deinstitutionalisation.

Finally, by putting the emphasis on the (re)appearance of indirect, discontinuous governmentalities, we can highlight the changes under way in the relationship between the public and private. These modifications do not automatically doom public action, nor do they necessarily indicate loss of control by state authorities. Instead they underscore the fact that the public–private dichotomy proposed by actors as crucially important to Africa as aid donors is inoperative. The boundaries between these spheres are not just ill-defined, situations in Africa also typically involve overlapping practices and, above all, multiple forms of ownership, regulation, legitimacies, interventions and even conceptions of what is public and what is private. This research shows that, liberal discourse notwithstanding, privatising does not mean granting autonomy to private actors or mutual autonomy to the political and economic spheres but indeed restructuring ways of being and acting in the political and economic realms.[16] Concretely, what we observe in economic and political practices is a plurality of mixed forms that blur the markers and boundaries, along with a wide variety of principles of legitimacy that characterise the actual processes of economic liberalisation, reform and privatisation. This is not specific to Africa alone, by the way, as examples in Eastern Europe show.[17]

Privatising the state: between globalisation and historicity

The process of "privatising the state" has become generalised today partly due to the internationalisation of economies and, more broadly, globalisation. In every country, one observes the rapid development of private actors and, even more, of discourses and interpretations promoting the "private sector", the "market", the privatisation of public companies, economic and financial liberalisation and disengagement of the state. Likewise, transnational flows have become a reality everywhere, even in supposedly marginalised economies like those of African countries. "Privatisation" has also become important as a mode of power. Due to the emergence of other economic powers (international institutions, multinational firms, financial markets), the state appears more decentralised and fragmented, reacting to events rather than actively shaping them and sharing its regulatory authority with other actors or entities.

The meaning of this new global mode of indirect government, which increasingly calls upon the private sector, depends on the country and the history of each state and the specific relationships between that state and society. However similar current situations may seem, they make sense only in relation to the past and the possible futures of the society in which they are situated. Indeed, the method of private indirect government and delegation are not new phenomena. Historically, they have been common practices in Africa and elsewhere, as Sinologists have shown, as well as specialists on Morocco and its Makhzenian governmentality.[18] In Africa, globalised "discharge" can only be understood by going back to historical processes that existed during colonisation and even in the pre-colonial period, as Mamadou

Diouf and Achille Mbembe have shown (see Chapters 9 and 10 of this book). Yet, as these authors also point out, privatisation before "globalisation" was very different from privatisation after it. Moreover, privatisation must be interpreted today in the context of duplicating power and developing a shadow economy.[19] This specific feature of state privatisation in Africa also needs to be qualified and narrowed down. There are major differences in the extent, the terms and, above all, the meanings of privatisation from one country to the next. These differences depend, once again, on national historical specificities. Delegation and the intensive use of private intermediaries can lead either to state consolidation or fragmentation, to centralised or decentralised state interventionism.

As we saw earlier, privatising the state also means modifying the relationship between the public and the private and between economics and politics. In the case of Africa, politics – at least since the colonial era – has been based on straddling positions of power and positions of accumulated wealth, the public and the private, what is legal and what is illegal. Yet this permanent feature in no way excludes significant transformations. In the 1930s, and again from the post-war years to the end of the 1970s, public actions referred to publicising political sovereignty and economic regulation as well as territorialisation of state authority, on the one hand, and to subordination of the economy to politics on the other. Although the practices failed to live up to these principles, the legitimate institutions at the time were nevertheless represented by public companies and public banks, the administration, stabilisation or compensation funds and other offices. Today, on the contrary, the prevailing principles are unquestionably liberalisation and privatisation, disengagement of the state from economic and social spheres from and greater autonomy for the economic sphere than for the political, in line with the liberal standards adopted by the international community and articulated in the discourse of the developed countries. Henceforth, the legitimate institutions are the market, the private sector and civil society. Although the practices are often the same, the standards by which they are assessed have radically changed. This is the shift that has led to seeing these transformations in terms of "privatisation"; the name is also an ironic allusion to international institutions and the "idea kits" that circulate in the "international community". But the allusion also harbours a critical analysis of dominant ideas. The so-called Weberian image these institutions have of the state (in Africa and elsewhere) has undoubtedly altered our understanding of reality and clouded our thinking.[20] Thus, privatisation should not be under-stood as the objective rise of private actors, the hegemony of a well-defined private sector over an equally circumscribed public sector or the emergence of new actors competing with the state. It merely reflects a break, first, from the references and standards of the neo-mercantile period (even if this break has oc-curred within the continuity of African historical trajectories) and, second, from the international environment and previous ideas about how its constraints and opportunities should be dealt with.

Once again, it is important to emphasise that this break can be under-stood only within the continuity of modes of government and subjectifica-tion. Today, the privatisation of the state, no matter how new and original it may be, is necessarily rooted in colonial governmentality. It is not an accident that the inspection, verification, testing and certification management com-panies resemble white concession owners of the past, that aid donors and western NGOs adopt, even unconsciously, the tone of nineteenth-century Christian missions and that violence is being used once again as a means of appropriation and upward social mobility.

Clearly, "privatising the state" is not a concept or a notion, let alone a new theory of the state. The research work on the generic topic of privatisation simply claims to bring to the fore and discuss the multiplicity of modes of government, regardless of whether they are actually new or merely appear to be new; it is our way of perceiving them that have changed. This work tries to identify the current breaks in modes of government and in the nature of the state and its interventions, and endeavours to open up new avenues of research by questioning and enriching phenomena that are often analysed in strictly univocal terms.

Endnotes

1 This article is part of a much broader reflection, begun in 1996, which resulted in various events and publications: a comparative seminar at CERI (SciencesPo, Paris) on 5 December 1997, and a seminar of African scholars at CEAN, Bordeaux on 22–23 October 1998; a special issue of the journal *Critique internationale,* no. 1, October 1998, and an edited book, B. Hibou (ed.), *La privatisation des États,* Paris: Karthala, coll. "Recherches internationales", 1999 (translated in English as *Privatizing the State,* New York: Hurst and Columbia University Press, 2004).

2 M. Weber, *General Economic History* (trans. F. H. Knight), London: George Allen & Unwin, 1927. Weber also speaks of it indirectly in *Economy and Society: An Outline of*

Interpretive Sociology (trans. E. Fischoff et al.), G. Roth and C. Wittich (eds.), 3 vols, New York: Bedminster Press, 1968 in connection with the ideas of appropriation (Vol. I, pp. 122 ff), forced loans (Vol. I, pp. 194 ff), tax farming (Vol. I, pp. 194 ff) and concessions (Vol. I, pp. 231 ff).

3   J.-F. Bayart, *The State in Africa. The Politics of the Belly,* London and New York: Longman, 1993 (Second Edition, Polity Press, 2009).

4   J. Roitman, "The pluralisation of economic regulatory authority in the Chad Basin", in B. Hibou (ed.), *Privatizing the State,* op.cit.

5   D. Harvey, *The Condition of Postmodernity. An Enquiry into the Origins of Cultural Change,* Cambridge MA: Basil Blackwell, 1990; K. Bennafla, "Mbaiboum: un marché au carrefour de frontiers multiples", *Autrepart,* no. 6, Éditions de l'Aube, 1998, pp. 53–72; J. Roitman, "The garrison-entrepôt", *Cahiers d'études africaines,* no. 150–52, XXXVIII (2-4), 1998, pp. 297–329.

6   C. Messiant, "La Fondation Eduardo Dos Santos: à propos de l'*'*investissement' de la société civile par le pouvoir angolais", *Politique africaine,* no. 73, March 1999, pp. 82–102; R. Marchal, "Des contresens possibles de la globalisation: privatisation de l'État et bienfaisance au Soudan et en Somalie", *Politique africaine* 73, March 1999, pp. 68–81.

7   S. Berry, *No Condition Is Permanent. The Social Dynamics of Agrarian Change in Sub-Saharan Africa,* Madison: University of Wisconsin Press, 1993.

8   I. Kopytoff (ed.), *The African Frontier: The Reproduction of Traditional African Societies,* Bloomington, IN: Indiana University Press, 1987.

9   R. Marchal, "Les mooryann de Mogadiscio. Formes de la violence dans un espace urbain en guerre", *Cahiers d'études africaines,* no. 130, XXXIII (2–3), 1993, pp. 295–320; R. Marchal and C. Messiant, *Les Chemins de la guerre et de la paix. Fins de conflit en Afrique orientale et australe,* Paris: Karthala, 1997; P. Richards, *Fighting for the Rain Forest. War, Youth and Resources in Sierra Leone,* Portsmouth, Heinemann, 1996; C. Geffray, *La Cause des armes au Mozambique. Anthropologie d'une guerre civile,* Paris, Karthala, 1990.

10   C. Tilly, "War making and state making as organised crime", in P. B. Evans, D. Rueschmeyer and T. Skopol (eds.), *Bringing the State Back In,* Cambridge, Cambridge University Press, 1985; F. Braudel, *The Mediterranean and the Mediterranean World in the Age of Philippe II,* London: University of California Press, Ltd., 1995, Vol. 2.

11   A. Mbembe, 'Du gouvernement privé indirect', *Politique africaine* 73, March 1999, pp. 103–21 ; J.-F Bayart, "La guerre en Afrique: dépérissement ou formation de l'État?", *Esprit,* no. 247, November 1998, pp. 55–73.

12   O. Vallée, 'La dette publique est-elle privée?' *Politique africaine* 73, March 1999, pp. 50–67.

13   B. Hibou, *L'Afrique est-elle protectionniste? Les chemins buissonniers de la libéralisation extérieure,* Paris: Karthala, coll. "Les Afriques", 1996.

14 For the concept, see Paul Veyne, *Bread and Circuses. Historical Sociology and Political Pluralism*. New York: Penguin, 1990.

15 J. Migdal, *Strong Societies and Weak States: State–society Relations and State Capabilities in the Third World,* Princeton: Princeton University Press, 1988.

16 This is shown in an especially eloquent way in Y. Chevrier, "Tenants of the house: Privatisation and the historical paths of the political", in B. Hibou (ed.), *Privatizing the State,* op. cit.

17 D. Stark, "Recombinant property in East European capitalism", *American Journal of Sociology,* vol. 101, no. 4, January 1996, pp. 993-1027.

18 See Y. Chevrier, "L'empire distendu: esquisse du politique en Chine des Qing à Deng Xiaoping", in J.-F. Bayart (ed.), *La greffe de l'État,* Paris: Karthala, 1996, and M. Iozy, *Monarchie et islam politique au Maroc,* Paris: Presses de la FNSP, 1999.

19 J.-F. Bayart, S. Ellis and B. Hibou, *The Criminalisation of the State in Africa,* London: International African Institute, 1999.

20 B. Hibou, "The political economy of the World Bank's discourse. From economic catechism to missionary deeds and misdeeds" in *Les Etudes du CERI,* no. 39, 1998 (translation in English by Janet Roitman, January 2000.

9

✳

Privatisation of African States and Economies: Comments from a historian

Mamadou Diouf

Introduction

There have been multiple and sometimes contradictory analyses of the current economic and political restructuring taking place in Africa. New concepts and expressions have developed to depict the contemporary African state as a criminal, privatised and failed political entity, incapable of exercising its territorial sovereignty, inadequately bureaucratised and prey to social actors who are either totally beyond its control, accomplices or merely indifferent. Some observers maintain that changes in the state modes of intervention in society, the economy and the bureaucracy have led to a loss of legitimacy, sovereignty and authority and an unmistakeable deterioration of the state's status and functions. From an economic standpoint in particular, the state is said to have relinquished its leadership role and control over its main instruments, i.e. land management and development. Worse still, it is said to be powerless to avoid outside pressure and the negative effects of global processes as well as the confiscation of certain state and bureaucratic functions by donors and NGOs, resulting in the irreversible decline of public administrations already undermined by policies that have left them understaffed.

Other observers, on the contrary, claim that this analysis – in line with welfare-state standards – reflects the trajectory of European countries since the eighteenth century and the developmentalist ideology of the 1950s and makes no sense when applied to developing countries. Béatrice Hibou asserts that what we are witnessing is less a withdrawal of the state than new modes of action in the form of private, indirect government.[1] The state is "adapting", as it were, to internal and external pressures through privatisation operations. This form of privatisation, at once intentional and imposed by circumstances, is an updated version of indirect government via private intermediaries. It also produces a diversified social structure and new actors positioned outside the state, the bureaucracy and the ruling class, which they "duplicate".[2] To be sure, the duplication of state infrastructures and functions has important consequences; it calls into question the notion of property and blurs the boundaries between the public and private spheres. According to this view, the economy remains under political control and is redirected as needed to keep pace with changes in the economic situation without surrendering to market laws or forces. This set of political, economic and social operations is interpreted as a new form of what Max Weber called "discharge".

At this stage of our discussion, it is worth taking a closer look at Weber's concept. In his view, "discharge" is the dominant form assumed by a government suffering from "weak bureaucratisation" and ineffectual administration.[3] These two problems were characteristic of the early period of colonial governance, from territorial conquest to the late 1930s, in contrast to the ensuing period, beginning in 1940 and ending in decolonisation, in which modernising bureaucrats[4] adopted a universalist, scientific approach in an attempt "to imagine a future" for African societies and institutions.[5] The first period was marked by administrative authoritarianism and the creation of "decentralised despotisms."[6] During the second period, a shift took place. At first, it was dominated by a centralising, interventionist approach (later upheld by the nationalists) and then, on the eve of independence, by decentralising techniques that "discharged" or delegated policymaking and responsibility for taxation to each colonial territory and sometimes to African elected officials.[7]

The concept of "discharge" effectively frees the study of African societies from analyses framed in terms of pathology, dysfunction and deviation from a universal standard.[8] It demands that the complexity of African societies be taken seriously. It means acknowledging the ability of the stakeholders to influence the course of events (and their own history) and to divert, circumvent and pervert them by various means, thus setting the state, its partners and its opponents on bumpy, unstable trajectories. Together, these trajectories form a "rhizome state" with a logic of mutual co-opting by elites, "duplication" of the ruling class and "constant renegotiation".[9]

Hibou's interpretation may well necessitate a historical analysis highlighting deeply rooted trends showing that "discharge" and/or delegation have in fact been instrumental in creating and building African states and their leaderships over the long term. While it is difficult to identify the elements that illustrate "discharge" in pre-colonial times, some traces of it can nevertheless be found. Although these traces pertain only to state formation (particularly the West African kingdoms), they offer a starting point for discussion. On the one hand, the state (the ruling class) did not establish a boundary between the public and private spheres. The absence of a centralised government, coupled with a small, widely scattered and amazingly mobile population affected the ability of the ruling class to derive a surplus from economic activities to a greater or lesser extent, depending on the degree of political centralisation or decentralisation.[10] On the other hand, when communities, as opposed to territories, had to be managed, there was no other way to set up an administration except by resorting to the patrons and clients belonging to the hierarchical systems of rulers and subordinates in the region. The control of administration, taxation and security was delegated to the territories.

This mode of governance relied on armed coercion to extract resources and/or guarantee the payment of tributes. The administrations used violence, kinship ties, slavery and the leasing of state functions to establish strict, systematic control over the areas where wealth was generated (gold and salt mines, Atlantic and trans-Saharan trade routes for luxury goods, etc.). The focus on controlling long-distance trade resources during the period of trans-Saharan trade and later transatlantic slave trade (17th and 18th centuries) in the context of political fragmentation after the collapse of the great Sudanese empires explains the success of the slave trade and the difficulty of imagining alternative ways to appropriate an economic surplus. As Frederick Cooper notes, it was easier to catch people than to put them to work.[11]

These issues of political and economic governance, trade and production were at the core of the controversies over modes of production initiated in the 1970s by French Marxist anthropologists. They were definitely the basis for Catherine Coquery-Vidrovitch's[12] theory of an African mode of production. Frederick Cooper had the same questions in mind when he examined the low level of business taxation (volume and level of business, extraction and appropriation of surplus) by the African states, the relationship between trade and production and the labour issue. Finally, meticulous studies inspired by the work of Indian historians might well lead us to view the Islamic social movements that developed in the Sahelian belt of West Africa from the late 18th century to the late 19th century as intellectual, armed, economic, political and social ways of separating the public sphere from the private in an attempt to foster the emergence of a civil society or at least to ensure the autonomy of certain groups.

The political and administrative control delegated to communities was taken over by colonial governance, because conquest and command replaced the values of the bourgeois world, the market and bureaucratic rationality in the colonies.[13] Several authors have pointed out the contradiction between bourgeois values and imperial violence.[14] In their studies on colonisation, Cooper and Ann Laura Stoler reached several conclusions that apply here as well. After identifying the main approaches to colonial economies and states, they give priority to two theories that challenge the views of world-systems theorists (particularly Samir Amin and Immanuel Wallerstein). The first theory considers the colonial economy a distinct entity based on two fundamental components: first, a mercantilist colonial conception (an exclusive agreement with the colony) according to which the home country secured privileged access to markets and raw materials by imposing drastic restrictions on the colony's freedom to trade with other partners and, second, a conception of the colony as an area in which the state may act differently, particularly by using force to obtain land for settlers and work for companies.[15] Similarly, they refer to the studies of Bruce Berman and John Lonsdale, who assert that the distinct nature of the colonial state stemmed precisely from its connection to the contradictory, indeterminate structure of colonial economies. Cooper and Stoler argue that "by endorsing the idea of a 'semi-autonomous capitalist state' in vogue in the 1970s, they [Berman and Lonsdale] show that the colonial state had to cope with different problems from those of the metropolitan or autonomous state". In any capitalist society, they add:

the state must settle disputes between the different factions of capital and ensure that the process of wealth accumulation does not derail or jeopardise the stability of power. The colonial state had to adjudicate not only between factions of capital and social classes, but also between metropolitan and imperial interests, between social relations of production and between capitalist and non-capitalist trade systems and networks. To maintain order and above all to recruit a labour force, a colonial state was needed, incapable of operating by force alone yet capable of forging alliances with the traditional authorities that preceded it.[16]

This oscillation between metropolitan values and imperial demands, between coercion and organisation along earlier lines of inequality and domination, was precisely what opened up spaces in which "discharge" and delegation could develop, because economic procedures were embedded in politics and administration.

"Discharge" was even more obvious in administrative governance. Due to economic concerns, imperial managers refused to invest in an administrative supervisory staff, at least during the first period. Colonial administration was delegated to local authorities. The case of Senegal provides a good illustration of this process. In the late nineteenth century, when the colonial conquest came to an end, the colonial authorities used traditional leaders to control and administer communities while continuing to harass the *marabouts* with deportation, house arrest, etc. When the chiefs were found to be embezzling and the *marabouts* and their communities engaging in groundnut production, the tasks of administration and taxation were delegated to religious clerics. These forms of delegated administration under direct rule became more visible under indirect rule. They were even more obvious in the colonies assigned to concessionary companies.[17]

The introduction of the concept of "discharge" in a historical perspective indeed confirms the theory of complex trajectories in the formation and building of the state. It nevertheless requires "historicising" the evolution of the state in terms of its economic manifestations and the development of its public and private domains. Historians divide the colonial era into three periods, the last of which is closed by decolonisation. The first period, extending from the territorial conquest to the outbreak of World War II, was a period of total "discharge", driven by a mercantilist approach, in which the chiefs were incorporated into the colonial administrative apparatus. It gave priority to colonial traditions that assigned roles to non-state actors and institutions while supporting the colonial state. As Mahmood Mamdani shows in his excellent description, this form of governance demonstrated once and for all that it was impossible to build colonies in the image and serving the interests of the metropole while accommodating indigenous elements. The resulting forms of colonial rule laid the foundation for ethnic management of African societies. Mamdani refers to these modes of management as "decentralised despotisms" built on a structure of customary rule and the authority of state-appointed local leaders.[18] The latter were responsible for handling land, taxation and security issues as well as mobilising the labour force, negotiating wages, etc. Thus, governance was divided early on into "two publics" that blurred the notion of a public space freed from community customs and the separation between the public and the private.[19] Instead, "two domains" were established: sovereignty (colonial institutions) and spirituality (the inviolable, protected values essential to the colonised society itself).[20]

The second colonial episode began in the 1940s and ended in the 1950s. Known as the period of "bureaucratic modernisation", it set out to bolster the key role assigned to the colonial triangle of "responsible" trade unions, "respectable" politicians and an enlightened colonial administration in charge of the colony's scientific and technological needs (management, delivery of selected seeds, social policy, labour force modernisation, etc.).[21] To this end, Britain and France launched ambitious reform projects. Britain enacted the Colonial Development Welfare Act in 1940 and France created the Fonds pour l'investissement en développement économique et social (FIDES) [Fund for investment in economic and social development] in 1946. This reformist and interventionist approach met with opposition from the colonial settlers and the high ranks of the colonial administration.

Bureaucratic modernisation failed due to a combination of factors including high cost, negligible outcomes and pressure from international organisations, such as the International Labour Organisation, to improve working conditions (including forced labour) and compensation, as well as trade union and political demands closely linked to the particular features of African societies. Faced with these results, the advocates of the modernisation movement were forced to re-examine their approach. How could they increase colonial productive capacity while reducing state intervention? How could they remove the obstacle of colonial companies that earned so much (thanks to state subsidies) while producing so little? Was it possible to achieve greater productivity without a fundamental change in the operating modes of African societies? Could they make the colonies directly pay the cost of modernising the bureaucracy and adapting the welfare state to Africa?[22]

The failure of bureaucratic modernisation ushered in a new period of internal autonomy followed by independence. Colonial interests were delegated to sovereign African states, heralding a decolonisation process involving not only political dynamics but economic and social reconfiguration as well. The transfer of power did not challenge the mechanisms and structures introduced during the second colonial period. The idea of development, along with the political and institutional arrangements linking sovereignty to spirituality, perpetuated the old procedures and modes, having learned from the failure of bureaucratic modernisation how to build an integral state, separate public from private and privatise. In a way, decolonisation enshrined, among other things, the failure to question "discharge" as a mode of governance in African societies.

This brief article is an invitation to broaden the discussion of privatisation and "discharge" by viewing them in historical perspective. Above all, it is intended to help rethink the dialectics and interactions between imperial theories and practices and between the dynamics of the colonial productive and commercial contexts and the reactions of African societies – in contrast to the universalist views of metropolitan theories and practices. Using the concept of "discharge" in an approach emphasising instability, change and la longue durée, would certainly enrich our understanding of how the African state and its public space were formed and built.

Endnotes

1 B. Hibou, "De la privatisation des économies à la privatisation des États", in B. Hibou, *De la privatisation des États,* Paris: Karthala, coll. "Recherches internationales", 1999, pp. 7–13.

2 On this subject, see J-F. Bayart, S. Ellis and B. Hibou, *La Criminalisation de l'État en Afrique,* Brussels, Complexe, coll. "Espace international", 1997, pp. 105–58.

3 See the Introduction.

4 F. Cooper, "Modernizing bureaucrats, backward Africans and the development concept", in F. Cooper and R. Packard (eds.), *International Development and the Social Sciences: Essays on the History and Politics of Knowledge,* Berkeley: University of California Press, 1997, pp. 64–92.

5   Lonsdale and Low refer to this period as the "second colonial occupation", in "Introduction", *The Oxford History of East Africa*, vol. 3, London: Oxford University Press, 1976, pp. 1–64.

6   M. Mamdani, *Citizen and Subject: Contemporary Africa and the Legacy of Late Colonialism*, Princeton: Princeton University Press, 1996.

7   F. Cooper, *Decolonization and African Society. The Labour Question in French and British Africa*, Cambridge: Cambridge University Press, 1996, p. 406.

8   See related article by R. D. Kaplan, "The Coming of Anarchy", *The Atlantic Monthly Review,* 273, 2, 1994 and the issue entitled La Malédiction, *Cahiers d'études africaines*, vol. 31, no. 1–2, 1991.

9   B. Hibou, "Retrait ou redéploiement de l'État", *Critique internationale*, no. 1, Oct. 1998, p. 168.

10 J. Goody, "Population and polity in the Voltaic region", in J. Friedman and M. J. Rowlands (eds.), *The Evolution of Social Systems*, Pittsburgh: University of Pittsburgh Press, 1978.

11 F. Cooper, "Africa and the world economy", in F. Cooper, A. Isaacman, F. E. Mallon, W. Roseberry and S. J. Stern (eds.), *Confronting Historical Paradigms. Peasants, Labor and the Capitalist World System in Africa and Latin America*, Madison: University of Wisconsin Press, 1993, pp. 84–201. First published in *African Studies Review*, no. 24, June–Sept. 1981.

12 C. Coquery-Vidrovitch, "Recherches sur un mode de production africain", *La Pensée,* no. 44, 1969, pp. 61-78.

13 E. Hobsbawn, *The Age of Empire: 1875–1914*, London: Weidenfeld and Nicholson, 1987.

14 For a good grasp of these issues, see the superb introduction by F. Cooper and A. Stoler, "Between metropole and colony. Rethinking research agenda", in *Tensions of Empire. Colonial Cultures in a BourgeoisWorld*, Berkeley: University of California Press, 1997, pp. 1–56.

15 Ibid., p. 18.

16 Ibid., pp. 19–20.

17 See, in this regard, the pioneering work of C. Coquery-Vidrovitch, *Le Congo au temps des grandes compagnies concessionnaires, 1898–1930*, Paris: Mouton, 1972.

18 M. Mamdani, op. cit.

19 P. Ekeh, "Colonialism and the two publics in Africa. A theoretical statement", *Comparative Studies in Society and History*, vol. 17, no. 1, January 1975, pp. 91–112.

20 P. Chatterjee, *The Nation and Its Fragments. Colonial and Postcolonial Histories,* Princeton: Princeton University Press, 1993. See, in particular, the discussion on the relationship between citizenship and community and the fact that the aspects relating to sovereignty were derived exclusively from colonial knowledge and practices (including "discharge", delegation and coercion), whereas the aspects relating to spirituality,

linked to demands based on Western democratic proposals, were used to draw up of the nationalist agenda. At this level, too, the distinctions were blurred. From this point of view, it should be understood that "community", "citizenship", "state" and "nation-state" are all colonial constructs and thus strongly marked by the same blurring and the exclusionary patterns and violence it generates.

21 F. Cooper, *Decolonization and African Society,* op. cit., p. 400.

22 Along the same lines, see the reflections of J. Marseille on the low economic gains in colonial situations and the impact of "discharge" on colonial economic structures (archaic practices, low productivity, reliance on non-economic constraints imposed by the colonial state and complete protection against any form of competition) in J. Marseille, *Empire colonial et capitalisme français. Histoire d'un divorce,* Paris: Albin Michel, 1984. See also M. Cowen, "Early years of the colonial development corporation. British state enterprise overseas during late colonialism", *African Affairs,* no. 83, 1984, pp. 63–75.

10

✶

On Private Indirect Government

Achille Mbembe

Introduction

This chapter is underpinned by two hypotheses. The first is the notion of *enchevêtrement,* "entanglement". Grounded in a history far deeper than many analysts recognise, Africa is moving forward in several directions simultaneously. This progression does not follow a closed orbit. It is neither advancing smoothly nor along a single line. It is headed towards several outcomes at once. One of these outcomes is the "exit of the state" – the second hypothesis underlying this paper. This exit is neither total nor irreversible. Indeed, it takes various forms. For the moment, it is paving the way to the emergence of political actors never before seen in the public space, a proliferation of unexpected forms of social reasoning and the establishment of novel mechanisms intended to regulate the conduct of individuals and enable new modes of developing private property and inequality. We propose to use the expression "private indirect government" to designate these emerging systems of domination, which have fundamentally different forms, intrinsic qualities and end purposes from those seen in postcolonial African regimes up to now.

Sovereignty and property

African societies are being upended in a context marked by the gradual dismantling of the state and, in the name of efficiency gains, denial of the legitimacy of state intervention in the economy. It should be kept in mind that the policies that have led to this gradual dismantling of public authority are based on the idea that the state, as a productive organisation, has failed in Africa and that economic organisation governed by the free play of market forces represents the most efficient way to achieve optimum allocation of resources. Translated into the terms of political economy, this idea has led, among other things, to selling public assets, repealing legal monopolies, awarding concessions on public goods and services, modifying customs legislation, revising exchange rates – in short, to a partial or full transfer to private entities of what was essentially public capital.

From a purely economic standpoint, experience often encourages observers to minimise the consequences of a change in the ownership of capital and underscores the relatively secondary importance of ownership compared with other criteria (market structure, corporate organisational and strategic decisions, degree of competition, workforce availability, relationship between wage costs and productivity, quality of human capital, etc.). It is nonetheless true that, in the African context, these operations fundamentally alter the processes of wealth allocation (income distribution, regulation of ethnic and regional balances) and modify the essentially political concepts of "public good" and "general interest".

Furthermore, and in the absence of specific economic effects (gains from trade based on exploiting a comparative advantage), the policies we have just described have paved the way to fierce struggles aimed at concentrating and then privatising force and the means to enforce it. It makes sense that the struggles would become exacerbated, because control over these means is an advantage in other struggles underway to appropriate profits, percentages and utilities formerly concentrated in the hands of the state. In other words, in Africa there is now a direct link between the primacy of free market orthodoxy, rising violence and the creation of private military, paramilitary and jurisdictional entities.

Several questions follow from these observations. For one, how does the struggle for concentration of the means of coercion mentioned above take place, and what conditions are necessary for this struggle to engender any kind of political order on the ruins of the earlier one? Under what conditions might this struggle ultimately lead to the defeat of the state as a general technology of domination and what other mechanisms and forms of organisation will replace this type of state? Another question: as the economy is still underpinned by the use of legal or illegal force, under what conditions can coercion, once it is concentrated, be converted into work productivity? And under what other conditions might the violence that has been unleashed disintegrate into total disorder and plunder instead of taking an economic turn?

There are some indications that provide answers to these questions. On the one hand, it is difficult to achieve a concentration of the means of constraint using only traditional resources, i.e. those used until now by the state. These resources simply do not exist anymore, or they are no longer available in the same quantities as before. *In fine*, the state itself no longer exists as a general system of domination. A central government still exists in name. Its organisational structure remains more or less intact, along with its system of titles and formal rituals and declarations. In principle, an autocrat continues to hold the power of appointment. In some cases, an administrative imaginary survives, even though the institutions and bureaucracy that are supposed to embody it have collapsed. Quite often there is no longer any hierarchy or centralised pyramid organisation to speak of. Orders issued from high above are rarely executed, or if they are, they are always profoundly distorted and profoundly modified at the bottom. Interlocutors change constantly, at every level. Official remits do not always correspond to real and effective powers, and often enough higher authorities are accountable to authorities at a lower level.

Where real powers exist and are exercised, they are wielded not by virtue of a law or a rule but often on the basis of purely informal, tentative arrangements that can be revised at any time without warning. Governmental bodies that are low on the scale in legal and regulatory terms have powers and influence well beyond those of higher-placed bodies. Most transactions are carried out orally, and administrative activity is no longer systematically recorded in writing. In practice, functions no longer presuppose prior professional training, even if, in theory, it is still a prerequisite. Civil service no longer calls for complete dedication to the job. Civil servants can, in effect, hire out their labour power or use it for other purposes during the hours theoretically reserved for their government post. They can even market their government function and turn it into a source of emoluments and private income, in addition to their salary, if it is still being paid. As a result, civil servants have become increasingly self-serving. In some cases, their work is no longer even remunerated by a salary. A formal budget is drawn up, but it is followed and executed according to purely contingent and informal criteria. Indeed, there is a proliferation not of autonomous centres of power but of hubs and enclaves at the core of what represented, not long ago, the system itself. These hubs, and the series of enclaves, are intertwined, in competition with each other and, in some instances, form networks. In any event, they constitute the links in a weak, unstable chain in which parallel decisions coexist with centralised decisions. This leads to frequent short-circuits, frequent changes and twisting of rules, structurally unforeseeable actions and situations characterised by inertia and sclerosis coupled with sudden, erratic, and accelerated movements.

While this state of affairs does not mean we can call certain postcolonial societies in Africa stateless societies, it has nevertheless fostered the emergence of situations of quasi-constitutional duplication of governing authority almost everywhere on the continent (parallel hierarchies alongside formal ones, hidden networks alongside public ones, etc.). In order to grasp the extent of the various forms of privatisation of sovereignty, let us recall once again that the struggle for concentration and then privatisation of the means of coercion is taking place in a setting characterised by global deregulation of markets and movements of money and by the incapacity of postcolonial African states to pay salaries or even levy taxes. Supposedly public functions and sovereign responsibilities are increasingly exercised by private operators for private purposes. Soldiers and police live off the inhabitants. Civil servants assigned to administrative tasks sell public documents and pocket the proceeds. How does this apparatus of domination become institutionalised, and is it ultimately part of the form of regulation that we call private indirect government?[1]

At this point, we can perhaps find help in the notion of "discharge" introduced by Max Weber. He used the term to designate transactions that were originally incumbent upon the state but were, at some point, taken over by henchmen and became the foundation of the oriental feudal system. According to Weber, the discharge system grew out of the decay of the monetary economy and the ensuing risk for oriental political regimes of falling back into a barter economy.[2] In fact, Weber distinguishes between several different types of discharge found in Ptolemaic Egypt, India, China and, from the tenth century onward, the Caliphate. In these models, tax collection might be put in the hands of private powers or soldiers who paid themselves out of the taxes collected. Levying taxes was carried out in the same way as drafting military recruits. In this way, a number of institutions were gradually set up, which, like vassal institutions in the feudal period, enjoyed a comfortable margin of autonomy upwards as well as downwards. In Weber's mind, the discharge system, as a technique of government and process of property formation, did not express a cultural trait specific to the East. It was this same type of domination, incidentally, that made it possible to administer Rome when the Empire evolved into a continental state. But, contrary to the West, the extortion of fees in the East eventually took precedence over exploitation through forced labour, thus aggravating the risk of returning to a barter economy.

The historical sequence under way in Africa is not identical to Weber's discharge model. On one hand, although there has been a return to a barter economy and actual demonetisation in several parts of the continent, the main phenomenon nevertheless remains the practice of barter within the money economy, as shown by examples of pre-financing state revenue (anticipated sales of mining resources in exchange for budgetary advances, widespread surrender of state mining or land holdings to companies or private operators that pay rents). On the other hand, the general context of the developments now taking place is one of extreme material scarcity. We are referring, first of all, to the subsistence crisis experienced by several countries. This crisis includes various forms of shortage and penury, as well as supply problems. The intensity of the crisis varies from region to region, and the contrasts are striking between the rich cities and rural areas and the less prosperous and poor areas, but nearly everywhere the resources available to the population have been reduced, sometimes drastically, while at the same time many other pressures have increased: taxes and miscellaneous payments, scattered and fragmented property ownership, indebtedness, pawn loans, the rising burden of rent and various forms of loss of position. The subsistence crisis is also tied, first, to the upheaval in the conditions affecting how Africans, since the latter part of the twentieth century, have determined the value and price they attribute to a wide range of activities and goods and, second, to the undermining of the established customary balances between people and things or even between life and death.

A central aspect of this crisis is the dynamics of the relationship between what could be called "real money" and its obverse, along with extreme volatility of prices. Currency depreciation has led to a drastic drop in the price of non-tradeable goods virtually everywhere. This is the case for the real remuneration of work in particular. The inflation of the cost of basic foodstuffs has set off a chain reaction. A change in the parity of currencies very often has had no effect on economic competitiveness, whereas the cost of imports needed for production has risen. Price fluctuations and increases go hand in hand with an unprecedented shortage of money. Entire regions are caught up in a process of eviction from the monetary economy at a time when the capacity of states to obtain cash payments in the form of taxes has never been so low.

The conditions for setting up private powers have been gradually established due to armed conflict and the intensive deployment of violence across the region imposed by the processes of restoring authoritarianism and economic deregulation. In the context of war, this development takes the form of dominating unarmed populations who are unable to find refuge and safety elsewhere. In some instances, large-scale systems of production based on forced labour and informal taxes (contributions of food or firewood, portage, services and fees) are introduced. Warfare activities encourage the constitution of property holdings. Sometimes the population is simply massacred, as postcolonial warriors are not interested in becoming a class of "masters of bodies" for the purpose of exploiting the labour power of human property or reducing it to a state of dependence. Under these conditions, the aim of war is not economic exploitation.

A different economy and other forms of exercising power appear in refugee camps and in places where people are forcibly grouped together. In these cases, revenues are amassed by collecting fees levied, in large part, for individual protection. Instead of granting fiefdoms to their warriors, who are increasingly children, the warlords guarantee them the right to reap benefits and dispensations in kind. These rights are exercised by looting stores, homes and plantations and by confiscating property belonging to war victims. Due to the periodic and fluctuating nature of their rewards, the warriors do not have the option of subjecting the unarmed population to forms of forced labour. Moreover, a culture of impunity flourishes in time of war – and not only then – which accounts for the fact that private actors guilty of proven crimes are afforded protection. For example, troops claim the right to plunder and rape. Towns and villages are sacked. Natural resources are auctioned off. People are put to death publicly. Populations are deliberately terrorised, and no one is ever prosecuted.

Tax exemptions and judicial immunity are also granted to those who have found a way to convert their high posts in what is left of the state apparatus into lucrative positions in national, regional and even international channels of the parallel economy. The same is true for a number of foreign brokers, shadow networks and so-called humanitarian organisations, whether long established or recently introduced in these countries. Depending on the circumstances, war and austerity also create the conditions for extending domination beyond the bounds of lineage affiliation. They are conducive to formalising new types of servitude and dependence. The question is not whether there are signs that a system of discharge and allocation of fiefdoms exists. The question is under what conditions the private powers now being set up will succeed in using force to accumulate wealth, usurp the rights of public authority and legal jurisdiction and acquire sufficiently solid immunity, so as to ensure consolidation, over time, of productive servitudes and thus become the originators of a novel model of capitalism.

Violence and territoriality

Although we cannot answer these questions yet, we can point to the creation of large, armed contingents in many countries of the region, ranging from official and semi-official organisations specialised in the use of violence to private structures in charge of security and protection – in short new institutions charged with administering violence. In fact, these armed forces fulfil not only the functions of war but also serve as an armed instrument for amassing property and restoring authoritarian forms of power. To counter the social protest movements that have erupted everywhere in support of political pluralism, most African regimes have given free rein to armed elements of various kinds (police, gendarmes, political police, so-called domestic security services, and if need be, the presidential guard). They have allowed these elements to live off the people, first under cover of operations purportedly intended to re-establish order and then through coercion administered on a daily basis (roadblocks, raids, forced tax collection, illegal property seizure, racketeering and other special privileges). Encouraged by lack of discipline, links have been set up between rank-and-file troops and organised crime and fraud. In some countries, the situation has reached a point that can be called, without exaggeration, "*tonton-macoutisation*".[3]

The gradual slide into "*tonton-macoutisation*" has taken several forms. Property seizures and confiscations have become increasingly frequent in order to loosen the hold that economic and civil disobedience campaigns put on public finances in some countries. Under the pretext of tax collection, the destruction or resale of goods has also become widespread. In some cases, production facilities and redistribution sites are militarily occupied. To punish shopkeepers, transport operators and other social categories that have been active in protest movements, marketplaces and administrative buildings have been periodically burnt down in order to erase traces of corruption and other incriminating documents or to provoke shortages and monopolise sources that supply essential foodstuffs. Troops are often sent to close shops when small businesses and trades, the source of livelihood for the lower classes in the cities, come under attack. More than previous forms of coercion, these exactions stem from economic pressures, but they also help to implement new methods of political exclusion. In a context in which the accumulation of overdue payments, advances on mining revenues and upfront financing of the interest from annuities mean that the state can no longer refinance itself, the state can no longer pay out salaries to ensure that the members of society remain beholden to it. This is now mainly achieved by controlling access to the parallel economy. Paid employment has been replaced by "occasional payments" as the prime method of turning society into a patronage system, altering the bases on which rights, transfers and obligations had been pegged until now and thereby transforming the very definition of postcolonial citizenship. Henceforth, a citizen is someone who has access to the parallel economy and to the forms of livelihood afforded by this economy.

On the other hand, the daily administration of coercion has become increasingly decentralised and privatised, giving rise to local cliques that take advantage of the situation to rake in illicit gains and settle personal scores. Using positions in the bureaucracy as sinecures is no longer the only way to bring in extra income; influence peddling in government now includes the notion of offices as goods to be bought and sold. In some cases, the situation is so acute that each bureaucrat levies a tax on his or her subordinates and on the users of a public service, with the army, police forces and the bureaucracy running an extortion operation to sponge off the citizenry. As Paul Veyne noted of the late Roman Empire, "[w]hen things reach this point, we can no longer speak of abuses or corruption; it must be admitted that we are looking at an original historical formation",[4] a specific way of regulating the behaviour of the population, distributing penalties and enjoying services.

Here we are confronted with a mode of deploying force and constraint that has its own positive dynamic. Relationships of subjugation specific to times of penury and deregulation are being created and institutionalised. These relationships are established via toll points, extortion and levies, which are, in turn, tied to a particular conception of the chain of command and the circulation of orders throughout society. This sort of subjugation replaces the former system consisting of exchanges of goods and services. People were bound not necessarily by contracts or pacts but by networks of reciprocal obligations, favours, tributes and honours that were often manifested by ostentatious spending.[5] In contrast, extortion, tolls and various forms of utilities appropriation specific to times of austerity are rooted in a climate of violence in which spoils, capture and plunder become the prime modes of acquisition and consumption of wealth. Granting favours as a method of government is henceforth replaced by debt, forcible levies, generalised taxation and various other fees.

In breaking the ties built on relative reciprocity and transfers of different kinds and resorting to unilateral constraint, the actors who control what is left of postcolonial African states seek to establish the state on other grounds. Those who possess the means of constraint have a distinct advantage over all the others in the struggles triggered by this mutation. In practice, they assume the attributes of a private lordship, with the public authority of a potentate extending over people as well as goods. Command over people becomes inseparable from using their belongings. Taxation is transformed into a broad category that requires no assent and is claimed without any reference to precise notions of the public interest or the common good. Furthermore, levying taxes is no longer an aspect of state monopoly on constraint but rather a feature of the loss of this monopoly, now scattered throughout society. There is no longer any difference between taxation and exaction.

Lastly, the privatisation of public violence and its deployment for private enrichment have a corollary: the accelerated development of a shadow economy over which members of the police, the army, customs and tax administration attempt to assert control (drug trafficking, counterfeit currency, arms and toxic waste, customs fraud, etc.). Should this control be achieved, it could precipitate the eviction from this parallel economy of broad swathes of society that, pushed by austerity policies, ensure their daily subsistence outside the legal economy, outside work for wages or salary and outside the direct patronage of official powers. What is at stake here is the opportunity for new modes of subjection and control of people.

The decisive nature of the international support that has been given to this process of entrenching authoritarianism has not been sufficiently underscored. The extraordinary reach of private "networks" and lobbies, the weight of the military and the perversion of bureaucratic systems have allowed situations of economic rents to be consolidated in many countries, rents that go not only to indigenous potentates but also to a long list of brokers, traders, mercenaries and handlers who maintain ties with intelligence services, the army and sometimes with organised crime. In countries where the influence of France prevails, for instance, the hustling and cosy wheeling and dealing that was a trait of the Gaullist networks have amplified and intensified under the auspices of managing privatisations, debts, donations, loans, advances and subsidies, tax deductions and various other claims. Today hardly any sector is exempt from corruption and venality, not even diplomatic services.

Spurred by privatisation and structural adjustment programmes, an economy of concessions is emerging made up of lucrative monopolies, secret contracts, private deals and exceptions to the law (in the tobacco sector, transport, agribusiness, major infrastructure works, oil, uranium, lithium, manganese, arms purchases, training and command structures for armies and tribal militias and recruitment of mercenaries). This is not a process of marginalisation, as has been claimed, but a junction and intertwining of international trafficking rings, foreign brokers and handlers, local traders and "technocrats" at work pushing broad segments of international economic relations in Africa into the underground economy.

It is symptomatic, in this respect, that what we are seeing looks very much like the exhaustion of the model of the territorial state, a model characterised by differentiated institutions, central and vertical political relationships, spatial demarcation and monopoly over the exercise of legitimate force and authorised tax levies.[6] The dogma of the "integrity" of the borders inherited from colonisation no longer holds. This does not mean we are witnessing an uncontrollable escalation of separatist fever that will shatter irreversibly the territorial framework of postcolonial states as in former Yugoslavia (except in the case of Ethiopia). Rather, it means that identity pressures, the dynamics of autonomy and differentiation, the diverse forms of ethnic regionalism, pressures to migrate, the growing influence of religion and the accelerated shift of African societies into the so-called parallel economy are profoundly altering the spatial and social organisation of the continent, the distribution of populations and the real operation of markets and, in the process, shifting the material foundations of power.

In all the countries where socio-political configurations were already sharply delineated before European penetration, regional differentiations have been accentuated, first driven by colonial policies for "extracting value" from the territories conquered in the nineteenth century and then by the forms of political control adopted since the end of direct rule in the colonies. In a great many instances, the divergence between the formal rigidity of borders and their economic and cultural mutability has been increasing. Situations of structural conflict have appeared nearly everywhere that ethnic groups claiming a territorial birthright feel they have been economically shunted aside by "outsiders". A sense of belonging is emerging, and identities are being reinvented via disputes over heritage and the manipulation of the ideologies of indigenous and ancestral rights.

The true map of the continent is being redrawn through the forces propelling the regrouping of territories and spatial dislocation along regional and international trade and trafficking routes, which to a large extent correspond to and transcend the historic pathways and zones of the dynamic mercantile expansion of the nineteenth century.[7] This can be seen along the old caravan routes traced around the Sahel, the routes to the Atlantic Ocean, the trade routes for ivory and precious stones that linked the Senegambia and Katanga regions[8] and later linked Katanga to southern Africa, the trading itineraries around the Red Sea and Indian Ocean and trade networks in the Nile basin. Vast areas where multiple currencies coexist and are exchanged alongside official structures, sometimes encouraged by formal bureaucracies, are increasingly controlled by what is left of fiscal and judicial systems and, above all, by military forces.

As for the rest, the economic and social importance of borders is taking on political significance insofar as these borders no longer merely separate one state from another but are becoming internal boundaries within states, as seen in parts of the Republic of Congo, Angola, Uganda, Sudan and countries on the edge of the Sahel.[9] The autonomy acquired by entire regions, the abandonment of pockets of land more or less emptied of their inhabitants, the existence of intermediate gaps and spaces within a single state, the concentration of population in river basins and other regional environmental sectors – these are the distinctive traits found in more and more countries. Similarly, we are seeing entire provinces of some states being gradually transformed into satellites of neighbouring states. In several places, these processes go hand in hand with an unprecedented resurgence of territory-based identity, an extraordinary insistence on family and clan antecedents and birthplace and a renewed fervour in ethnic imaginary representations. In most large urban centres confronted with property ownership issues, differentiation between non-native people (those who come from somewhere else, who migrated) and indigenous people (those who were born on the land and have always lived in the same place) has become commonplace.[10] The proliferation of internal borders – whether imaginary, symbolic or related to economic or power struggles – and the exacerbation of local affiliations that is its corollary have given rise to exclusionary practices, identity-based boundaries and persecutions that can turn into veritable pogroms and even genocide.[11]

Along with these movements of re-territorialisation, a specific form of violence is developing: war. Let us note that, in a context of economic contraction and depression, most of these wars, although they have disastrous short- and long-term consequences, are nonetheless on a small scale. Even if they engage the armed forces of one or several countries, in general they remain wars between gangs and quite often are wars of plunder opposing one group of predators to another. Like some medieval wars, they make use of small numbers of troops and relatively primitive weapons. But while their tactics may be fairly rudimentary, they nonetheless lead to catastrophes. Military pressure is sometimes exerted for the sole purpose of destroying the means of survival of the civilian population (food stores, livestock, farming implements). Plunder and extortion are not uncommon. In some cases, these wars enable gang leaders to wield relatively continuous control over more or less large areas of territory. This control gives them access not only to the people of these territories but also to local resources and the goods produced there. The financing of the wars under way is quite complex. Ransom, living off the land and plundering it is not enough.

In addition to funds furnished by those living abroad and the tapping of the local workforce to perform chores and forced labour for porterage and troop supply, we should mention the recourse to loans, appeals to private financiers, the letting of concessions (forests, mines, etc.) and the emergence of special forms of taxation. To recruit men, and above all to equip them, funds are obtained from companies that exploit resources in the portion of territory controlled by a given faction. In return for exploiting resources that they subsequently export to the world market, these companies transfer large sums to those who control the area by bills of exchange or other means (cash disbursements, allocations in kind, etc.). This war tax system also includes other financial expedients such as fines, licenses and extortion, confiscation of fixed assets and forcible contributions from occupied or conquered territories.

Wherever it has taken root, warfare has reshaped the administration of lands, goods and people and transformed the ways in which resources are levied and distributed and even the framework of dispute resolution. In the places where war breaks out, it does not necessarily lead to the development of the state apparatus or a state monopoly on the use of force within its boundaries as in Europe. Under today's conditions, there is no automatic connection between war and the emergence of an undisputed central power. It is true, however, that along with other factors, the military enterprise is one of the ways whereby new forms of military domination materialise on the continent. In some cases, a reconfigured form of the state prevails and transforms itself, as needed, into the main technology of this domination. Here, as in other areas, intertwining local and international stakes must be taken into account. In any case, situations of war force a renegotiation of the relationships between individual and community, the foundations of the exercise of authority and relationships to time and space, to profit and to the invisible. [12]

The public good and tax regulation

The distinction between the state of war and the state of peace is itself increasingly artificial. Extortion, or more broadly the power to dispose of people and property at will, is not limited to settings where war is rife. These activities are often only distantly related to fiscal action *per se*, as they are embedded in the sphere of mere subsistence. Effective and economically oriented violence, whether in a warfare mode or for plunder, is directly related to the notion of taxation and consequently to the issues surrounding construction or destruction of the state. Throughout history, taxation has been the decisive factor in the economic foundation of the state in the same way that the monopoly on legitimate violence has been one of the key steps in the creation of states. It was by means of taxation that force and arbitrary rule were transformed into authority and violence into exchange. In the Western world, for example, taxation has always been more than just a price to be paid for public services. In paying taxes, the individual subject does indeed contribute as an individual to public expenditures on behalf of all members of society. The taxpayer can, of course, take personal satisfaction from this, but it is never the individual who decides what share of his or her income goes to the state. The financial and economic calculations required by taxation always involve that other authority and other power – the state – and, beyond the state, the different social groups that oppose each other, fight among themselves and make compromises. Lastly, the collective pressure inherent in the fiscal relationship never completely rules out the possibility of a relationship of exchange between taxpayers and the state. It is through this relationship of exchange that the fiscal subject "purchases" rights on the state and democratic political systems are distinguished from those based on coercion and arbitrary action. In the latter, the common good or the public interest is never meant to be a topic for genuine public debate.

But let us come back to the dimension of violence as such to note that, at the origin of tax levies, there is always a relationship of coercion. In African history, war has been – and continues to be – the prime locus for the manifestation of this relationship of violence. This relationship showed itself in the form of the plunder that conquerors carried off after their victory. Plunder paid off the warriors and fed them, and warfare could on occasion also become an enterprise of enrichment. In most cases, however, and despite all sorts of protocols, spoils were taken in a disorderly fashion, often in the form of pillage, and the plundering lasted only as long as the raid or the razzia. In the long term, its productivity was uncertain, because successive pillages exhausted capital without necessarily leading to the creation of goods. Razzias were purely destructive in nature. The goods of the raided population – everything they most treasured – ceased to exist. Their work destroyed, and, even if they managed to save their lives, only terror and fear were left in the land. In some cases, the material devastation was such that the transfer of wealth, the acquisition of profit and the prospect of ransom by pillage often led to disorganisation of trade and credit. Moreover, this relationship created ties that lasted only a short time, the time of conquest, although sometimes conquest was followed by occupation or the creation of a protectorate subject to payment of tribute. Warfare was a strictly lapidary act, almost without compensation.

Taxation is always a political issue, insofar as it attempts to limit disorder, lay down the law, control private violence and produce order. Historically, the problem of controlling private violence could be resolved by exacting tribute, requisitioning goods or enrolling forced labour. In these three cases, the subjugated groups might retain the freedom to pursue their livelihoods, although they were often deprived of the fruits of their daily labour when forced to work without any compensation. In all cases, a portion of their resources, time, labour and the products of their labour was ceded to their masters, either in kind or later in monetary form. This was a feature of this sort of trade and of its arbitrariness. The political significance of taxation emerged at the dawn of modern times when the need to convert this arbitrariness into a mutual obligation between sovereign and subject became a concern. As a result, a close relationship was established between the institution of taxation, on the one hand, and, on the other hand, the process of gaining political freedom and becoming citizens.

As we know, this process extended over a long period of time in the Western world. It was tied to profound changes in social structure, trade, means of warfare and systems of law, in how the public good and the public interest were conceptualised and in the relationships between the state, society and the market. Let us take France as an example. Originally the royal tax was called "aid", "hearth tax" or "subsidy". It was only later that it acquired the name "*tallage*" or "*taille*". The hearth tax differed from aid in that it was a fee levied on "fire" or hearth, whereas a "subsidy" was a supplement paid to an individual or a group as support or as remuneration for services rendered.[13] This was also the way customary law worked. The relationship between suzerains and vassals dictated that the king had to draw his revenue from his domain like all the other lords of the time, but the feudal rules also provided that, in case of need, and notably to supplement the revenue of the royal domain, the monarchy could appeal for temporary aid in a framework set by customary law. The "*tallage*" or "*taille*" was a sort of tax levied by the lords, an integral part of feudal institutions. It was only later that the royal authority became involved, when it succeeded in supplanting the customary authorities, breaking down their resistance and transgressing the obligation of receiving authorisation from the non-elected representative assembly [*États généraux*]. The entire non-combatant population became subject to this tribute.

Three ideas underpinned this fee. First, in paying *tallage*, the non-combatant population was, in a sense, buying back its obligation under conscription, thereby earning exemption from direct participation in the incessant wars of the period. At the same time, it bought a guarantee of continued possession of the rest of their holdings that were thereby protected from pillage. Second, the *taille* was raised only exceptionally and temporarily, at least in the beginning. It was an extraordinary "tax", an institution specific to times of war. In theory, there was no reason for it to survive once it has served its purpose. Lastly, it was not one of the royal rights. As it was not a regular duty owed by subjects to the sovereign, it could not be levied without the assent of the taxpayers.[14] It is thus clear that, originally, one of the functions of taxation was to acquire the means of war – men, supplies, money and arms. Taxation fulfilled a capital function in the very formation of Western states, inasmuch as the institution of taxation was inseparably linked to setting up and financing a vast military apparatus and the means of collection. The development of this centralised apparatus was part of a long process, spanning the passage from the right to private warfare (claimed and exercised by feudal lords up to the end of the Middle Ages) to the notion of a monopoly on the right to wage war, which devolved to the king as sovereign and guarantor of public order. To this extent, taxation was one of the instruments of the birth and development of two related concepts, public authority and the common good.

These two concepts took hold in opposition to the customary recourse to private violence to obtain justice. The notion of public authority exercised in the interest of the common good slowly gained precedence over the right to private violence.[15] The monopoly on violence and the monopoly on taxation mutually justified and reinforced each other.[16] However, in the history of the West as in that of Africa, there has never been taxation without a degree of organised coercion, in other words, a certain way of "mistreating one's subjects", of administering them, of ensuring extraction, of exploiting and dominating the people. To organise coercion as efficiently as possible, stable control must be exercised over the population of a given territory. This control is meaningful only if it ensures access to a share of the resources, goods and services produced in the territory.

We are thus confronted with two contradictory movements of ideas. On one hand, the principle of the *right to raise taxes*, unanimously accepted since Roman times and invoked by legal specialists whenever necessary, was established as one of the attributes of a sovereign power (taxation authority). On the other hand, the principle of *assent to taxation*, which gradually became a principle of public law, held that the sovereign had no right to levy taxes outside his own domain simply of his own volition. To obtain the assent of lords and provincial states, the sovereign had to prove exceptional needs. There is thus a tension between the constraint of binding taxation and the free and voluntary acceptance of taxation. These two principles of taxation were opposed until finally reconciled in democratic regimes. The prevailing current in the colonies in the nineteenth century was the tradition in which the state, in the figure of the king, was the master of the life, honour and goods of his subjects. In this tradition, the subjects possessed only the usufruct of their holdings. In reality, property belonged by sovereign right to the king and to the state, leaving only the right of use to the subjects. In some cases, the sovereign prince could dispose of this property against the wishes of the individual holders. In demanding taxes, the state and the king were merely taking back what was theirs by right. Again in this tradition, taxation was justified partly by the necessity of ensuring public prosperity and the common good and partly by the need to keep subjects subservient. In this sense, it was the very hallmark of subjection. Taxes kept the subjects from losing sight of their condition; in the words of Richelieu, "if they were free of tribute they would think they were freed of obedience". Like a donkey, they had to become accustomed to their burden.[17]

Coming back to the case of Africa, it is important to emphasise, in the contexts described earlier, that a new form of power organisation based on control over the main means of coercion (armed force, intimidation, imprisonment, expropriation, slaughter) has arisen within the framework of territories to which the traditional notion of the state no longer applies, states whose borders are only vaguely defined and, in any case, vary with the vagaries of military encounters. These states exercise the right to "tax", i.e. to exact supplies, tributes and tolls of all sorts, which then provide support for bands of warriors and a semblance of civil apparatus and means of coercion. At the same time, they participate in formal and informal networks in which currency and wealth (ivory, diamonds, wood, ore, etc.) circulate abroad. This has been the case especially in countries where the process of privatisation of sovereignty has been combined with war and has arisen from an unprecedented interlacing of the interests of international brokers, handlers and traders with those of local plutocrats.[18]

What we are witnessing in Africa is indeed the creation of another type of political economy and the invention of other systems of coercion and exploitation strategies. The question is, first, whether these processes will ultimately lead to a system of capitalised coercion sufficiently coherent to impose changes in the organisation of production and the class structure of African societies and, second, whether the submission these processes require on the part of Africans, the exclusion and inequalities they entail – with socialised violence as their corollary – can be legitimised to the point of once again becoming a public good. One might also wonder to what extent the violence (pillage, rioting, extortion, etc.) and inequality inherent in these processes risks precipitating the destruction of "civility" as a salient feature of belonging to society. The taxation crisis, penury and population migrations that accompany these reconfigurations suggest that, for the time being, what we are seeing is simply a struggle between predators, but there is no reason to think that this crime could not give birth to prosperity and democracy in the long term. Meanwhile, below the state level, new forms of social belonging and incorporation are in gestation in the form of "leagues", "corporations" and "coalitions". There can be no doubt that most of the religious and spiritual movements flourishing in Africa today constitute (among other things) spaces of visibility, albeit ambiguous, where new normative systems and new common languages are negotiated and where new authorities are formed. Here, once again, there is no reason to think that the proliferation of these separate spheres and their affirmation in the public space reflect anything other than a fragmented, heteronomous conception of the "political community".

The fundamental question concerning the emergence of a legal subject remains unanswered. The history of other regions of the world shows that taxation, beyond creating interpersonal allegiances, has served to define the bonds between the governors and the governed. The state does indeed have the means to "obligate" its subjects, but, in theory at least, it cannot obligate subjects except by obligating itself. It has the right to levy taxes only insofar as its subjects, represented in assemblies, exercise their right to have a say in how the taxes are collected, assessed and spent. It is through this process that the state has been able to define itself as a common good and not merely as a relationship of domination. Through this process the state also converts its power to obligate others by obligating itself into the power to lay down the law. Finally, it is through this process that the subject acquires a status in the political order by paying taxes and exercising a right over the use of tax monies, thereby giving legal existence to the subject's political and civic capacity. This objectification is part of the exchange of rights and obligations with the state through which it gains public credit precisely because it has used its sovereign power in compliance with the law. Perhaps there is no other path to political modernity.

Endnotes

1   Regarding this type of functioning, see the notes in A. Mbembe and J. Roitman, "Figures of the subject in times of crisis", *Public Culture,* no. 16, 1995, pp. 341–4.

2   Weber uses this notion in an effort to compare the West to the East and shows that no form of exploitation of forced labour developed in the East, where extortion of fees was dominant. See M. Weber, *Histoire économique. Esquisse d'une histoire universelle de l'économie et de la société,* trans. by C. Bouchindhomme, Paris: Gallimard, 1991, pp. 87–9.

3   The expression *tonton-macoute* is drawn from the history of Haiti. Originally this Creole term referred to a cruel and terrifying phantasmagoric figure, one of whose most visible features was that it carried a straw bag (*macoute*). Later it was used to designate the militia set up under the Duvalier regime that was assigned to doing dirty work for the ruling classes, among other functions.

4   P. Veyne, "Clientèle et corruption au service de l'État: la vénalité des offices dans le Bas-Empire romain", *Annales. Économies, sociétés, civilisations,* vol. 36, no. 3, May–June 1981, pp. 339–60.

5   J. P. Warnier, *L'Esprit d'entreprise au Cameroun,* Paris: Karthala, 1993; S. Berry, *No Condition Is Permanent,* Madison: University of Wisconsin Press, 1994.

6   See M. Weber, *Economy and Society,* New York: Bedminster Press, 1968; C. Tilly, *The Formation of National States in Western Europe,* Princeton: Princeton University Press, 1975.

7   J. R. Gray and D. Birmingham, *Pre-Colonial African Trade. Essays on Trade in Central and Eastern Africa Before 1900,* London: Oxford University Press, 1970; C. Meillassoux, *The Development of Indigenous Trade and Markets in West Africa,* London: Oxford University Press, 1971; P. Lovejoy and S. Baier, "The desert-side economy of the Central Sudan", *International Journal of African Historical Studies,* vol. 7, no. 4, 1975, pp. 551–81; A. J. H. Latham, "Currency, credit and capitalism on the Cross River in the pre-colonial era", *Journal of African History,* vol. 12, no. 4, 1971, pp. 249–60.

8   S. Bredeloup, "L'aventure des diamantaires sénégalais", *Politique africaine,* no. 56, 1994, pp. 77–93.

9   J. MacGaffey (ed.), *The Real Economy of Zaire,* London: James Currey, 1992.

10 See examples in S. Jaglin and A. Dubresson (eds.), *Pouvoirs et cités d'Afrique noire,* Paris: Karthala, 1993.

11 See also the reports of R. Lemarchand in *Burundi: Ethnocide as Discourse and Practice,* Cambridge: Cambridge University Press, 1994 and F. M. Deng in *War of Visions. Conflict of Identities in the Sudan,* Washington DC: The Brookings Institution, 1995.

12 See T. Allen, "Understanding Alice: Uganda's holy spirit movement in context", *Africa,* vol. 61, no. 3, 1991, pp. 370–99 and K. Wilson, "Cults of violence and counterviolence in Mozambique", *Journal of Southern African Studies,* vol. 18, no. 3, 1992, pp. 527–82.

13 Literally, aid is assistance given to a person or entity in need. The donor acts to help, contributing its efforts to those of the recipient. Aid is by nature a temporary form of assistance. If it is permanently levied, it becomes something else. Aid cannot be extorted. The recipient is bound by a relationship of dependence to the donor.

14 On these and preceding observations, see E. Esmonin, *La Taille en Normandie au temps de Colbert, 1661–1683,* Geneva: Mégariotis Reprints, 1978, pp. 2–10.

15 See *La France et l'Angleterre à la fin du Moyen Âge,* trans. by N. Genet and J.-P. Genet, Paris: Aubier, 1994, pp. 220–6.

16 N. Elias: "[...] armed force concentrated in the hands of the central government ensures collection of contributions, and the concentration of fiscal revenue in the coffers of the central administration consolidates the monopolisation of physical coercion, of military force, these two instruments of power mutually reinforcing each other," in *La Dynamique de l'Occident,* Paris: Calman-Lévy, 1975, p. 170. See also L.

von Stein, "On taxation", in R. A. Musgrave and A. T. Peacock, *Classics in the Theory of Public Finance,* New York: Macmillan, 1967, pp. 28–36.

17 On this debate, see Richelieu, *Testament politique,* vol. I; Bossuet, *Politique tirée de l'Écriture sainte,* VI, II, par. 3; Lebret, *De la souveraineté du roy,* livre III, chap. VII; Lacour-Gayet, *L'Éducation politique de Louis XIV,* livre II, chap. VIII; Bodin, *De la république,* livre I, chap. VIII; La Mothe Le Vayer, *La Politique du prince.*

18 See W. Reno, *Corruption and State Politics in Sierra Leone,* Cambridge: Cambridge University Press, 1995.